Top Cow Productions Presents

VOLUME 1

Created by
MOHSEN ASHRAF

Published by Top Cow Productions, Inc.
Los Angeles

For Top Cow Productions, Inc.
Marc Silvestri - CEO
Matt Hawkins - President & COO
Elena Salcedo - Vice President of Operations
Vincent Valentine - Production Manager

IMAGE COMICS, INC. • **Todd McFarlane**: President • **Jim Valentino**: Vice President • **Marc Silvestri**: Chief Executive Officer • **Erik Larsen**: Chief Financial Officer • **Robert Kirkman**: Chief Operating Officer • **Eric Stephenson**: Publisher / Chief Creative Officer • **Nicole Lapalme**: Controller • **Leanna Caunter**: Accounting Analyst • **Sue Korpela**: Accounting & HR Manager • **Marla Eizik**: Talent Liaison • **Jeff Boison**: Director of Sales & Publishing Planning • **Dirk Wood**: Director of International Sales & Licensing • **Alex Cox**: Director of Direct Market Sales • **Chloe Ramos**: Book Market & Library Sales Manager • **Emilio Bautista**: Digital Sales Coordinator • **Jon Schlaffman**: Specialty Sales Coordinator • **Kat Salazar**: Director of PR & Marketing • **Drew Fitzgerald**: Marketing Content Associate • **Heather Doornink**: Production Director • **Drew Gill**: Art Director • **Hilary DiLoreto**: Print Manager • **Tricia Ramos**: Traffic Manager • **Melissa Gifford**: Content Manager • **Erika Schnatz**: Senior Production Artist • **Ryan Brewer**: Production Artist • **Deanna Phelps**: Production Artist • **IMAGECOMICS.COM**

SYPHON VOLUME 1.
ISBN: 978-1-5343-2073-4

First Printing. December 2021. Published by Image Comics, Inc. Office of publication: PO BOX 14457, Portland, OR 97293. Originally published in single magazine form as SYPHON 1-3.

SYPHON
VOLUME 1

STORY BY
MOHSEN ASHRAF

Written by
PATRICK MEANEY & MOHSEN ASHRAF

Art by
JEFF EDWARDS

Colors by
JOHN KALISZ

Letters by
TROY PETERI

Edited by
MATT HAWKINS & ELENA SALCEDO

CHAPTER ONE

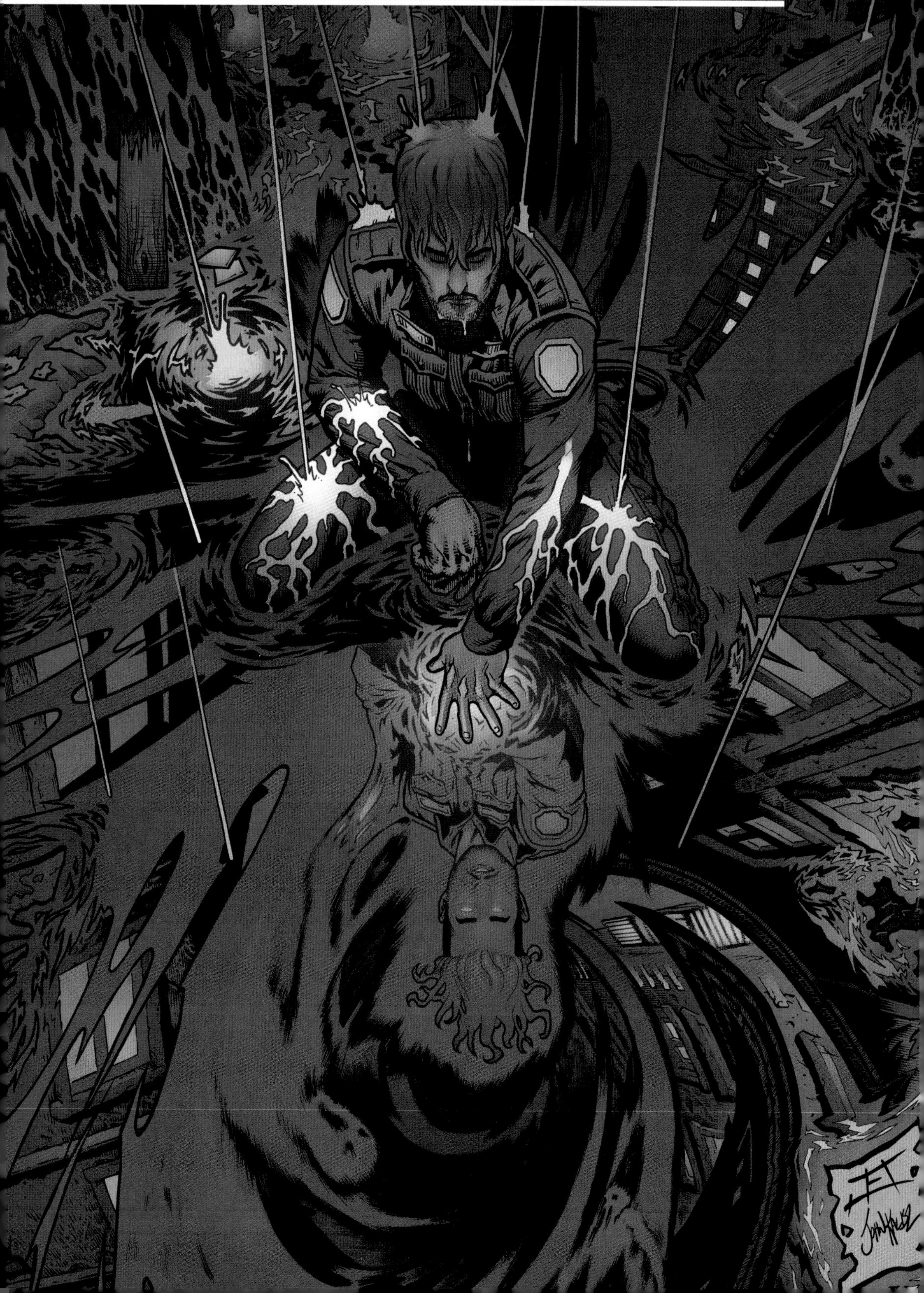

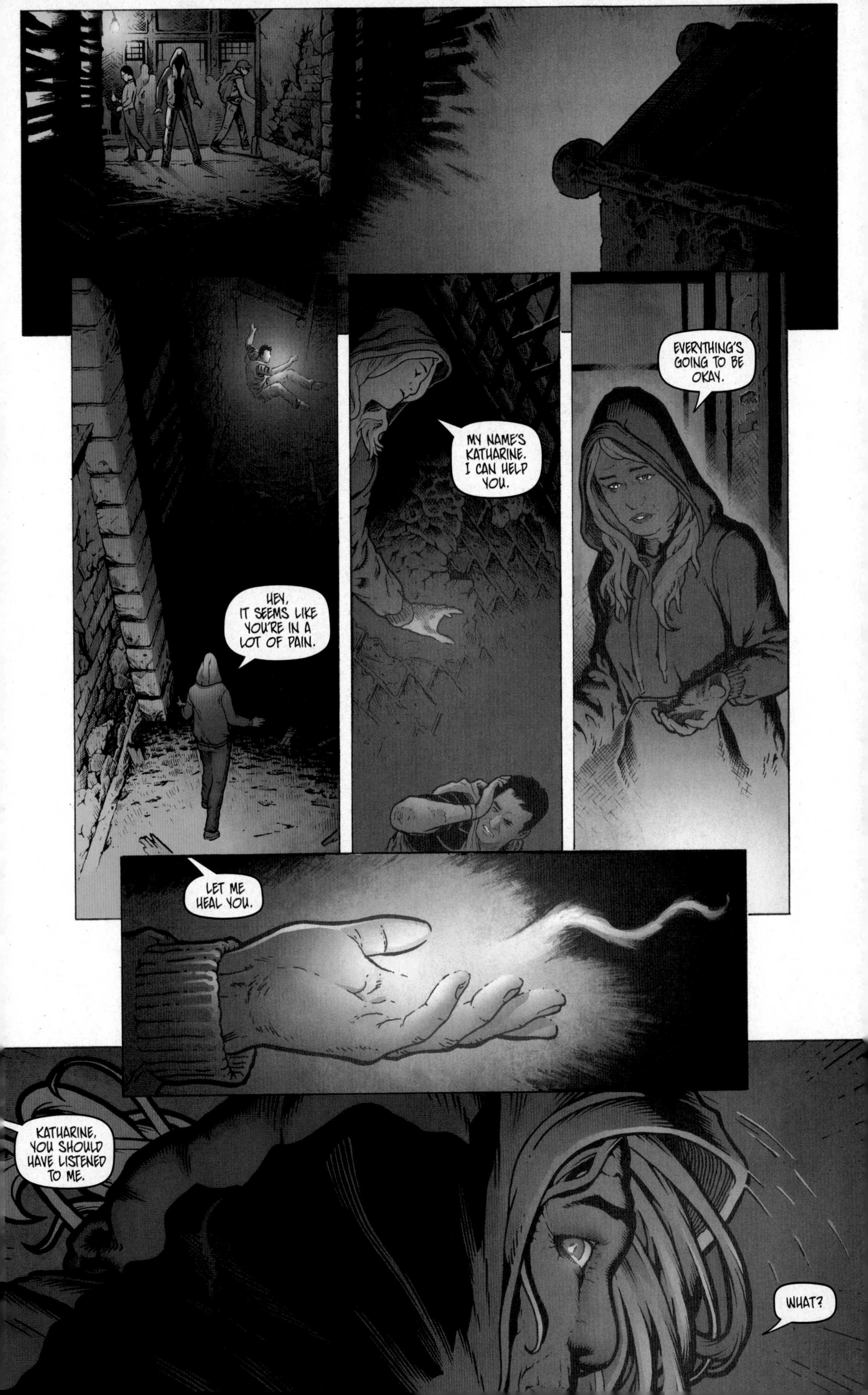
HEY, IT SEEMS LIKE YOU'RE IN A LOT OF PAIN.
MY NAME'S KATHARINE. I CAN HELP YOU.
EVERYTHING'S GOING TO BE OKAY.
LET ME HEAL YOU.
KATHARINE, YOU SHOULD HAVE LISTENED TO ME.
WHAT?

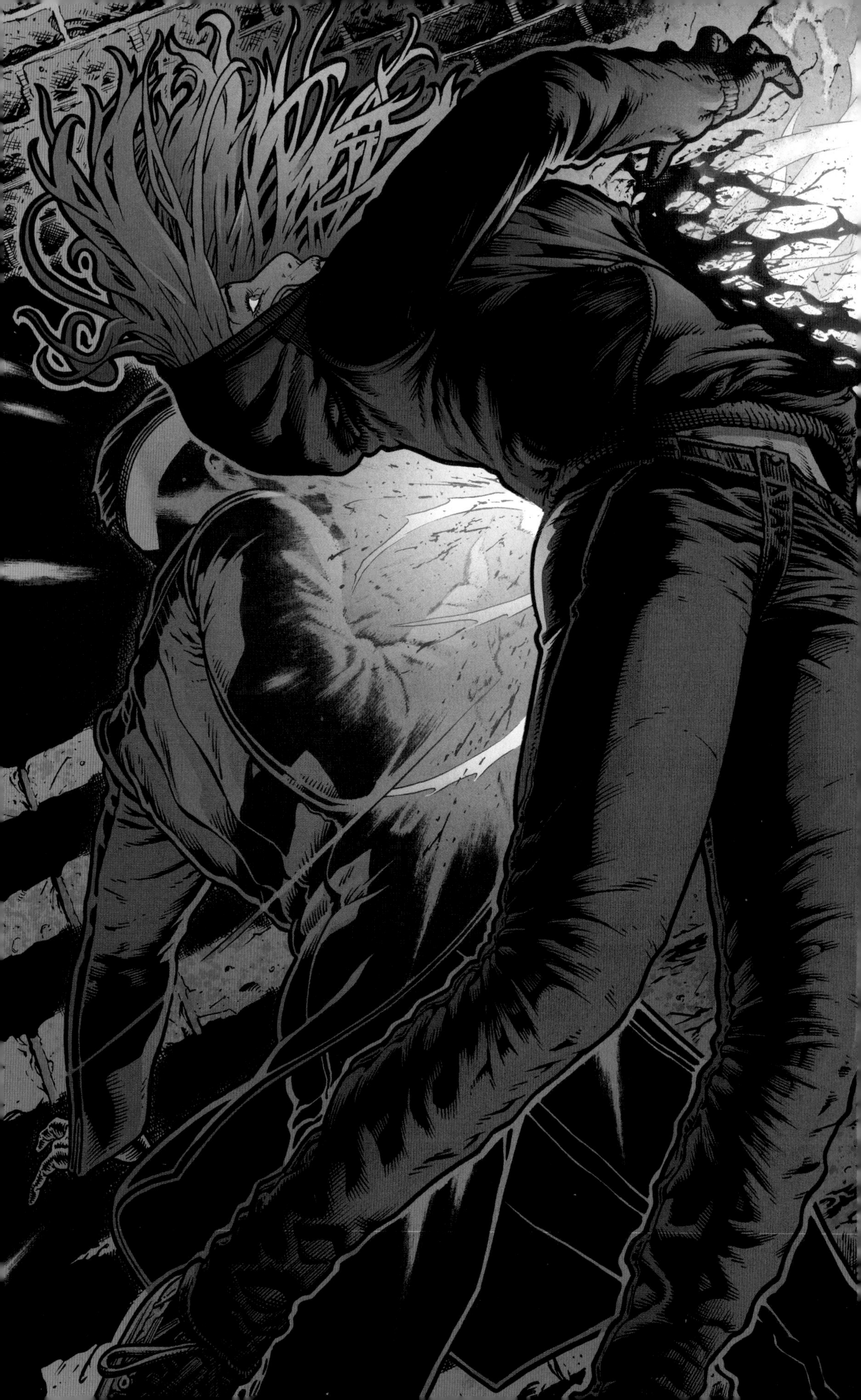

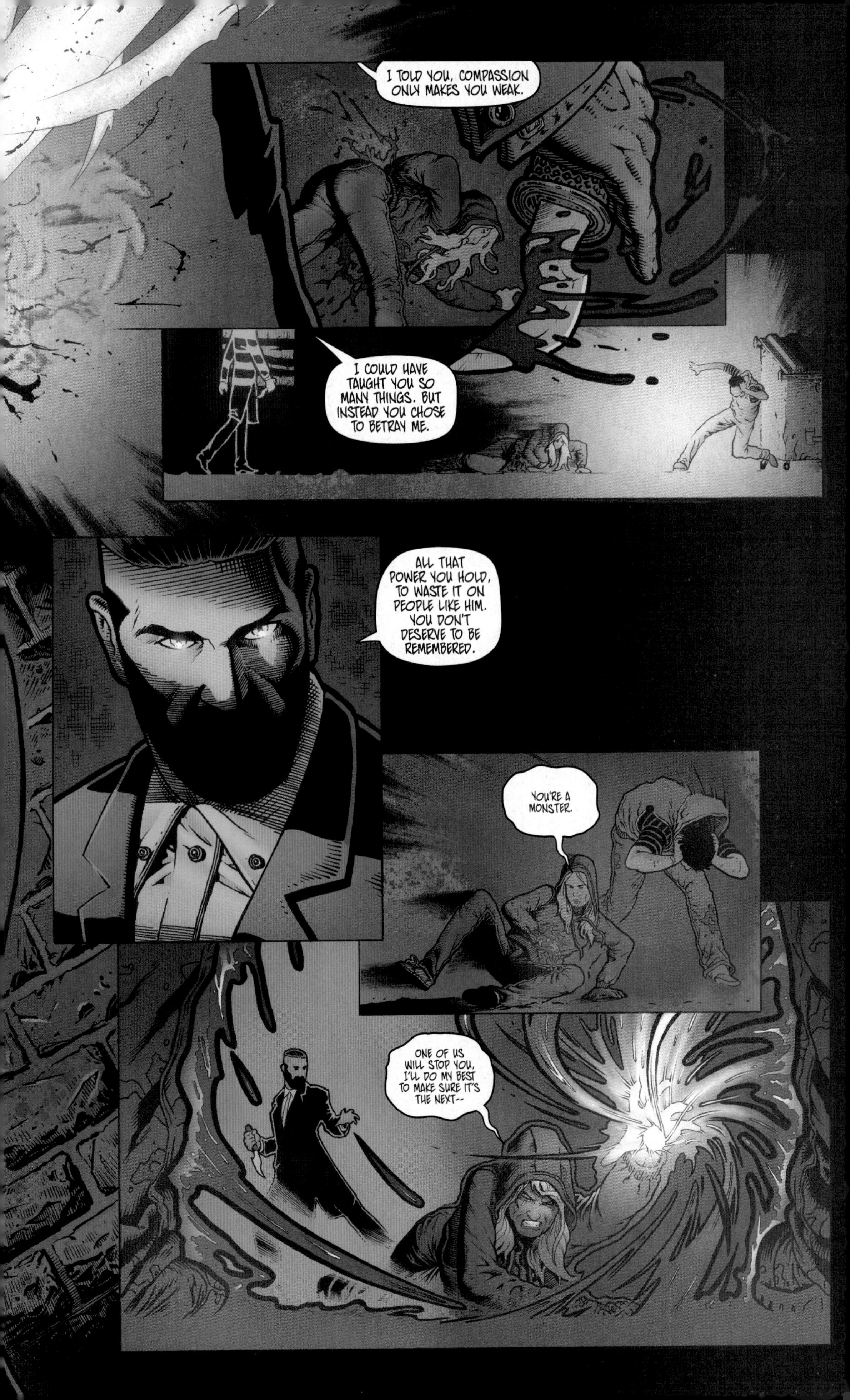
I TOLD YOU, COMPASSION ONLY MAKES YOU WEAK.
I COULD HAVE TAUGHT YOU SO MANY THINGS. BUT INSTEAD YOU CHOSE TO BETRAY ME.
ALL THAT POWER YOU HOLD, TO WASTE IT ON PEOPLE LIKE HIM. YOU DON'T DESERVE TO BE REMEMBERED.
YOU'RE A MONSTER.
ONE OF US WILL STOP YOU, I'LL DO MY BEST TO MAKE SURE IT'S THE NEXT--

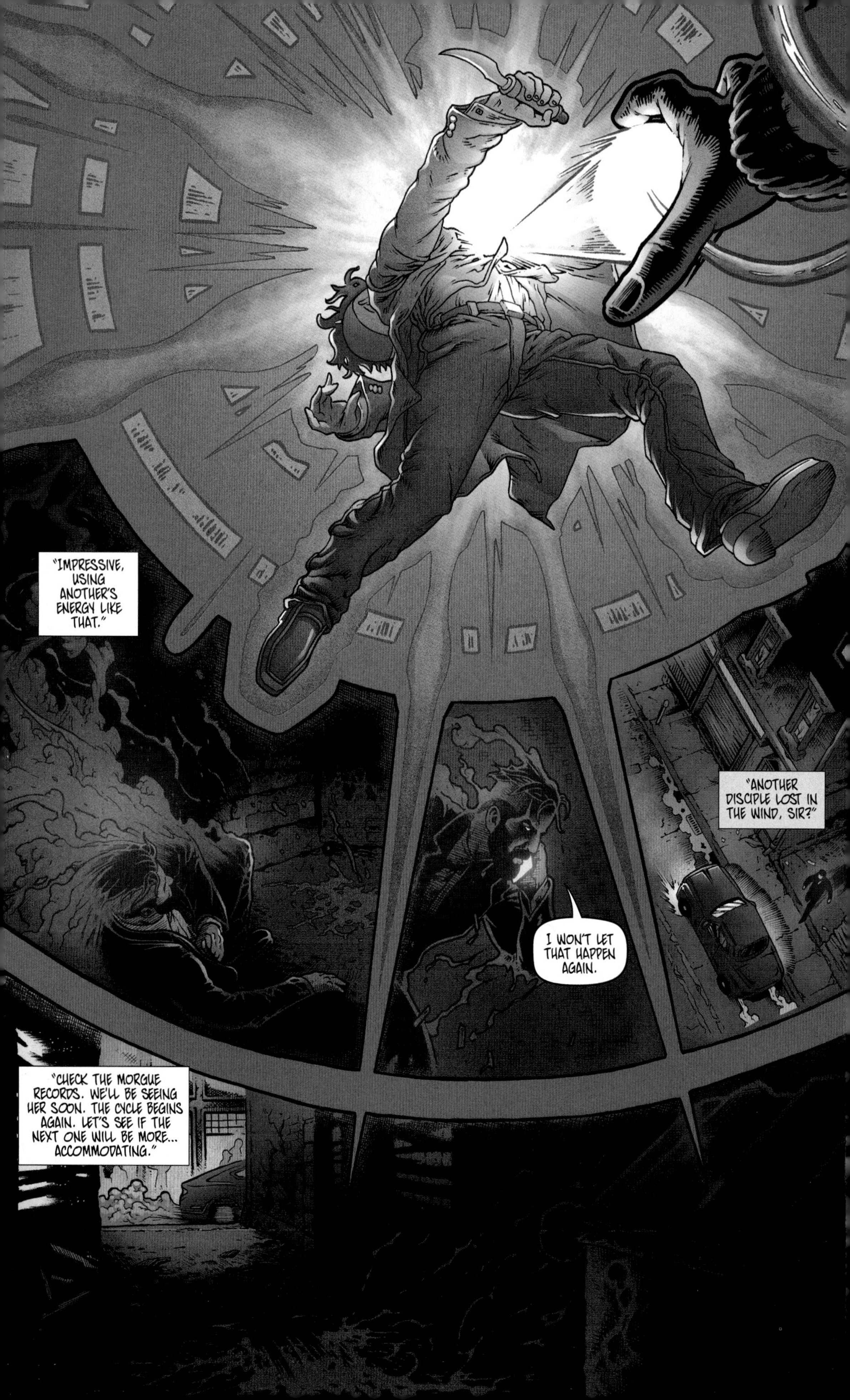
"IMPRESSIVE, USING ANOTHER'S ENERGY LIKE THAT."
"ANOTHER DISCIPLE LOST IN THE WIND, SIR?"
I WON'T LET THAT HAPPEN AGAIN.
"CHECK THE MORGUE RECORDS. WE'LL BE SEEING HER SOON. THE CYCLE BEGINS AGAIN. LET'S SEE IF THE NEXT ONE WILL BE MORE... ACCOMMODATING."

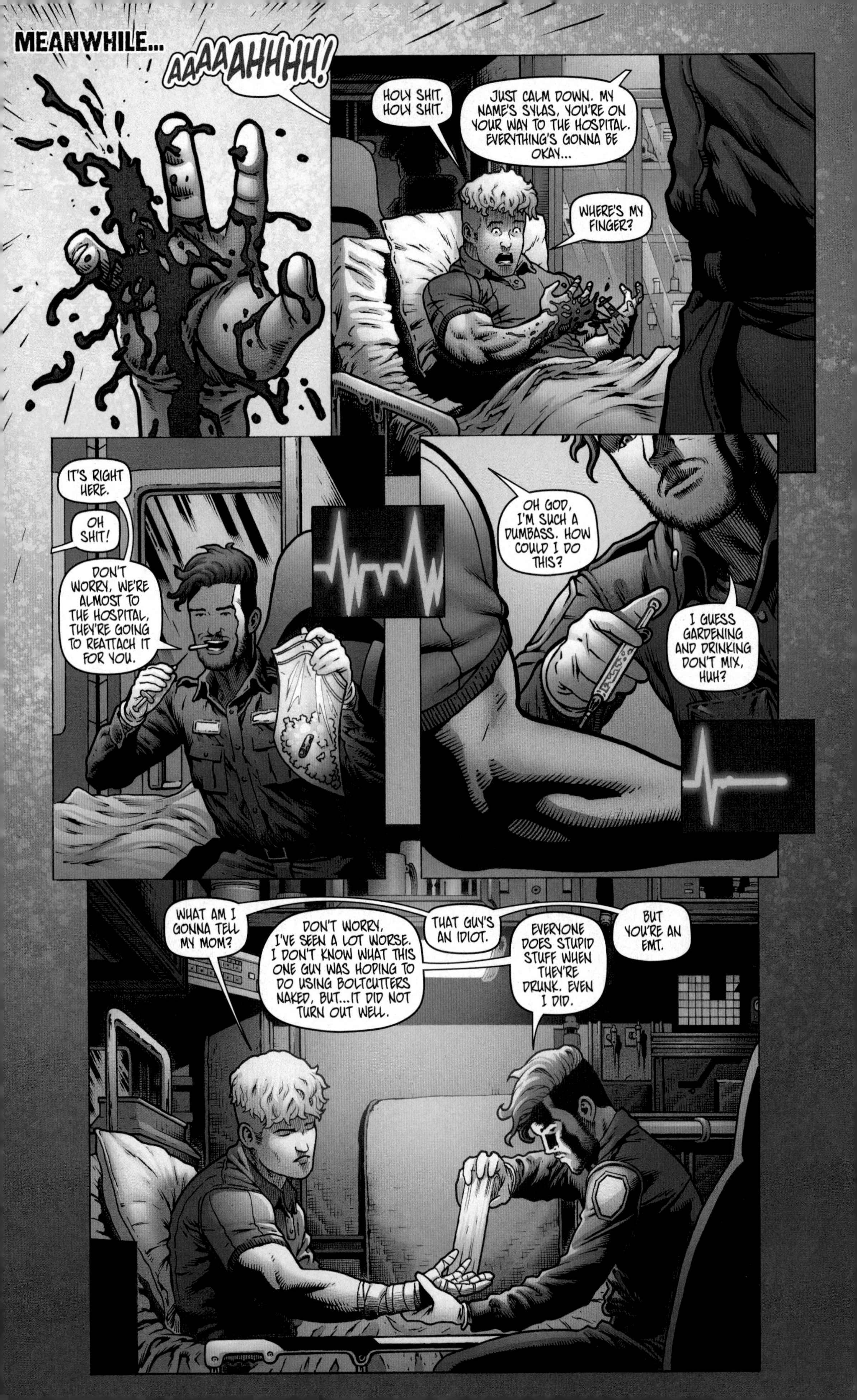
MEANWHILE...
AAAAAHHHH!
HOLY SHIT, HOLY SHIT.
JUST CALM DOWN. MY NAME'S SYLAS, YOU'RE ON YOUR WAY TO THE HOSPITAL. EVERYTHING'S GONNA BE OKAY...
WHERE'S MY FINGER?
IT'S RIGHT HERE.
OH SHIT!
DON'T WORRY, WE'RE ALMOST TO THE HOSPITAL, THEY'RE GOING TO REATTACH IT FOR YOU.
OH GOD, I'M SUCH A DUMBASS. HOW COULD I DO THIS?
I GUESS GARDENING AND DRINKING DON'T MIX, HUH?
WHAT AM I GONNA TELL MY MOM?
DON'T WORRY, I'VE SEEN A LOT WORSE. I DON'T KNOW WHAT THIS ONE GUY WAS HOPING TO DO USING BOLTCUTTERS NAKED, BUT...IT DID NOT TURN OUT WELL.
THAT GUY'S AN IDIOT.
EVERYONE DOES STUPID STUFF WHEN THEY'RE DRUNK. EVEN I DID.
BUT YOU'RE AN EMT.

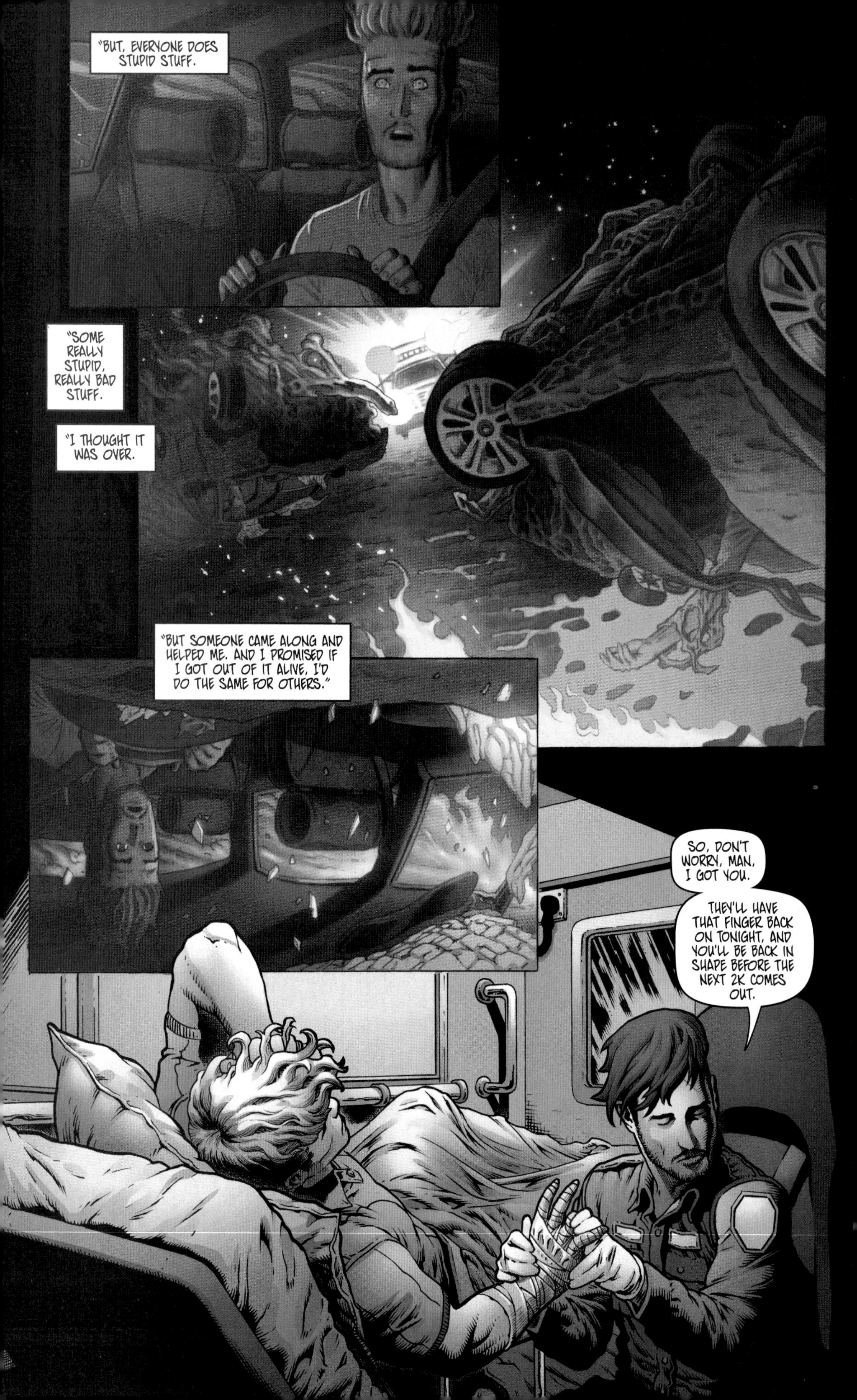
"BUT, EVERYONE DOES STUPID STUFF.
"SOME REALLY STUPID, REALLY BAD STUFF.
"I THOUGHT IT WAS OVER.
"BUT SOMEONE CAME ALONG AND HELPED ME. AND I PROMISED IF I GOT OUT OF IT ALIVE, I'D DO THE SAME FOR OTHERS."
SO, DON'T WORRY, MAN, I GOT YOU.
THEY'LL HAVE THAT FINGER BACK ON TONIGHT, AND YOU'LL BE BACK IN SHAPE BEFORE THE NEXT 2K COMES OUT.

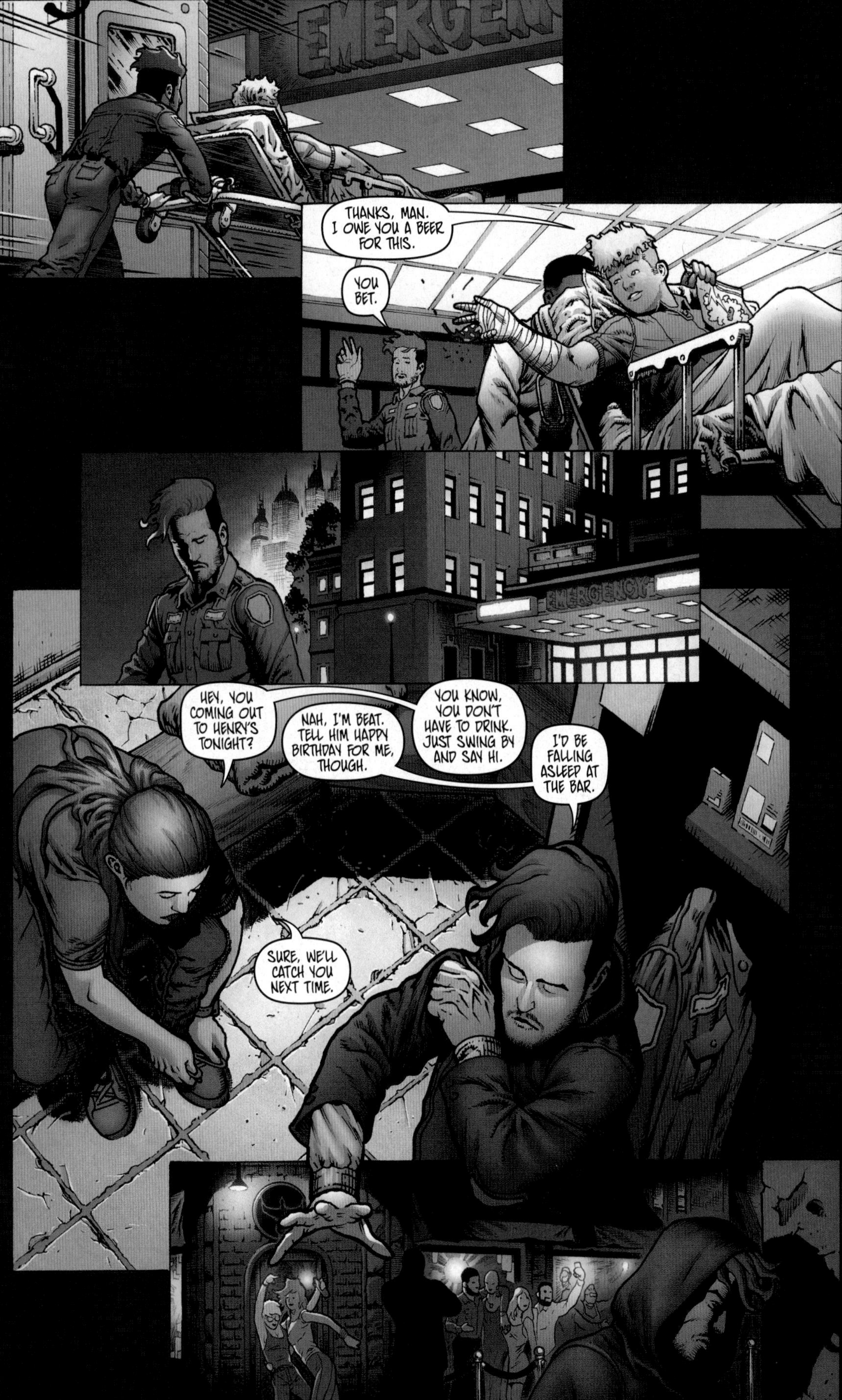
EMERGEN
THANKS, MAN. I OWE YOU A BEER FOR THIS.
YOU BET.
EMERGENCY
HEY, YOU COMING OUT TO HENRY'S TONIGHT?
NAH, I'M BEAT. TELL HIM HAPPY BIRTHDAY FOR ME, THOUGH.
YOU KNOW, YOU DON'T HAVE TO DRINK. JUST SWING BY AND SAY HI.
I'D BE FALLING ASLEEP AT THE BAR.
SURE, WE'LL CATCH YOU NEXT TIME.

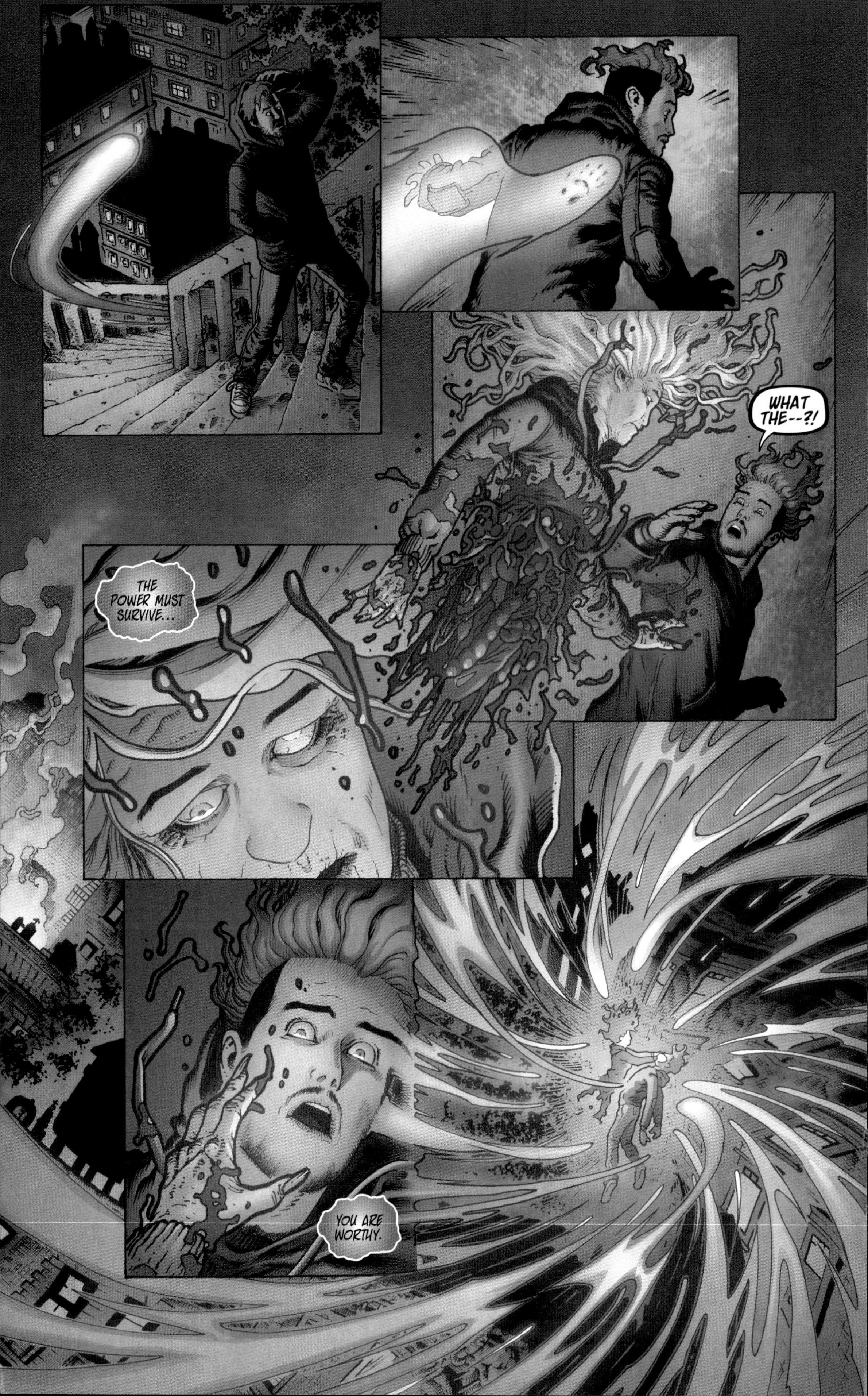
WHAT THE--?!
THE POWER MUST SURVIVE...
YOU ARE WORTHY.

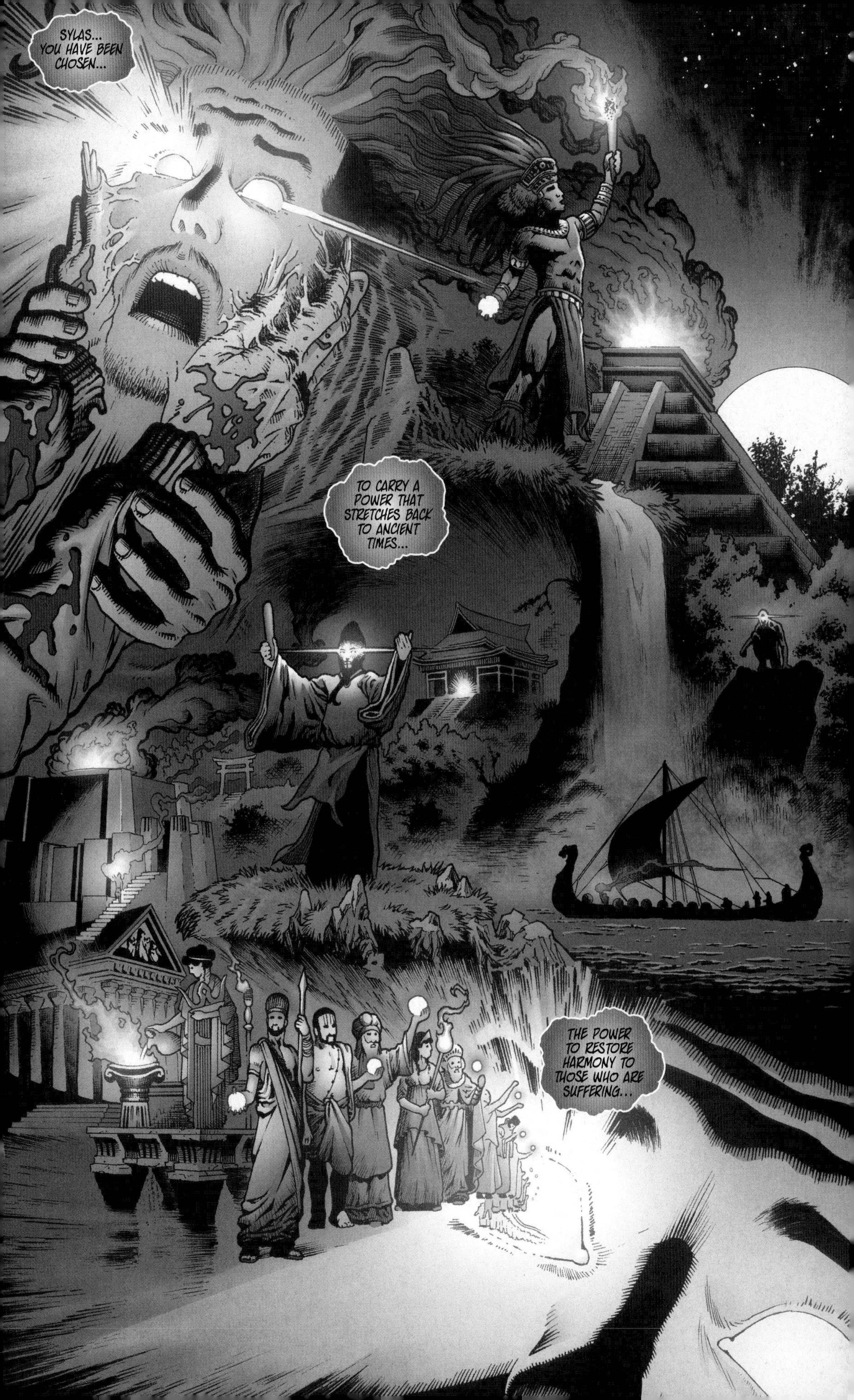

SYLAS... YOU HAVE BEEN CHOSEN...
TO CARRY A POWER THAT STRETCHES BACK TO ANCIENT TIMES...
THE POWER TO RESTORE HARMONY TO THOSE WHO ARE SUFFERING...

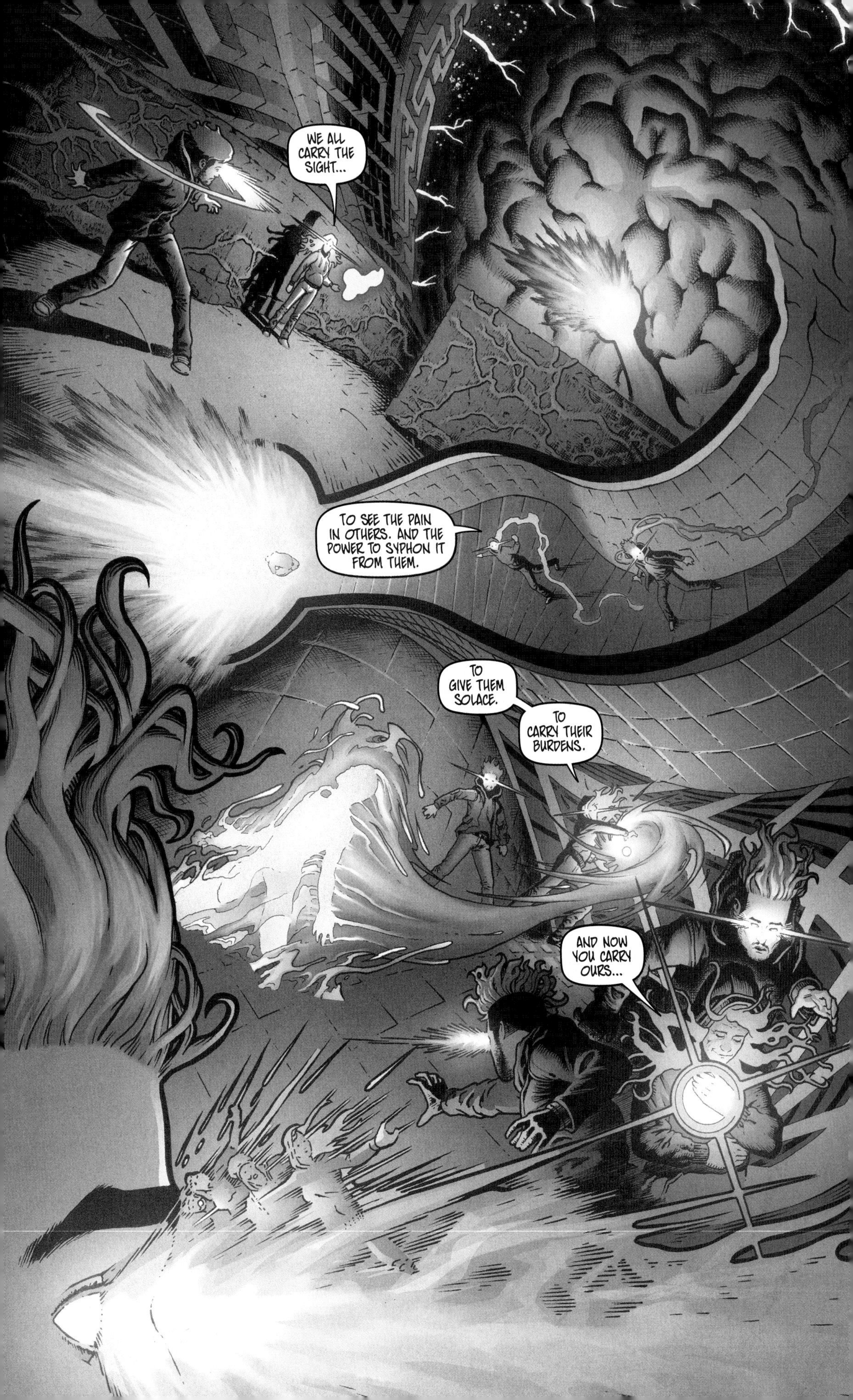
WE ALL CARRY THE SIGHT...
TO SEE THE PAIN IN OTHERS. AND THE POWER TO SYPHON IT FROM THEM.
TO GIVE THEM SOLACE.
TO CARRY THEIR BURDENS.
AND NOW YOU CARRY OURS...

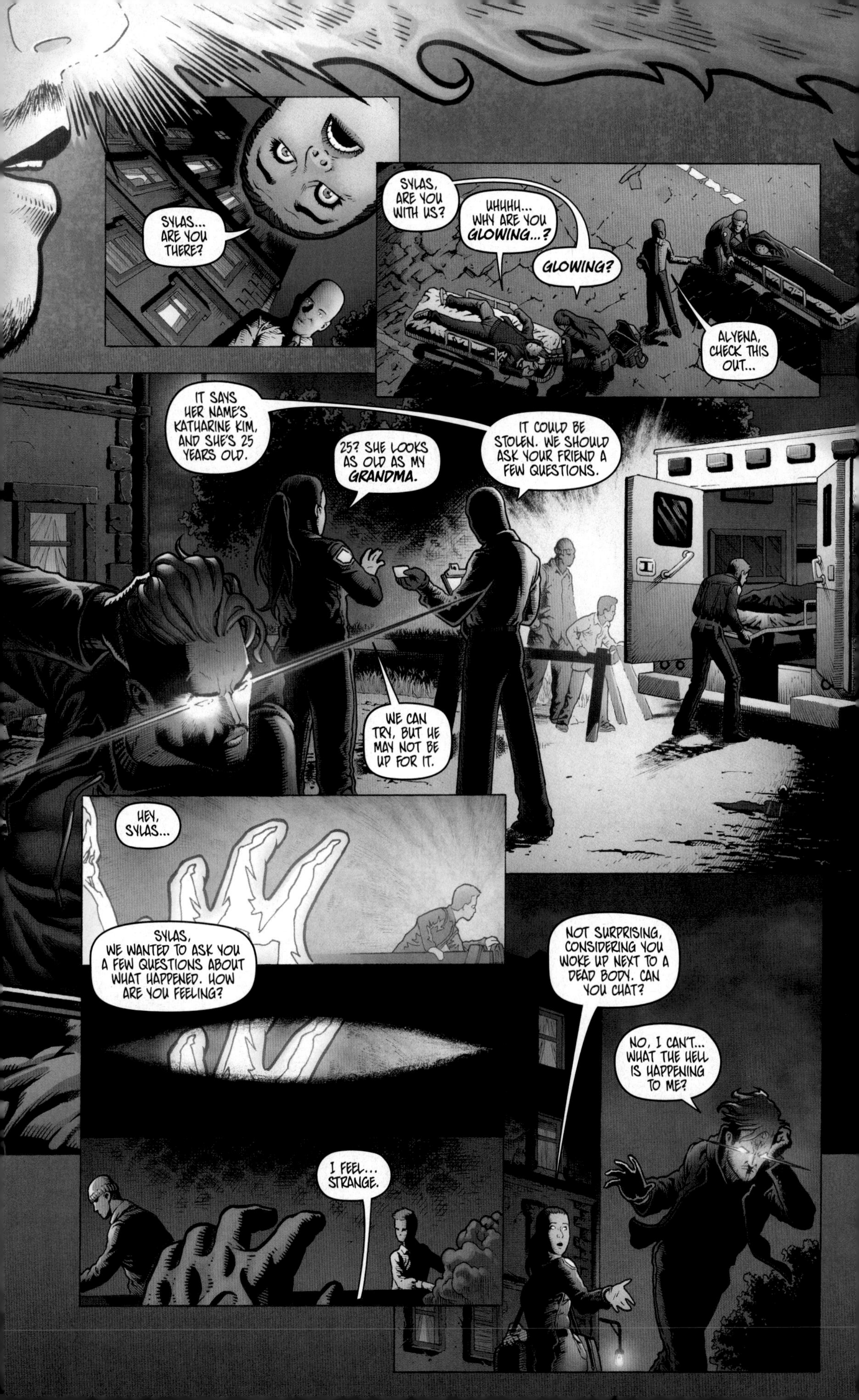
SYLAS... ARE YOU THERE?
SYLAS, ARE YOU WITH US?
UHHHH... WHY ARE YOU GLOWING...?
GLOWING?
ALYENA, CHECK THIS OUT...
IT SAYS HER NAME'S KATHARINE KIM, AND SHE'S 25 YEARS OLD.
25? SHE LOOKS AS OLD AS MY GRANDMA.
IT COULD BE STOLEN. WE SHOULD ASK YOUR FRIEND A FEW QUESTIONS.
WE CAN TRY, BUT HE MAY NOT BE UP FOR IT.
HEY, SYLAS...
SYLAS, WE WANTED TO ASK YOU A FEW QUESTIONS ABOUT WHAT HAPPENED. HOW ARE YOU FEELING?
I FEEL... STRANGE.
NOT SURPRISING, CONSIDERING YOU WOKE UP NEXT TO A DEAD BODY. CAN YOU CHAT?
NO, I CAN'T... WHAT THE HELL IS HAPPENING TO ME?

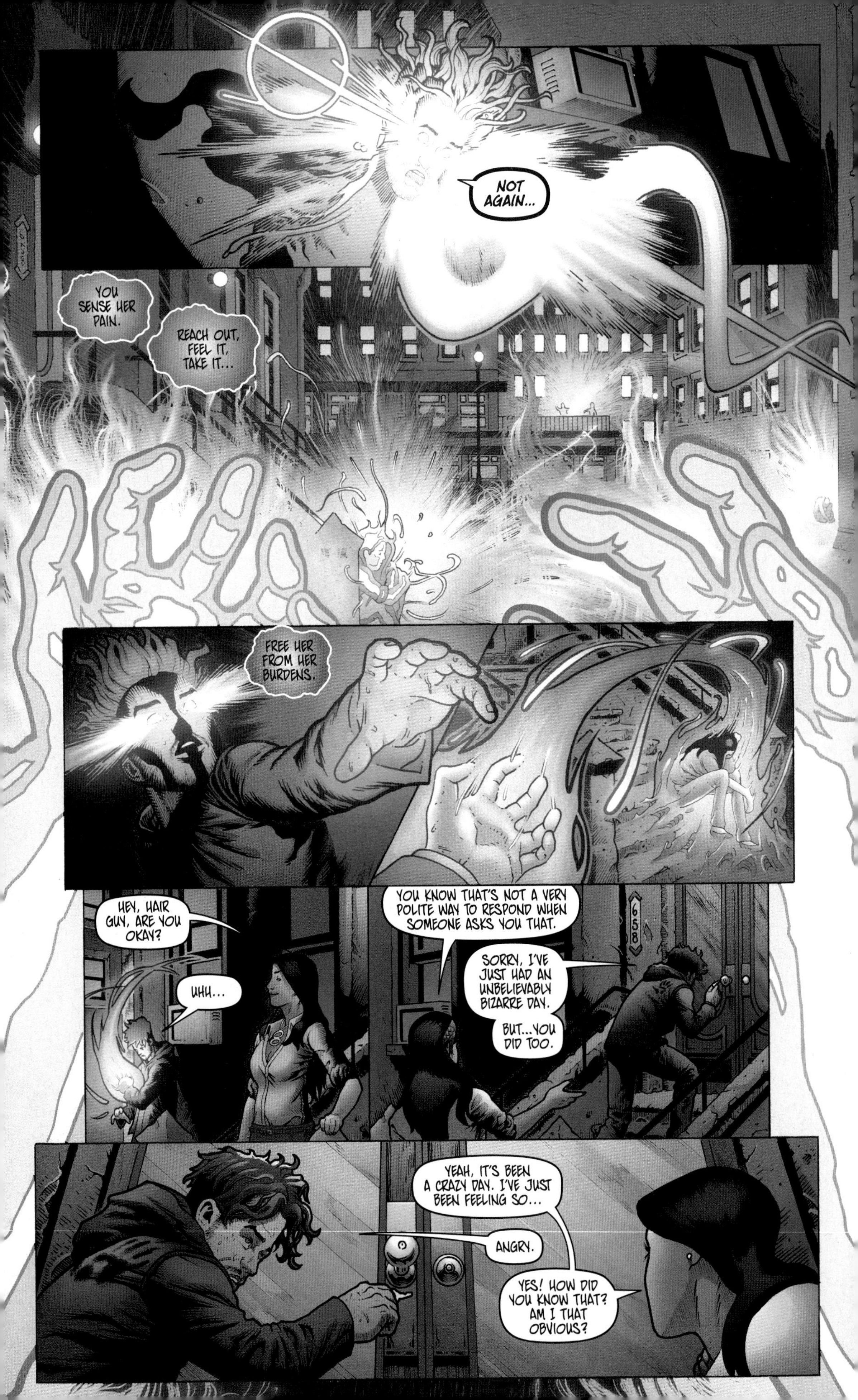
NOT AGAIN...
YOU SENSE HER PAIN.
REACH OUT, FEEL IT, TAKE IT...
FREE HER FROM HER BURDENS.
HEY, HAIR GUY, ARE YOU OKAY?
UHH...
YOU KNOW THAT'S NOT A VERY POLITE WAY TO RESPOND WHEN SOMEONE ASKS YOU THAT.
658
SORRY, I'VE JUST HAD AN UNBELIEVABLY BIZARRE DAY.
BUT...YOU DID TOO.
YEAH, IT'S BEEN A CRAZY DAY. I'VE JUST BEEN FEELING SO...
ANGRY.
YES! HOW DID YOU KNOW THAT? AM I THAT OBVIOUS?

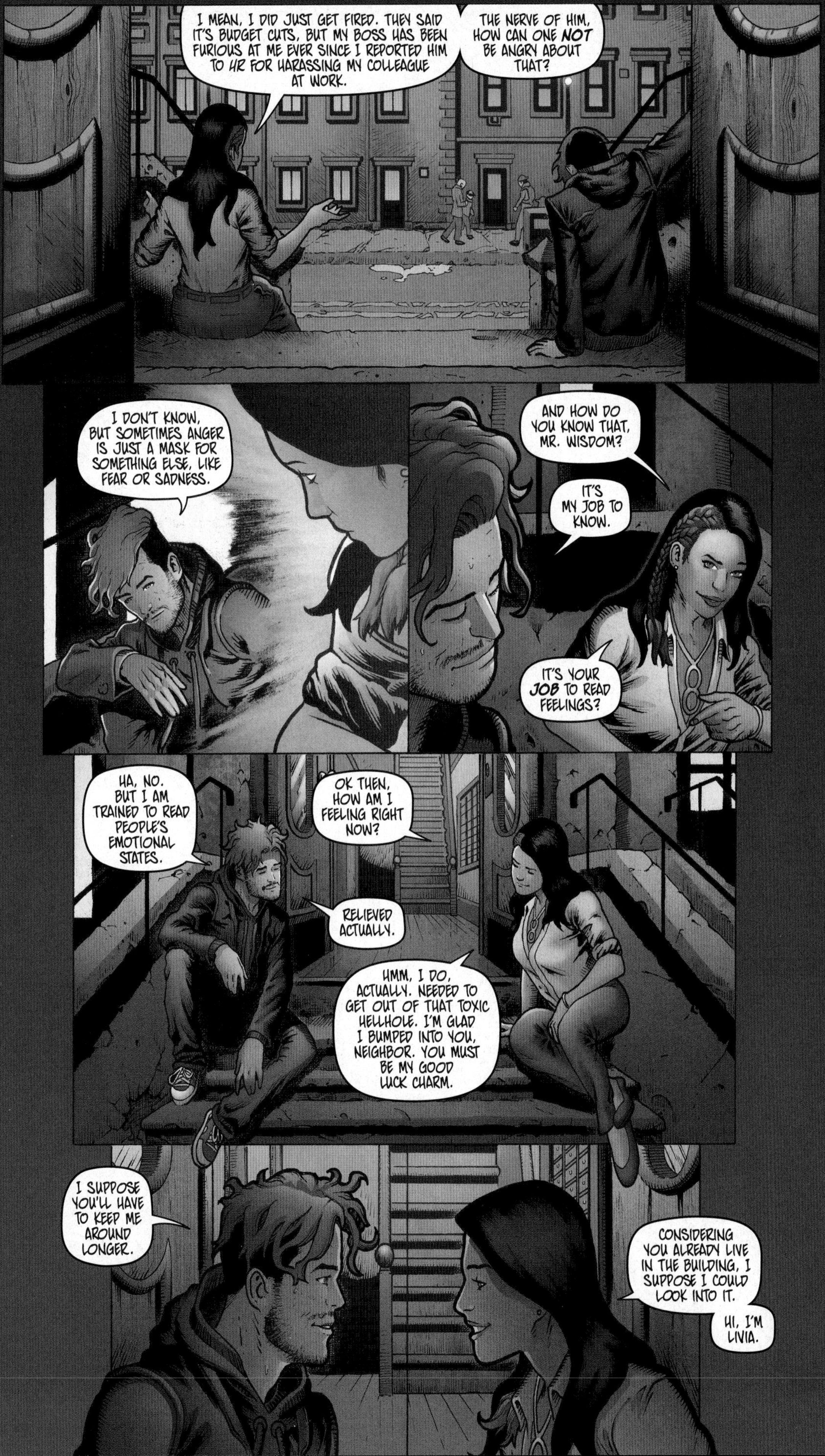
I MEAN, I DID JUST GET FIRED. THEY SAID IT'S BUDGET CUTS, BUT MY BOSS HAS BEEN FURIOUS AT ME EVER SINCE I REPORTED HIM TO HR FOR HARASSING MY COLLEAGUE AT WORK.
THE NERVE OF HIM, HOW CAN ONE **NOT** BE ANGRY ABOUT THAT?
I DON'T KNOW, BUT SOMETIMES ANGER IS JUST A MASK FOR SOMETHING ELSE, LIKE FEAR OR SADNESS.
AND HOW DO YOU KNOW THAT, MR. WISDOM?
IT'S MY JOB TO KNOW.
IT'S YOUR **JOB** TO READ FEELINGS?
HA, NO. BUT I AM TRAINED TO READ PEOPLE'S EMOTIONAL STATES.
OK THEN, HOW AM I FEELING RIGHT NOW?
RELIEVED ACTUALLY.
HMM, I DO, ACTUALLY. NEEDED TO GET OUT OF THAT TOXIC HELLHOLE. I'M GLAD I BUMPED INTO YOU, NEIGHBOR. YOU MUST BE MY GOOD LUCK CHARM.
I SUPPOSE YOU'LL HAVE TO KEEP ME AROUND LONGER.
CONSIDERING YOU ALREADY LIVE IN THE BUILDING, I SUPPOSE I COULD LOOK INTO IT.
HI, I'M LIVIA.

"THE NEXT FEW MONTHS WERE A BIT OF A BLUR.

OH MY GOD, JERRY, OH MY GOD...

IT'S OKAY. HE'S GOING TO BE JUST FINE. AND YOU WILL BE TOO.

"I NOW HAVE A GIRLFRIEND.

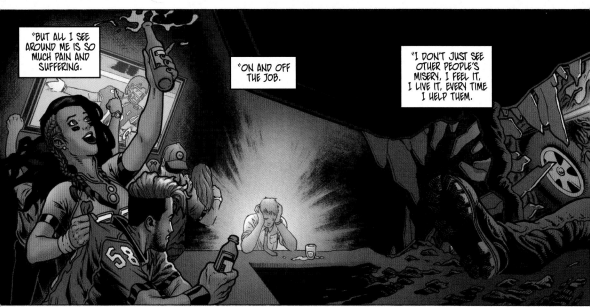

"BUT ALL I SEE AROUND ME IS SO MUCH PAIN AND SUFFERING.

"ON AND OFF THE JOB.

"I DON'T JUST SEE OTHER PEOPLE'S MISERY, I FEEL IT, I LIVE IT, EVERY TIME I HELP THEM.

"THERE'S JUST SO MUCH DARKNESS, AND THE MORE I HELP OTHERS, THE MORE IT EATS AWAY AT ME LIKE A PARASITE CONSUMING A HOST.

YOU DO NOT TALK TO ME LIKE THAT!

JUST GET THE HELL OFF ME! I DON'T WANT TO SEE YOU AGAIN!

"LIVIA TRIES TO KEEP ME UPBEAT, BUT SHE JUST WOULDN'T UNDERSTAND. NO ONE COULD.

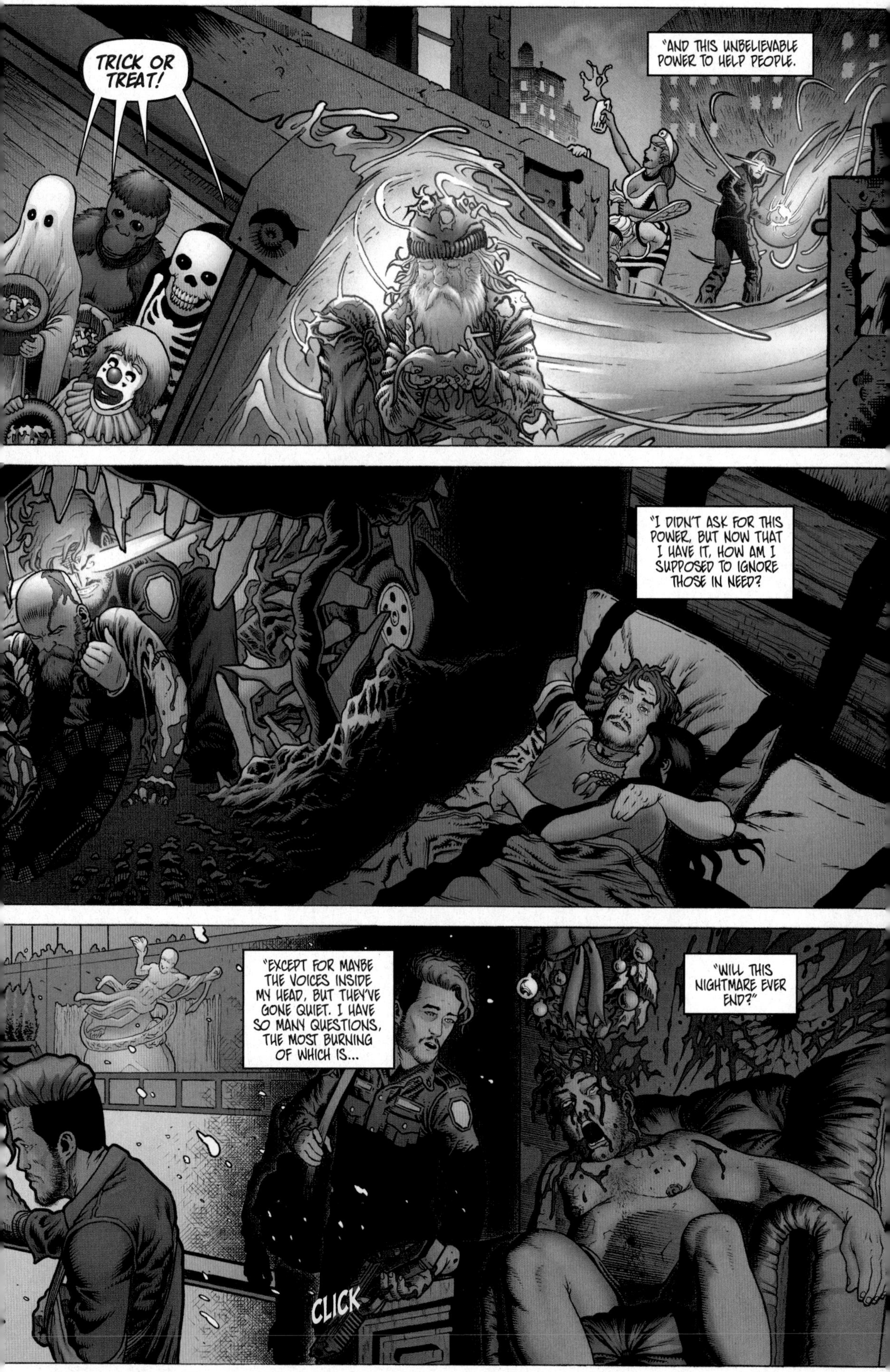
TRICK OR TREAT!
"AND THIS UNBELIEVABLE POWER TO HELP PEOPLE.
"I DIDN'T ASK FOR THIS POWER, BUT NOW THAT I HAVE IT, HOW AM I SUPPOSED TO IGNORE THOSE IN NEED?
"EXCEPT FOR MAYBE THE VOICES INSIDE MY HEAD, BUT THEY'VE GONE QUIET. I HAVE SO MANY QUESTIONS, THE MOST BURNING OF WHICH IS...
CLICK
"WILL THIS NIGHTMARE EVER END?"

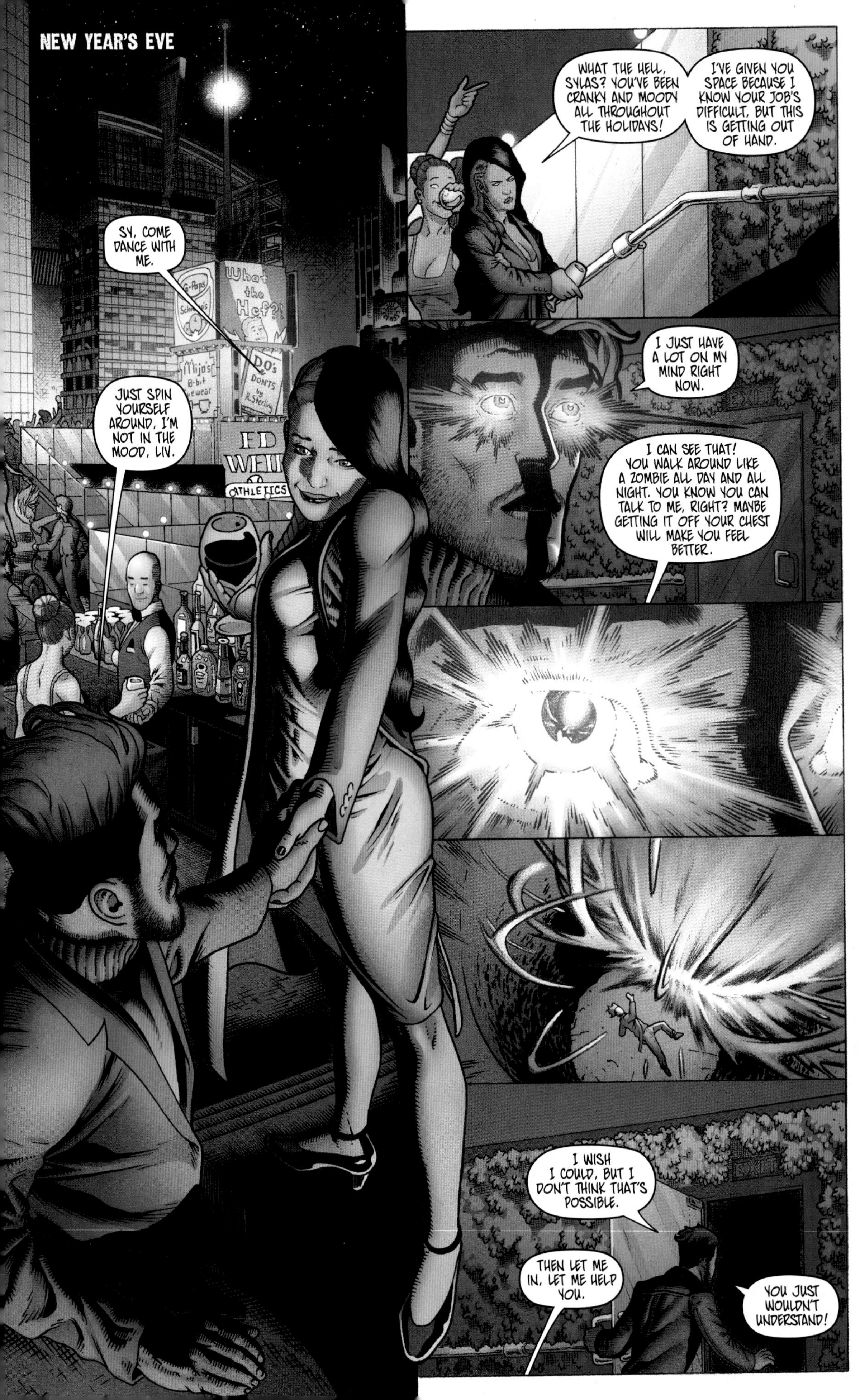
NEW YEAR'S EVE
SY, COME DANCE WITH ME.
JUST SPIN YOURSELF AROUND, I'M NOT IN THE MOOD, LIV.
What the Hef?!
DO's DONTS by R. Sterling
ED WEIN ATHLETICS
WHAT THE HELL, SYLAS? YOU'VE BEEN CRANKY AND MOODY ALL THROUGHOUT THE HOLIDAYS!
I'VE GIVEN YOU SPACE BECAUSE I KNOW YOUR JOB'S DIFFICULT, BUT THIS IS GETTING OUT OF HAND.
I JUST HAVE A LOT ON MY MIND RIGHT NOW.
I CAN SEE THAT! YOU WALK AROUND LIKE A ZOMBIE ALL DAY AND ALL NIGHT. YOU KNOW YOU CAN TALK TO ME, RIGHT? MAYBE GETTING IT OFF YOUR CHEST WILL MAKE YOU FEEL BETTER.
EXIT
I WISH I COULD, BUT I DON'T THINK THAT'S POSSIBLE.
THEN LET ME IN, LET ME HELP YOU.
YOU JUST WOULDN'T UNDERSTAND!

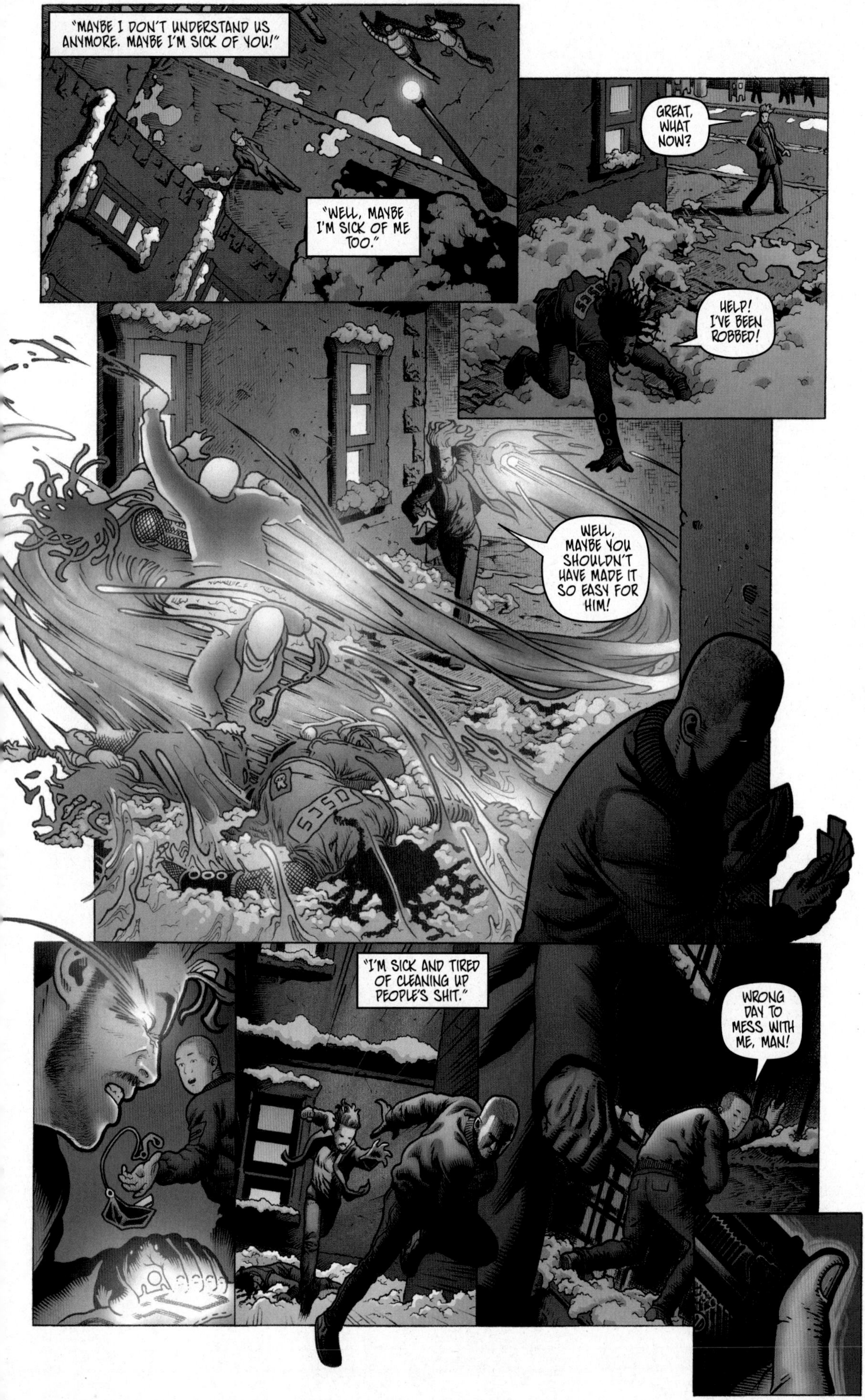
"MAYBE I DON'T UNDERSTAND US ANYMORE. MAYBE I'M SICK OF YOU!"
"WELL, MAYBE I'M SICK OF ME TOO."
GREAT, WHAT NOW?
HELP! I'VE BEEN ROBBED!
WELL, MAYBE YOU SHOULDN'T HAVE MADE IT SO EASY FOR HIM!
"I'M SICK AND TIRED OF CLEANING UP PEOPLE'S SHIT."
WRONG DAY TO MESS WITH ME, MAN!

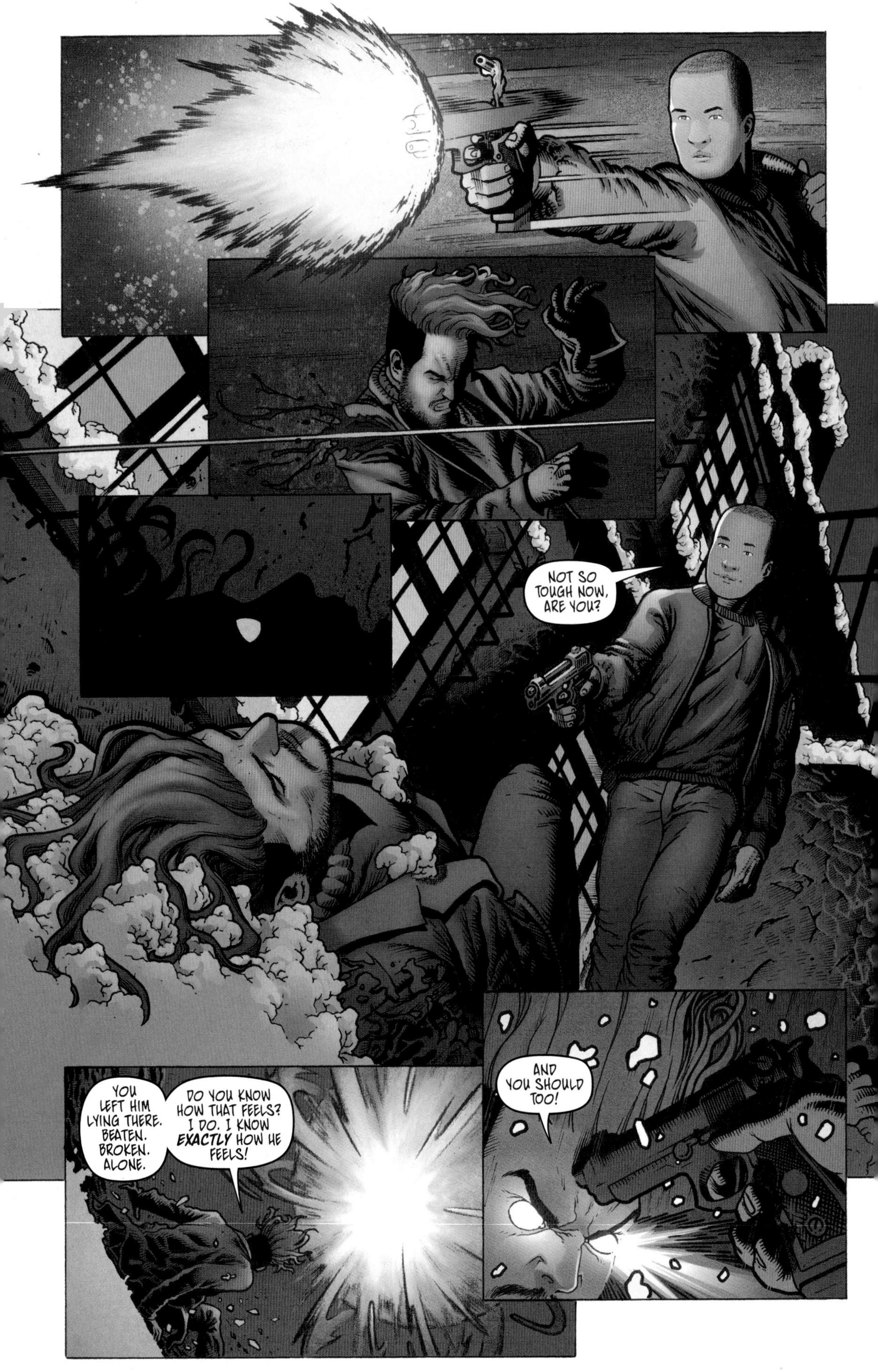
NOT SO TOUGH NOW, ARE YOU?
AND YOU SHOULD TOO!
YOU LEFT HIM LYING THERE. BEATEN. BROKEN. ALONE.
DO YOU KNOW HOW THAT FEELS? I DO. I KNOW *EXACTLY* HOW HE FEELS!

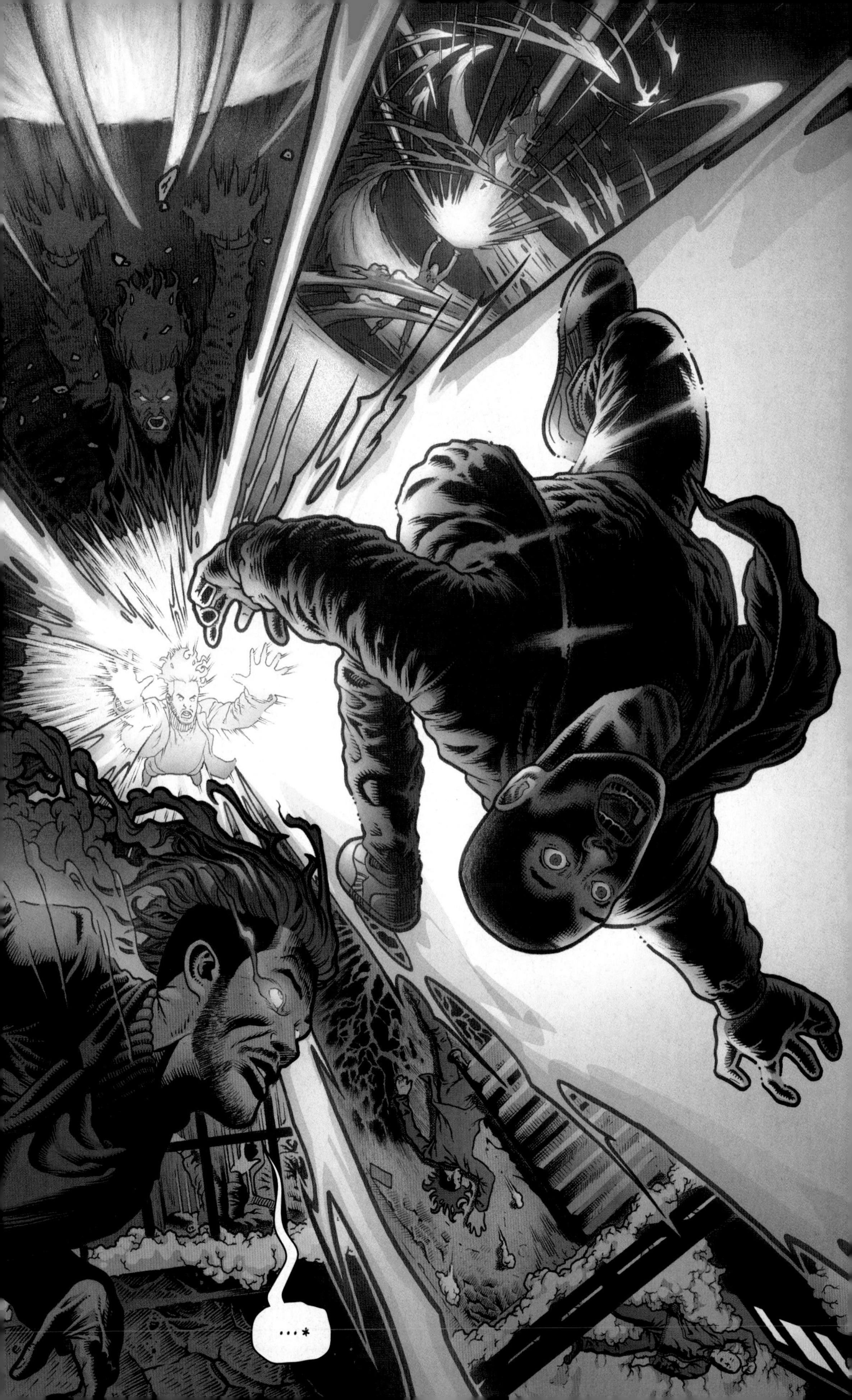
...*

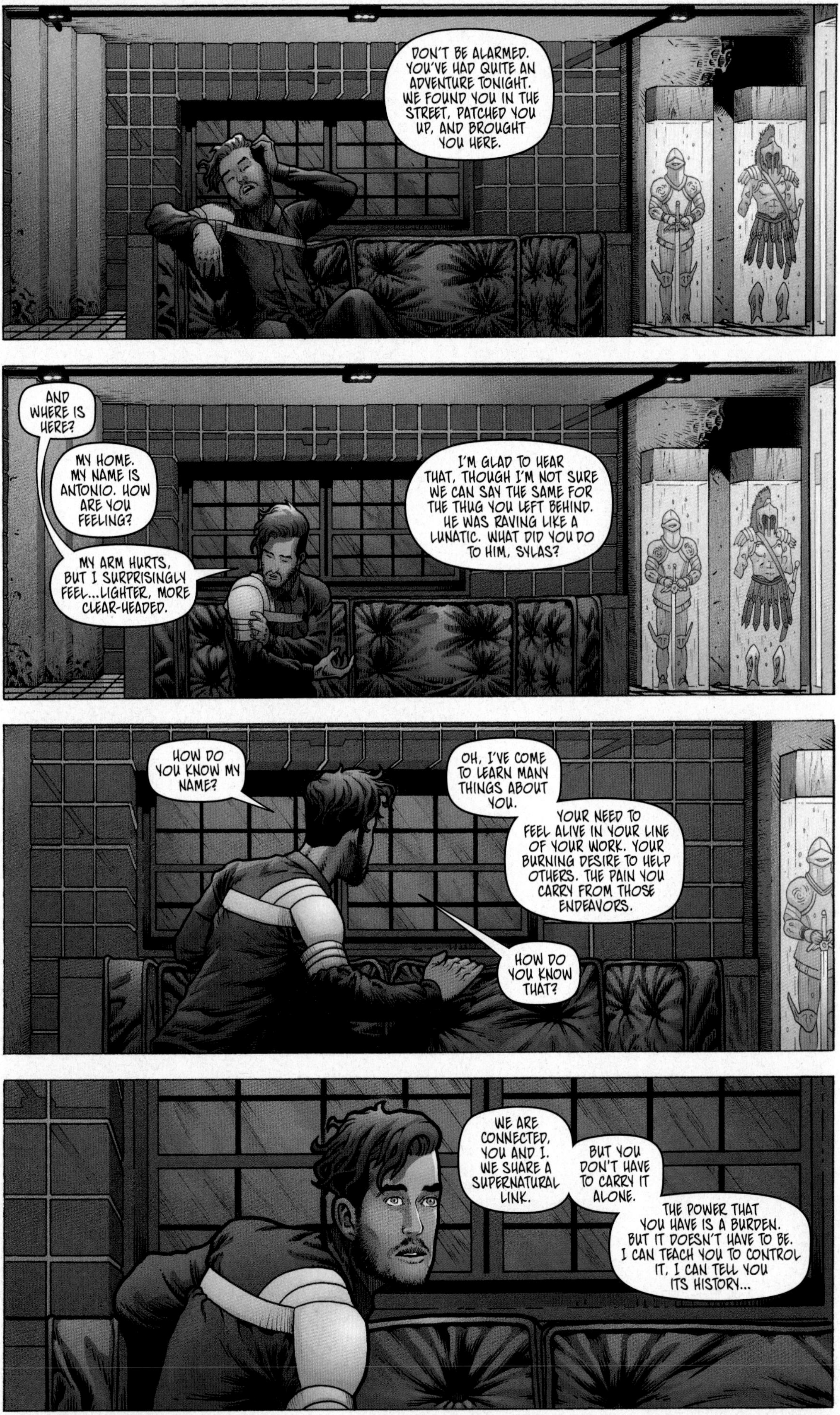
DON'T BE ALARMED. YOU'VE HAD QUITE AN ADVENTURE TONIGHT. WE FOUND YOU IN THE STREET, PATCHED YOU UP, AND BROUGHT YOU HERE.
AND WHERE IS HERE?
MY HOME. MY NAME IS ANTONIO. HOW ARE YOU FEELING?
MY ARM HURTS, BUT I SURPRISINGLY FEEL...LIGHTER, MORE CLEAR-HEADED.
I'M GLAD TO HEAR THAT, THOUGH I'M NOT SURE WE CAN SAY THE SAME FOR THE THUG YOU LEFT BEHIND. HE WAS RAVING LIKE A LUNATIC. WHAT DID YOU DO TO HIM, SYLAS?
HOW DO YOU KNOW MY NAME?
OH, I'VE COME TO LEARN MANY THINGS ABOUT YOU.
YOUR NEED TO FEEL ALIVE IN YOUR LINE OF YOUR WORK. YOUR BURNING DESIRE TO HELP OTHERS. THE PAIN YOU CARRY FROM THOSE ENDEAVORS.
HOW DO YOU KNOW THAT?
WE ARE CONNECTED, YOU AND I. WE SHARE A SUPERNATURAL LINK.
BUT YOU DON'T HAVE TO CARRY IT ALONE.
THE POWER THAT YOU HAVE IS A BURDEN. BUT IT DOESN'T HAVE TO BE. I CAN TEACH YOU TO CONTROL IT, I CAN TELL YOU ITS HISTORY...

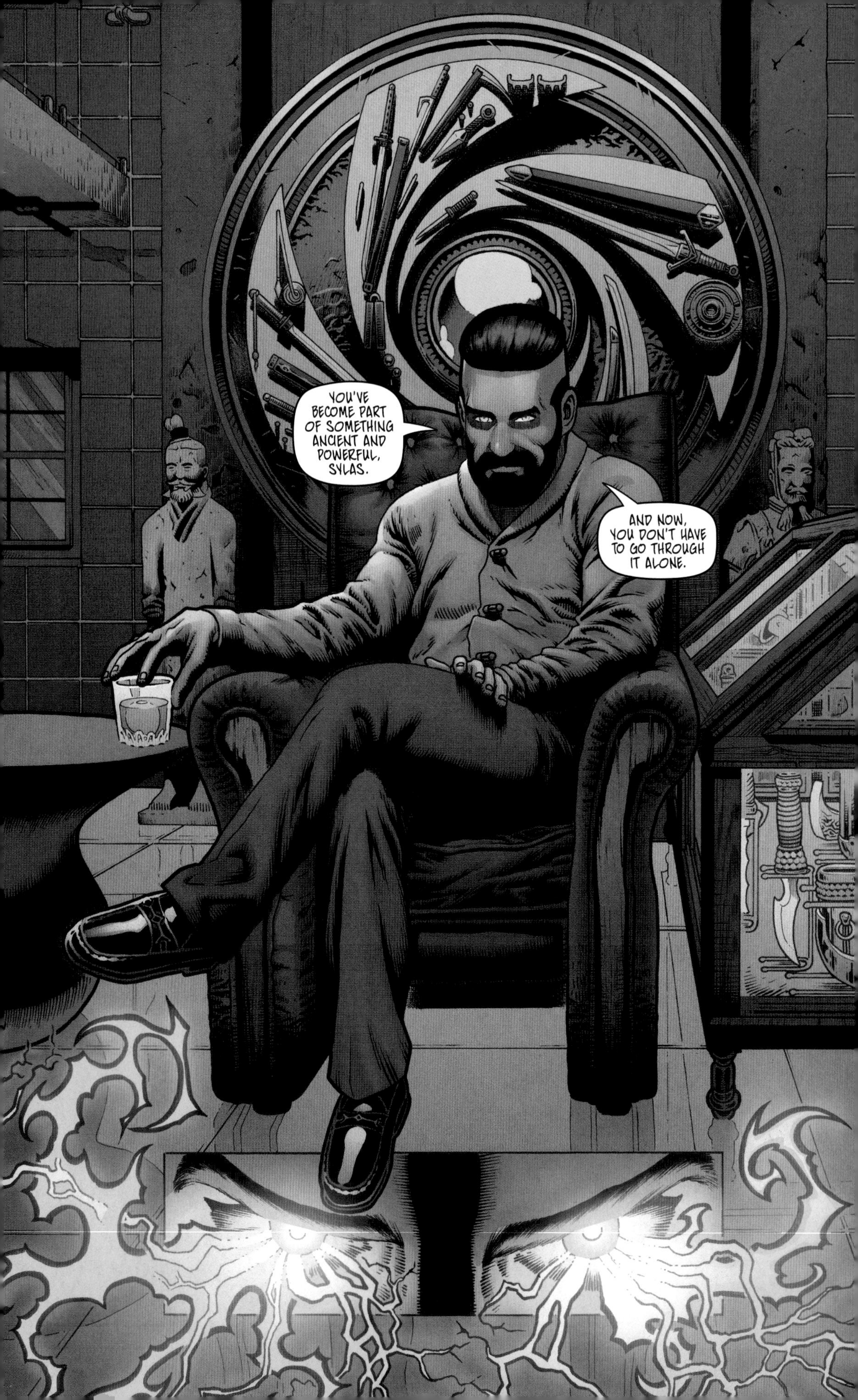
YOU'VE BECOME PART OF SOMETHING ANCIENT AND POWERFUL, SYLAS.
AND NOW, YOU DON'T HAVE TO GO THROUGH IT ALONE.

CHAPTER TWO

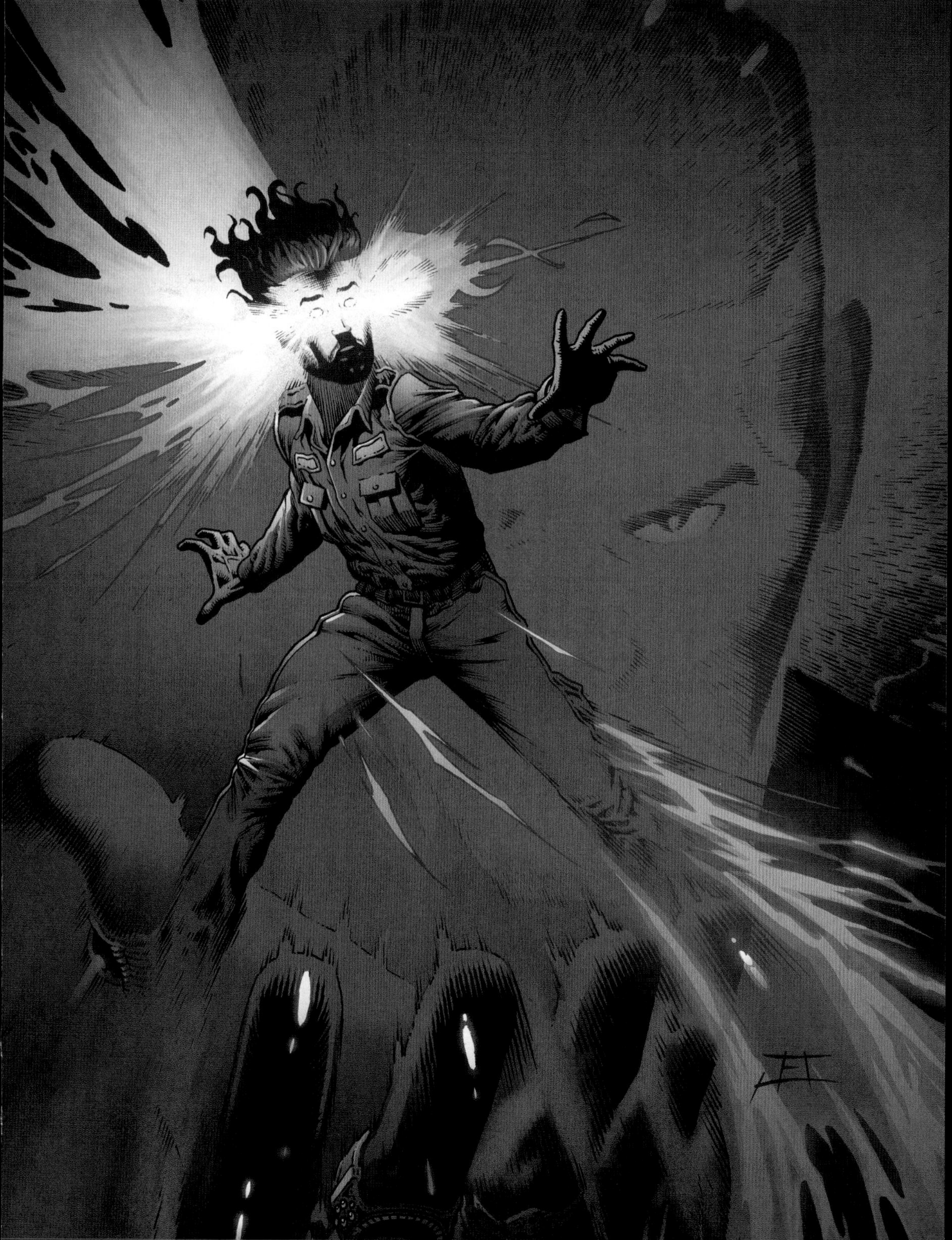

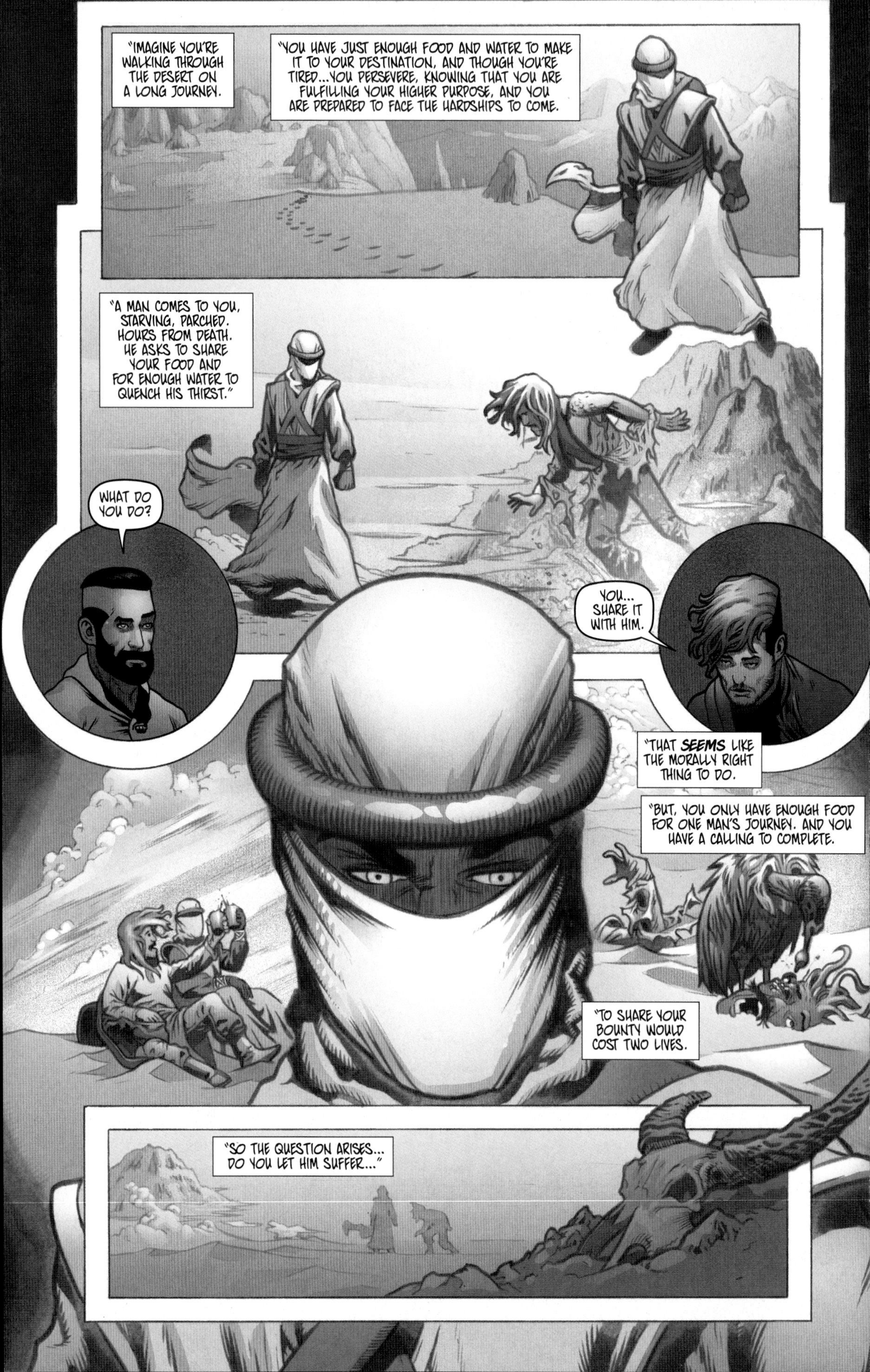
"IMAGINE YOU'RE WALKING THROUGH THE DESERT ON A LONG JOURNEY.
"YOU HAVE JUST ENOUGH FOOD AND WATER TO MAKE IT TO YOUR DESTINATION, AND THOUGH YOU'RE TIRED...YOU PERSEVERE, KNOWING THAT YOU ARE FULFILLING YOUR HIGHER PURPOSE, AND YOU ARE PREPARED TO FACE THE HARDSHIPS TO COME.
"A MAN COMES TO YOU, STARVING, PARCHED. HOURS FROM DEATH. HE ASKS TO SHARE YOUR FOOD AND FOR ENOUGH WATER TO QUENCH HIS THIRST."
WHAT DO YOU DO?
YOU... SHARE IT WITH HIM.
"THAT **SEEMS** LIKE THE MORALLY RIGHT THING TO DO.
"BUT, YOU ONLY HAVE ENOUGH FOOD FOR ONE MAN'S JOURNEY. AND YOU HAVE A CALLING TO COMPLETE.
"TO SHARE YOUR BOUNTY WOULD COST TWO LIVES.
"SO THE QUESTION ARISES... DO YOU LET HIM SUFFER..."

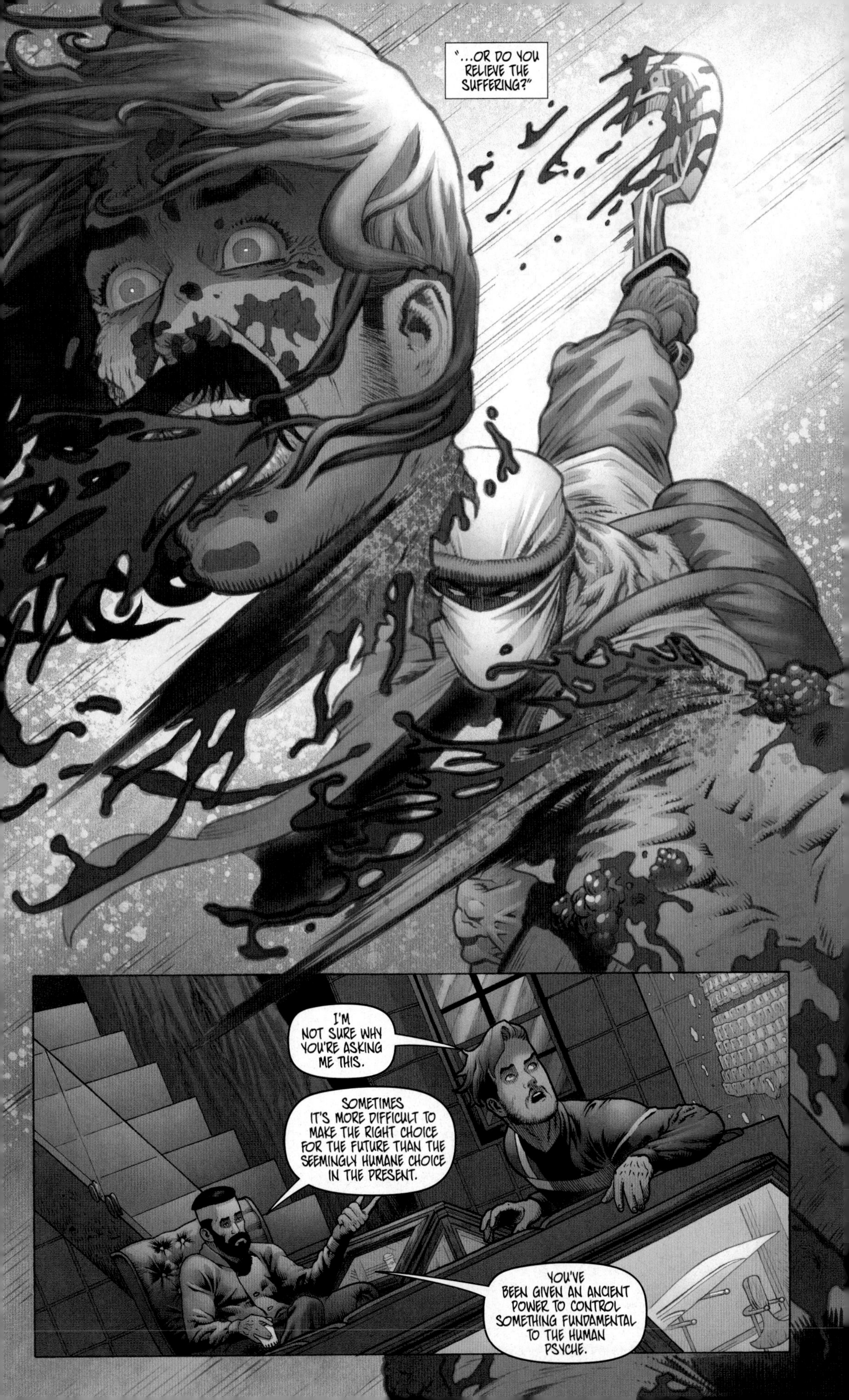
"...OR DO YOU RELIEVE THE SUFFERING?"
I'M NOT SURE WHY YOU'RE ASKING ME THIS.
SOMETIMES IT'S MORE DIFFICULT TO MAKE THE RIGHT CHOICE FOR THE FUTURE THAN THE SEEMINGLY HUMANE CHOICE IN THE PRESENT.
YOU'VE BEEN GIVEN AN ANCIENT POWER TO CONTROL SOMETHING FUNDAMENTAL TO THE HUMAN PSYCHE.

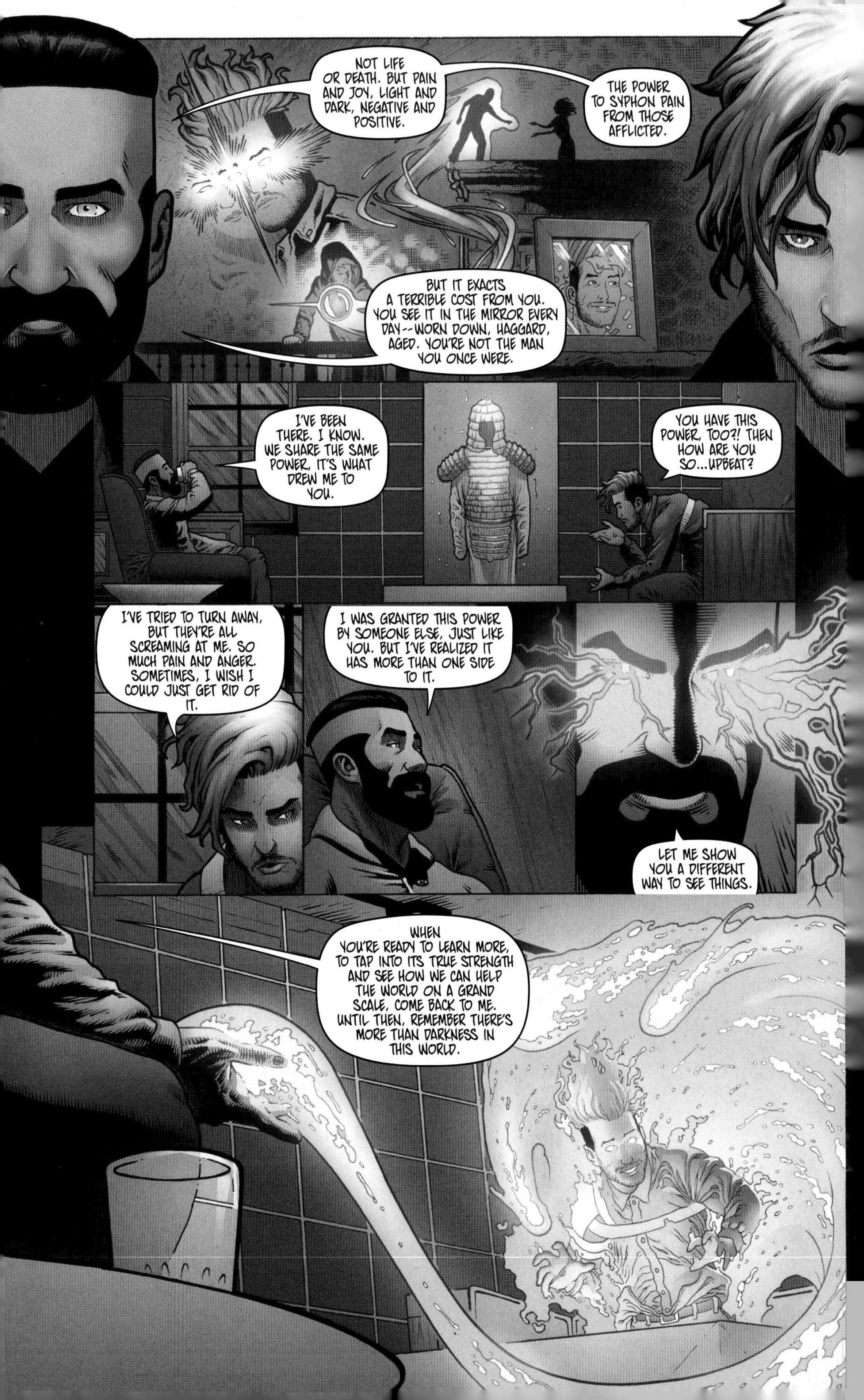
NOT LIFE OR DEATH. BUT PAIN AND JOY, LIGHT AND DARK, NEGATIVE AND POSITIVE.
THE POWER TO SYPHON PAIN FROM THOSE AFFLICTED.
BUT IT EXACTS A TERRIBLE COST FROM YOU. YOU SEE IT IN THE MIRROR EVERY DAY--WORN DOWN, HAGGARD, AGED. YOU'RE NOT THE MAN YOU ONCE WERE.
I'VE BEEN THERE. I KNOW. WE SHARE THE SAME POWER, IT'S WHAT DREW ME TO YOU.
YOU HAVE THIS POWER, TOO?! THEN HOW ARE YOU SO...UPBEAT?
I'VE TRIED TO TURN AWAY, BUT THEY'RE ALL SCREAMING AT ME. SO MUCH PAIN AND ANGER. SOMETIMES, I WISH I COULD JUST GET RID OF IT.
I WAS GRANTED THIS POWER BY SOMEONE ELSE, JUST LIKE YOU. BUT I'VE REALIZED IT HAS MORE THAN ONE SIDE TO IT.
LET ME SHOW YOU A DIFFERENT WAY TO SEE THINGS.
WHEN YOU'RE READY TO LEARN MORE, TO TAP INTO ITS TRUE STRENGTH AND SEE HOW WE CAN HELP THE WORLD ON A GRAND SCALE, COME BACK TO ME. UNTIL THEN, REMEMBER THERE'S MORE THAN DARKNESS IN THIS WORLD.

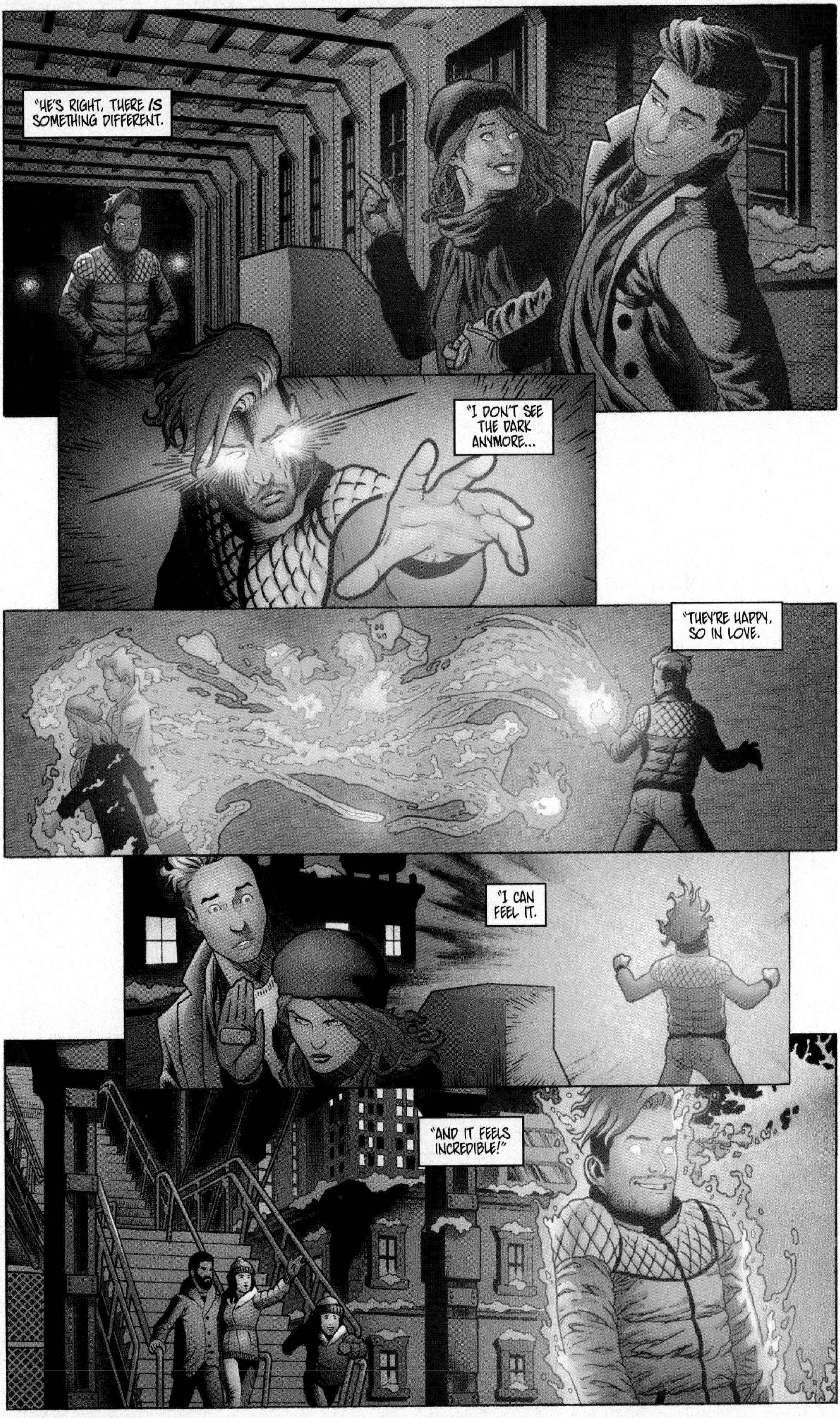
"HE'S RIGHT, THERE IS SOMETHING DIFFERENT.
"I DON'T SEE THE DARK ANYMORE...
"THEY'RE HAPPY, SO IN LOVE.
"I CAN FEEL IT.
"AND IT FEELS INCREDIBLE!"

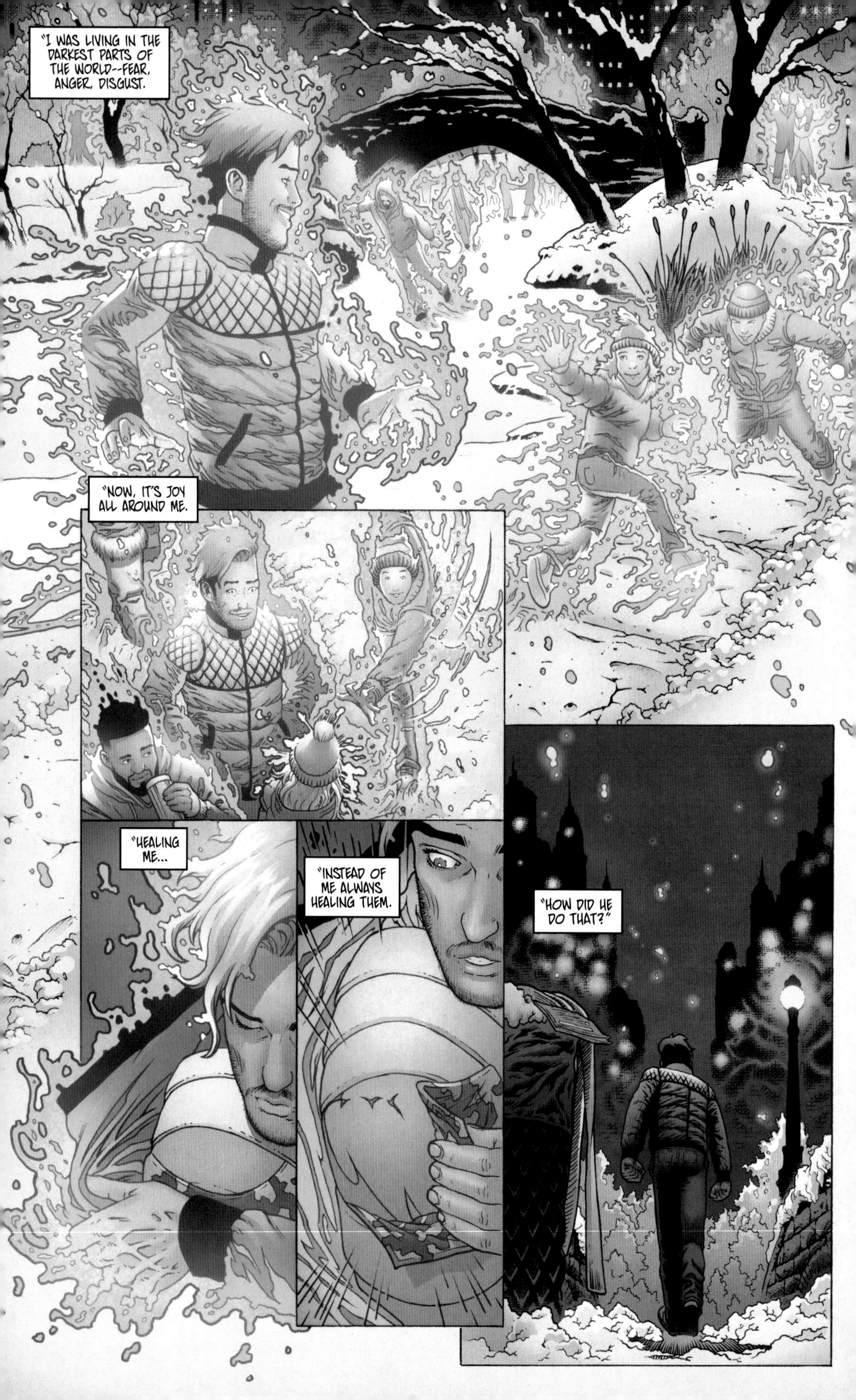
"I WAS LIVING IN THE DARKEST PARTS OF THE WORLD--FEAR, ANGER, DISGUST.
"NOW, IT'S JOY ALL AROUND ME.
"HEALING ME...
"INSTEAD OF ME ALWAYS HEALING THEM.
"HOW DID HE DO THAT?"

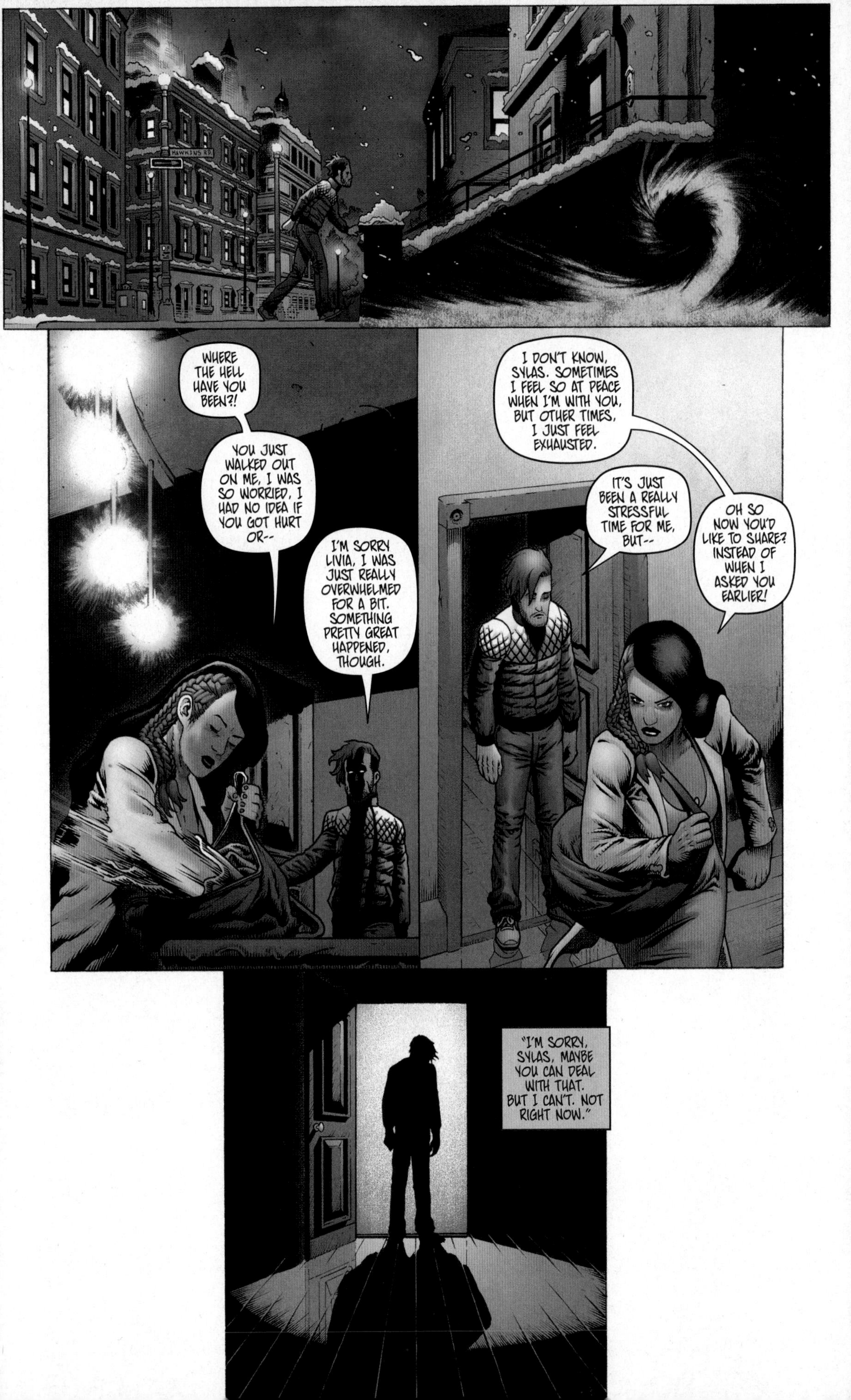
HAWKINS RD.
WHERE THE HELL HAVE YOU BEEN?!
YOU JUST WALKED OUT ON ME, I WAS SO WORRIED, I HAD NO IDEA IF YOU GOT HURT OR--
I'M SORRY LIVIA, I WAS JUST REALLY OVERWHELMED FOR A BIT. SOMETHING PRETTY GREAT HAPPENED, THOUGH.
I DON'T KNOW, SYLAS. SOMETIMES I FEEL SO AT PEACE WHEN I'M WITH YOU, BUT OTHER TIMES, I JUST FEEL EXHAUSTED.
IT'S JUST BEEN A REALLY STRESSFUL TIME FOR ME, BUT--
OH SO NOW YOU'D LIKE TO SHARE? INSTEAD OF WHEN I ASKED YOU EARLIER!
"I'M SORRY, SYLAS, MAYBE YOU CAN DEAL WITH THAT. BUT I CAN'T. NOT RIGHT NOW."

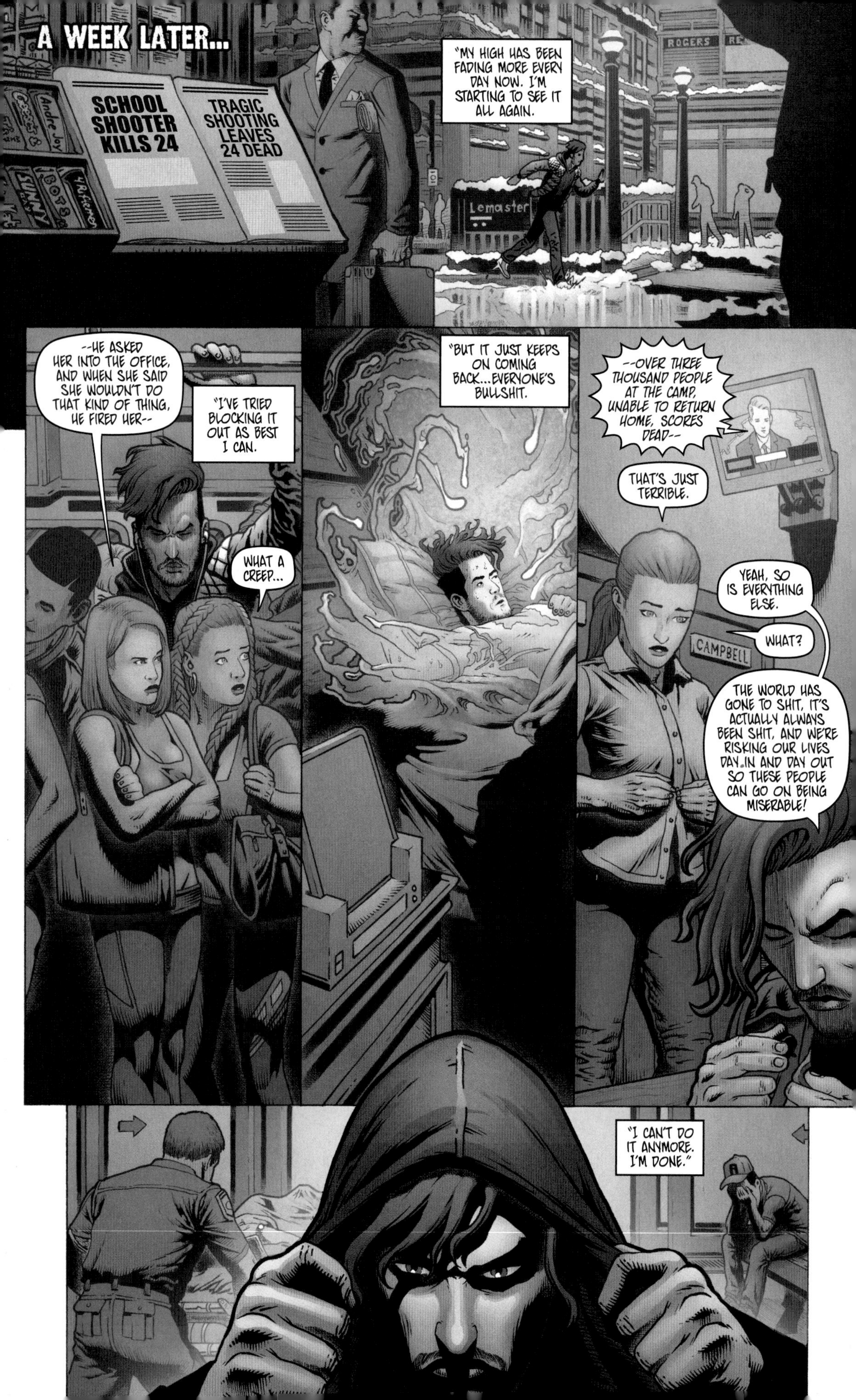
A WEEK LATER...
SCHOOL SHOOTER KILLS 24
TRAGIC SHOOTING LEAVES 24 DEAD
"MY HIGH HAS BEEN FADING MORE EVERY DAY NOW. I'M STARTING TO SEE IT ALL AGAIN.
ROGERS
Lemaster
--HE ASKED HER INTO THE OFFICE, AND WHEN SHE SAID SHE WOULDN'T DO THAT KIND OF THING, HE FIRED HER--
"I'VE TRIED BLOCKING IT OUT AS BEST I CAN.
WHAT A CREEP...
"BUT IT JUST KEEPS ON COMING BACK...EVERYONE'S BULLSHIT.
--OVER THREE THOUSAND PEOPLE AT THE CAMP, UNABLE TO RETURN HOME, SCORES DEAD--
THAT'S JUST TERRIBLE.
YEAH, SO IS EVERYTHING ELSE.
WHAT?
CAMPBELL
THE WORLD HAS GONE TO SHIT, IT'S ACTUALLY ALWAYS BEEN SHIT, AND WE'RE RISKING OUR LIVES DAY IN AND DAY OUT SO THESE PEOPLE CAN GO ON BEING MISERABLE!
"I CAN'T DO IT ANYMORE. I'M DONE."

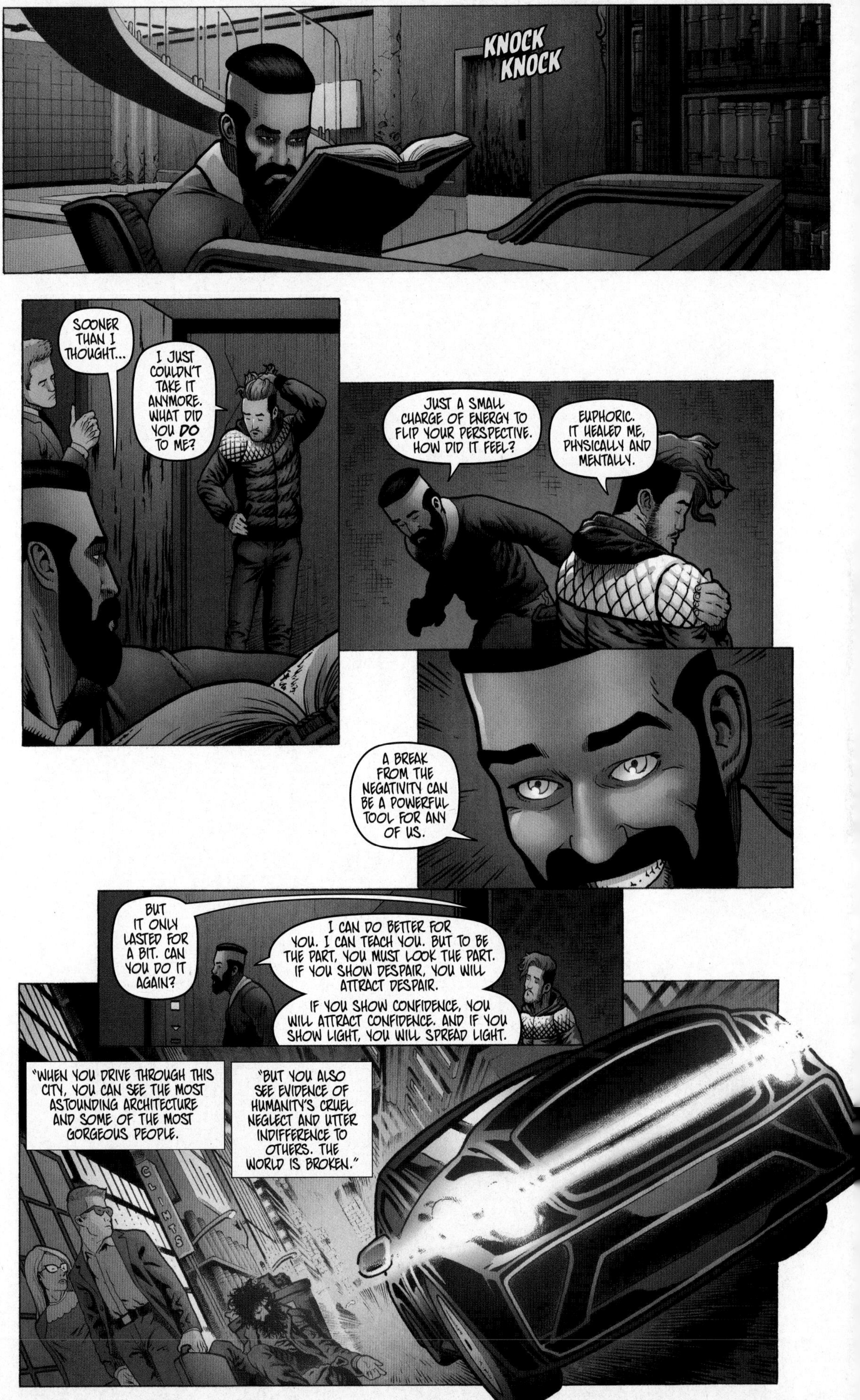
KNOCK KNOCK
SOONER THAN I THOUGHT...
I JUST COULDN'T TAKE IT ANYMORE. WHAT DID YOU DO TO ME?
JUST A SMALL CHARGE OF ENERGY TO FLIP YOUR PERSPECTIVE. HOW DID IT FEEL?
EUPHORIC. IT HEALED ME, PHYSICALLY AND MENTALLY.
A BREAK FROM THE NEGATIVITY CAN BE A POWERFUL TOOL FOR ANY OF US.
BUT IT ONLY LASTED FOR A BIT. CAN YOU DO IT AGAIN?
I CAN DO BETTER FOR YOU. I CAN TEACH YOU. BUT TO BE THE PART, YOU MUST LOOK THE PART. IF YOU SHOW DESPAIR, YOU WILL ATTRACT DESPAIR.
IF YOU SHOW CONFIDENCE, YOU WILL ATTRACT CONFIDENCE. AND IF YOU SHOW LIGHT, YOU WILL SPREAD LIGHT.
"WHEN YOU DRIVE THROUGH THIS CITY, YOU CAN SEE THE MOST ASTOUNDING ARCHITECTURE AND SOME OF THE MOST GORGEOUS PEOPLE.
"BUT YOU ALSO SEE EVIDENCE OF HUMANITY'S CRUEL NEGLECT AND UTTER INDIFFERENCE TO OTHERS. THE WORLD IS BROKEN."

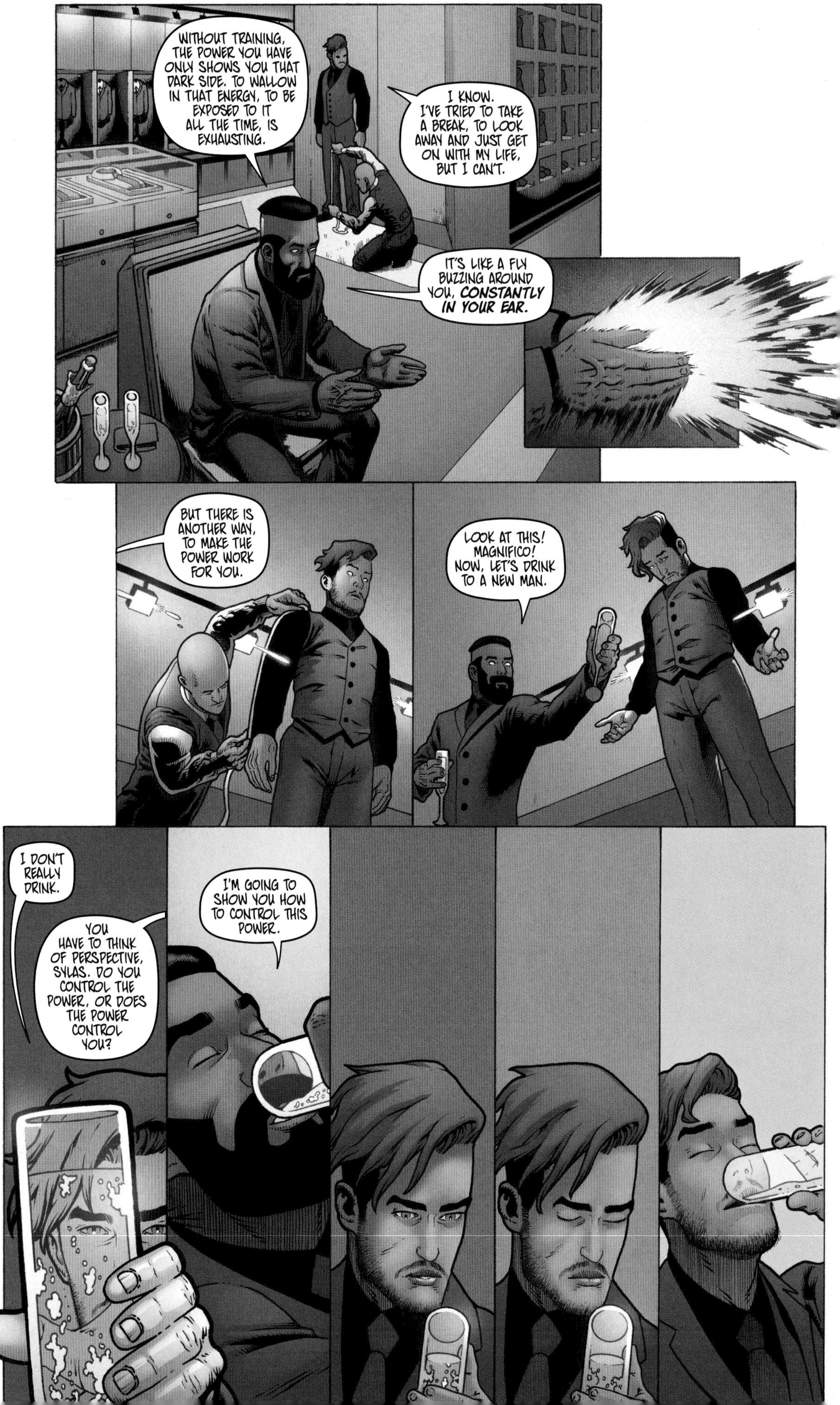
WITHOUT TRAINING, THE POWER YOU HAVE ONLY SHOWS YOU THAT DARK SIDE. TO WALLOW IN THAT ENERGY, TO BE EXPOSED TO IT ALL THE TIME, IS EXHAUSTING.
I KNOW. I'VE TRIED TO TAKE A BREAK, TO LOOK AWAY AND JUST GET ON WITH MY LIFE, BUT I CAN'T.
IT'S LIKE A FLY BUZZING AROUND YOU, **CONSTANTLY IN YOUR EAR.**
BUT THERE IS ANOTHER WAY, TO MAKE THE POWER WORK FOR YOU.
LOOK AT THIS! MAGNIFICO! NOW, LET'S DRINK TO A NEW MAN.
I DON'T REALLY DRINK.
YOU HAVE TO THINK OF PERSPECTIVE, SYLAS. DO YOU CONTROL THE POWER, OR DOES THE POWER CONTROL YOU?
I'M GOING TO SHOW YOU HOW TO CONTROL THIS POWER.

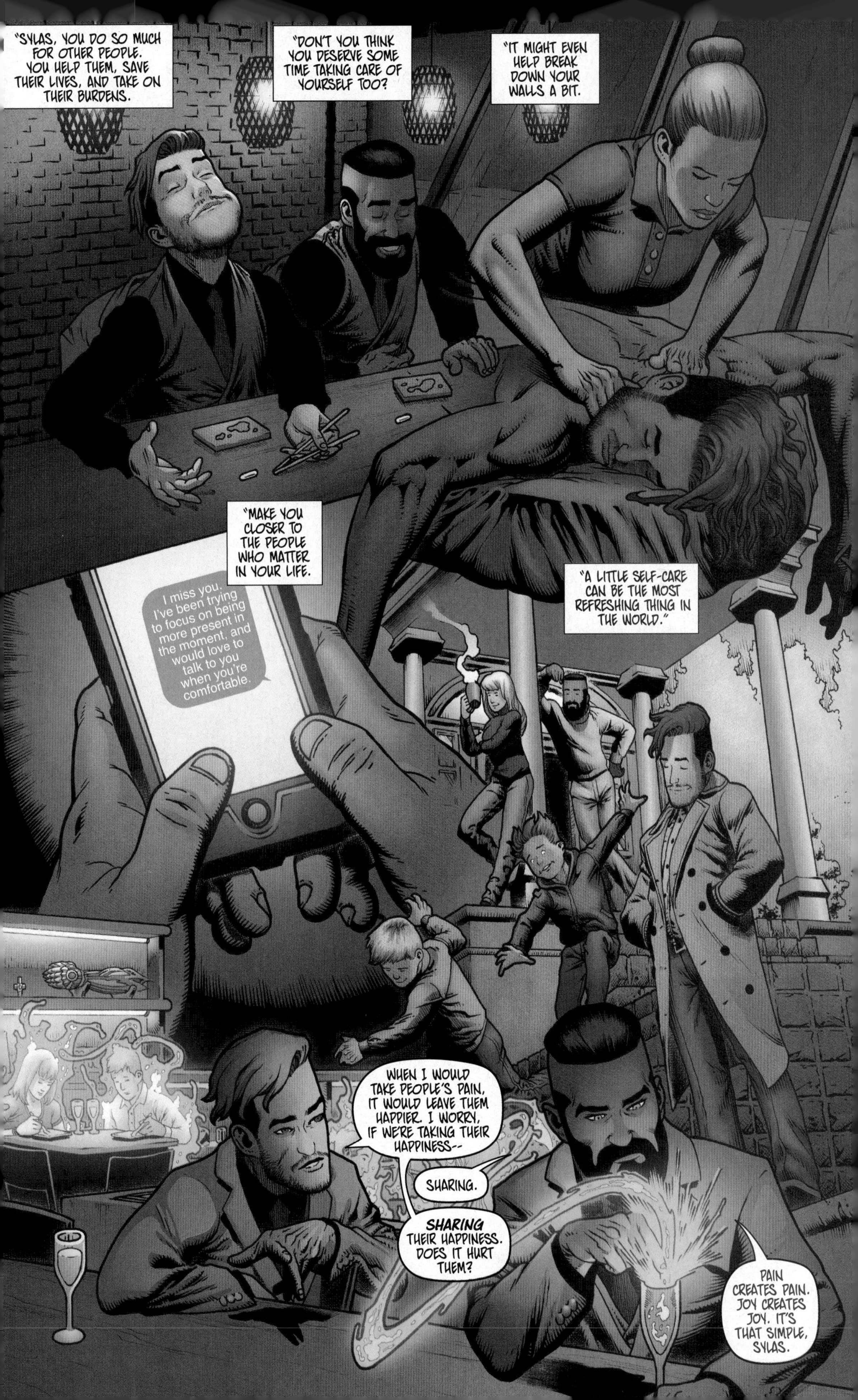
"SYLAS, YOU DO SO MUCH FOR OTHER PEOPLE. YOU HELP THEM, SAVE THEIR LIVES, AND TAKE ON THEIR BURDENS.
"DON'T YOU THINK YOU DESERVE SOME TIME TAKING CARE OF YOURSELF TOO?
"IT MIGHT EVEN HELP BREAK DOWN YOUR WALLS A BIT.
"MAKE YOU CLOSER TO THE PEOPLE WHO MATTER IN YOUR LIFE.
I miss you. I've been trying to focus on being more present in the moment, and would love to talk to you when you're comfortable.
"A LITTLE SELF-CARE CAN BE THE MOST REFRESHING THING IN THE WORLD."
WHEN I WOULD TAKE PEOPLE'S PAIN, IT WOULD LEAVE THEM HAPPIER. I WORRY, IF WE'RE TAKING THEIR HAPPINESS--
SHARING.
SHARING THEIR HAPPINESS. DOES IT HURT THEM?
PAIN CREATES PAIN. JOY CREATES JOY. IT'S THAT SIMPLE, SYLAS.

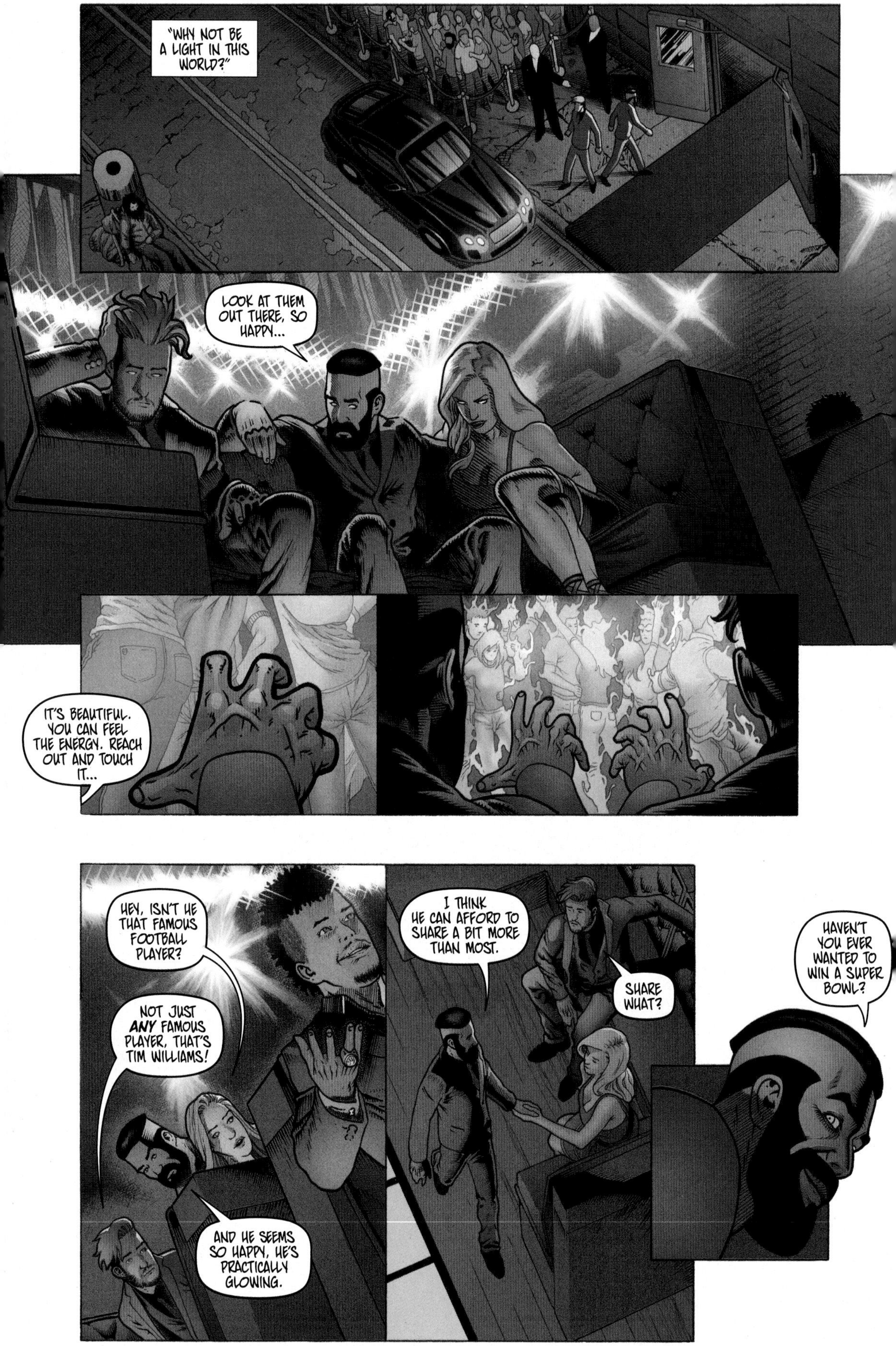
"WHY NOT BE A LIGHT IN THIS WORLD?"
LOOK AT THEM OUT THERE, SO HAPPY...
IT'S BEAUTIFUL. YOU CAN FEEL THE ENERGY. REACH OUT AND TOUCH IT...
HEY, ISN'T HE THAT FAMOUS FOOTBALL PLAYER?
NOT JUST **ANY** FAMOUS PLAYER, THAT'S TIM WILLIAMS!
AND HE SEEMS SO HAPPY, HE'S PRACTICALLY GLOWING.
I THINK HE CAN AFFORD TO SHARE A BIT MORE THAN MOST.
SHARE WHAT?
HAVEN'T YOU EVER WANTED TO WIN A SUPER BOWL?

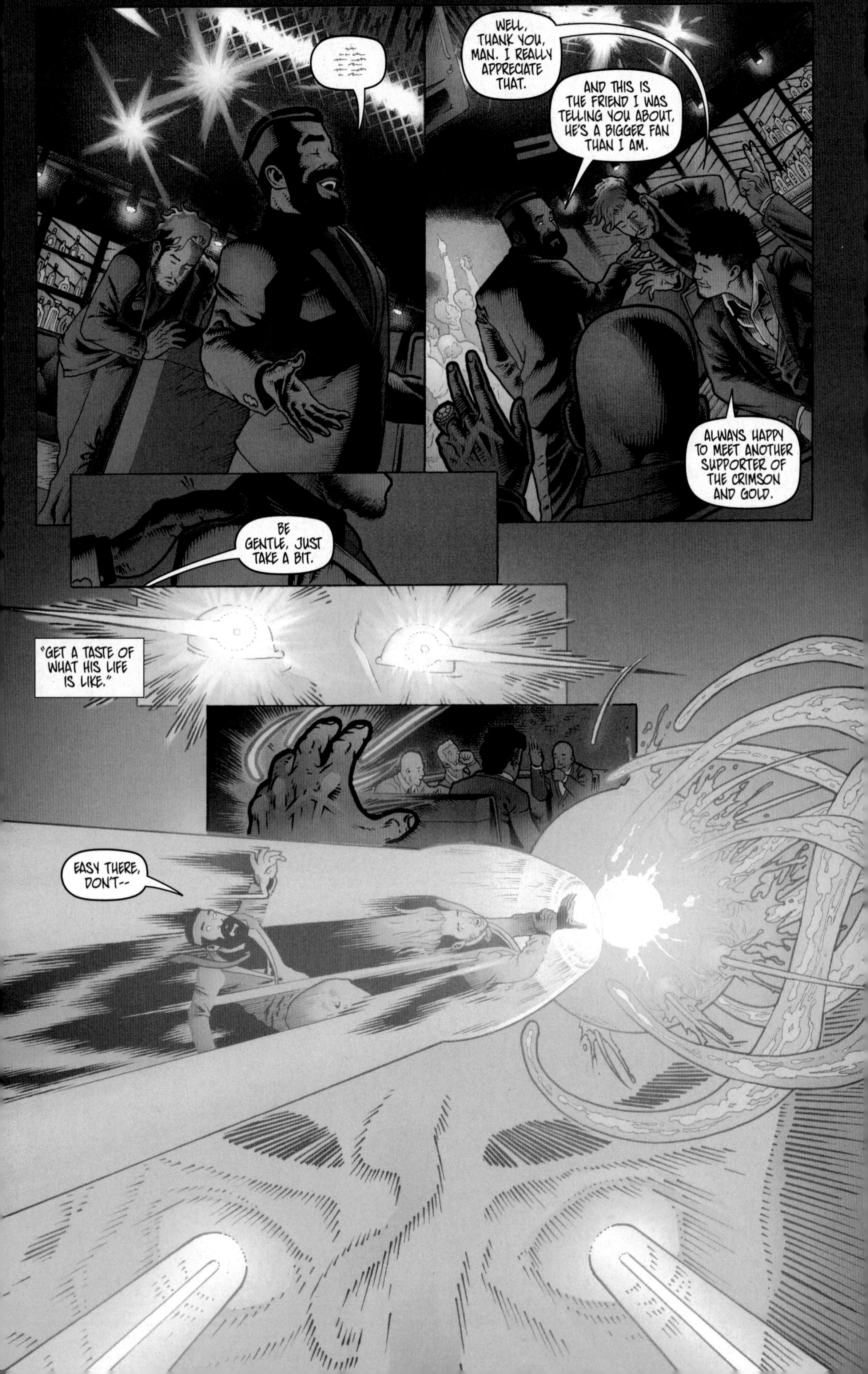
WELL, THANK YOU, MAN. I REALLY APPRECIATE THAT.
AND THIS IS THE FRIEND I WAS TELLING YOU ABOUT, HE'S A BIGGER FAN THAN I AM.
ALWAYS HAPPY TO MEET ANOTHER SUPPORTER OF THE CRIMSON AND GOLD.
BE GENTLE, JUST TAKE A BIT.
"GET A TASTE OF WHAT HIS LIFE IS LIKE."
EASY THERE, DON'T--

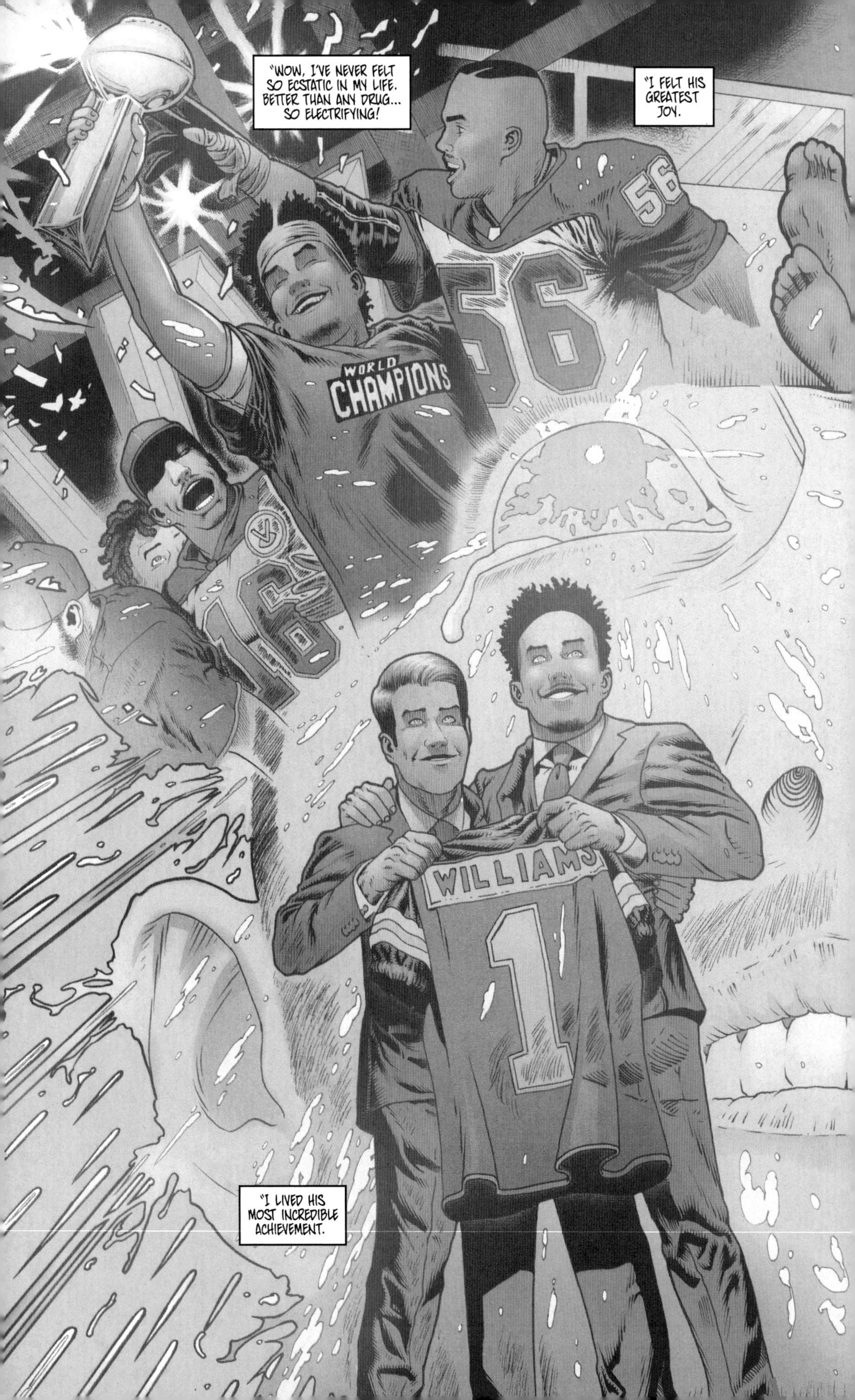
"WOW, I'VE NEVER FELT SO ECSTATIC IN MY LIFE. BETTER THAN ANY DRUG... SO ELECTRIFYING!
"I FELT HIS GREATEST JOY.
WORLD CHAMPIONS
"I LIVED HIS MOST INCREDIBLE ACHIEVEMENT.
WILLIAMS

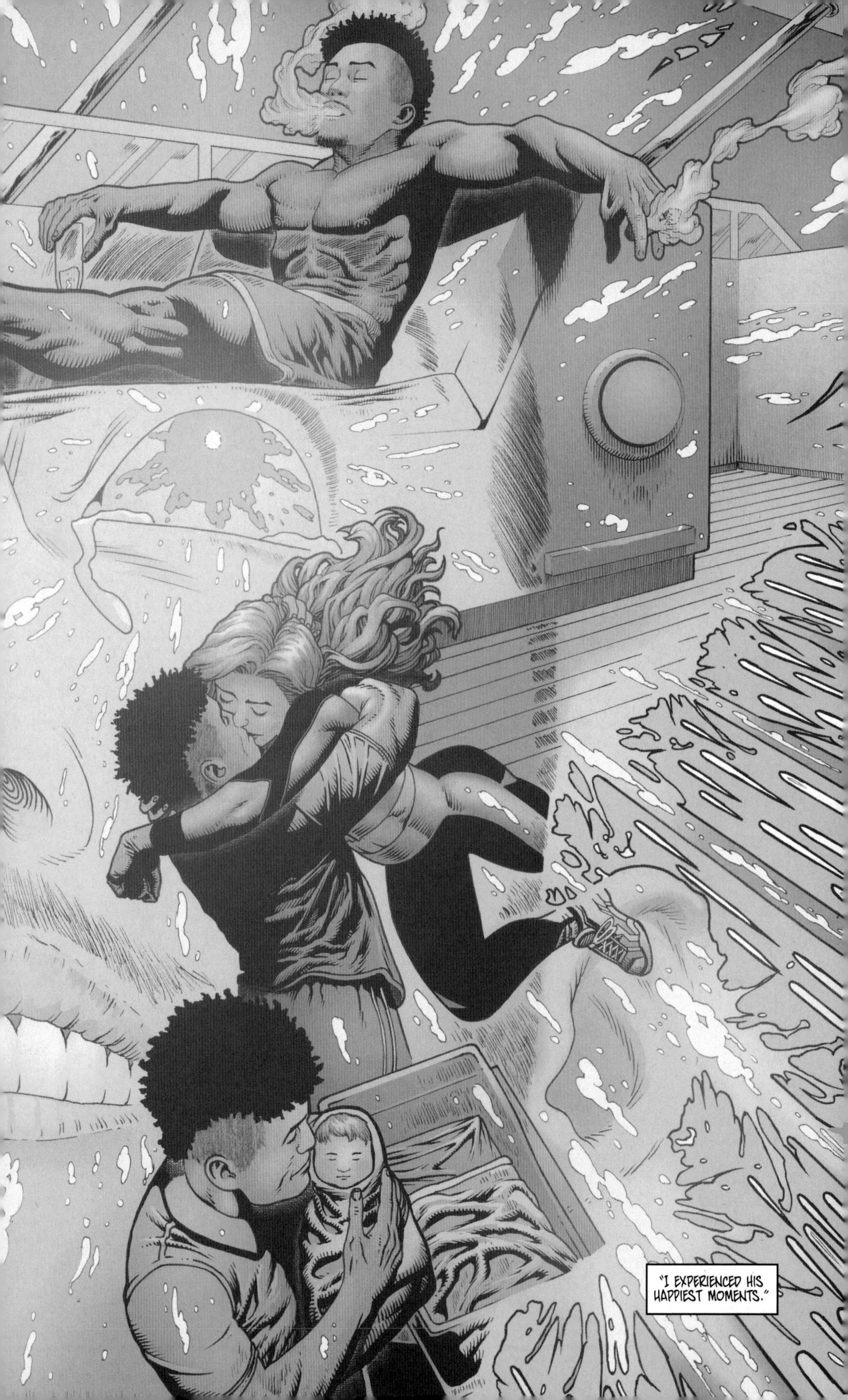
"I EXPERIENCED HIS HAPPIEST MOMENTS."

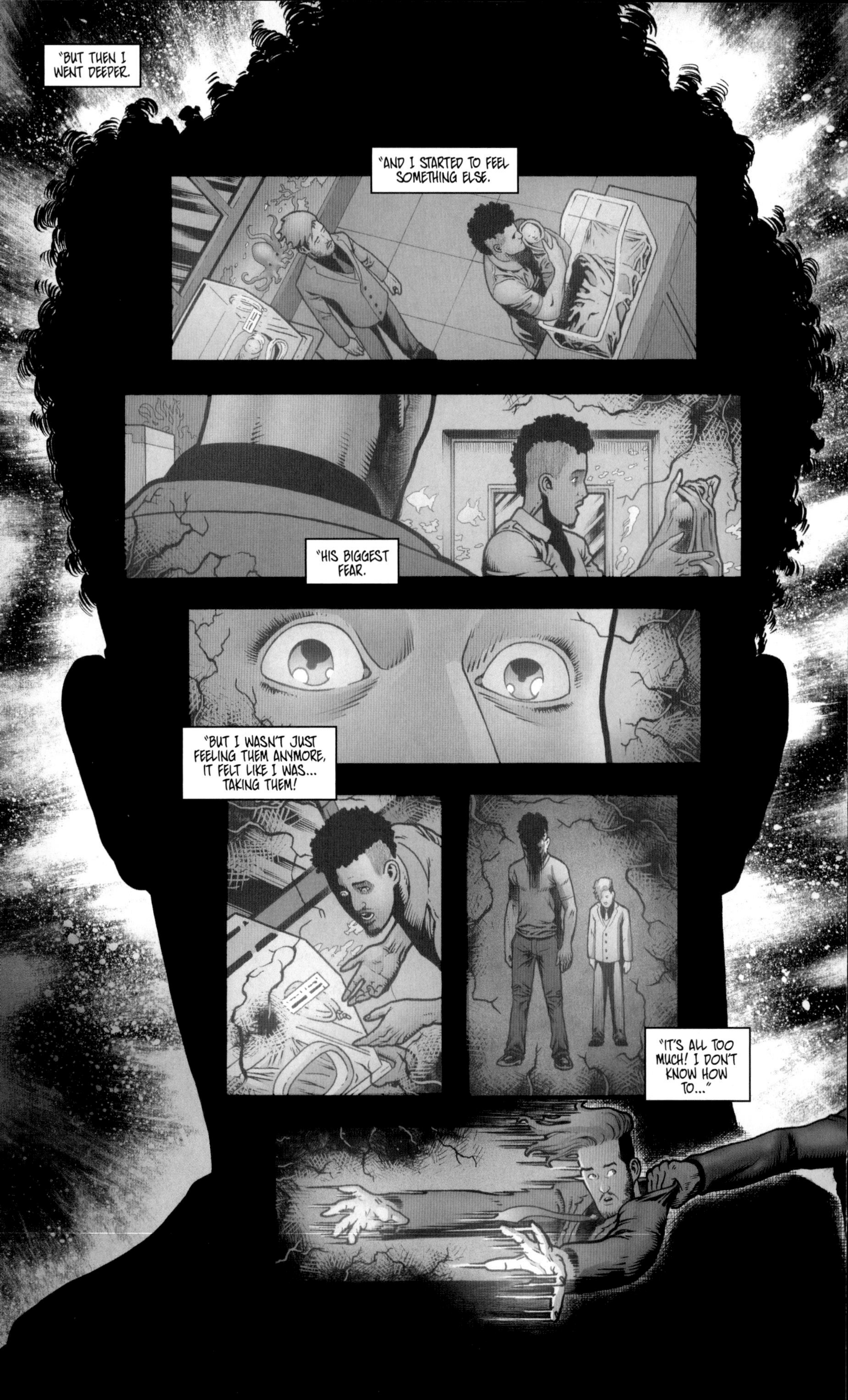
"BUT THEN I WENT DEEPER.
"AND I STARTED TO FEEL SOMETHING ELSE.
"HIS BIGGEST FEAR.
"BUT I WASN'T JUST FEELING THEM ANYMORE, IT FELT LIKE I WAS... TAKING THEM!
"IT'S ALL TOO MUCH! I DON'T KNOW HOW TO..."

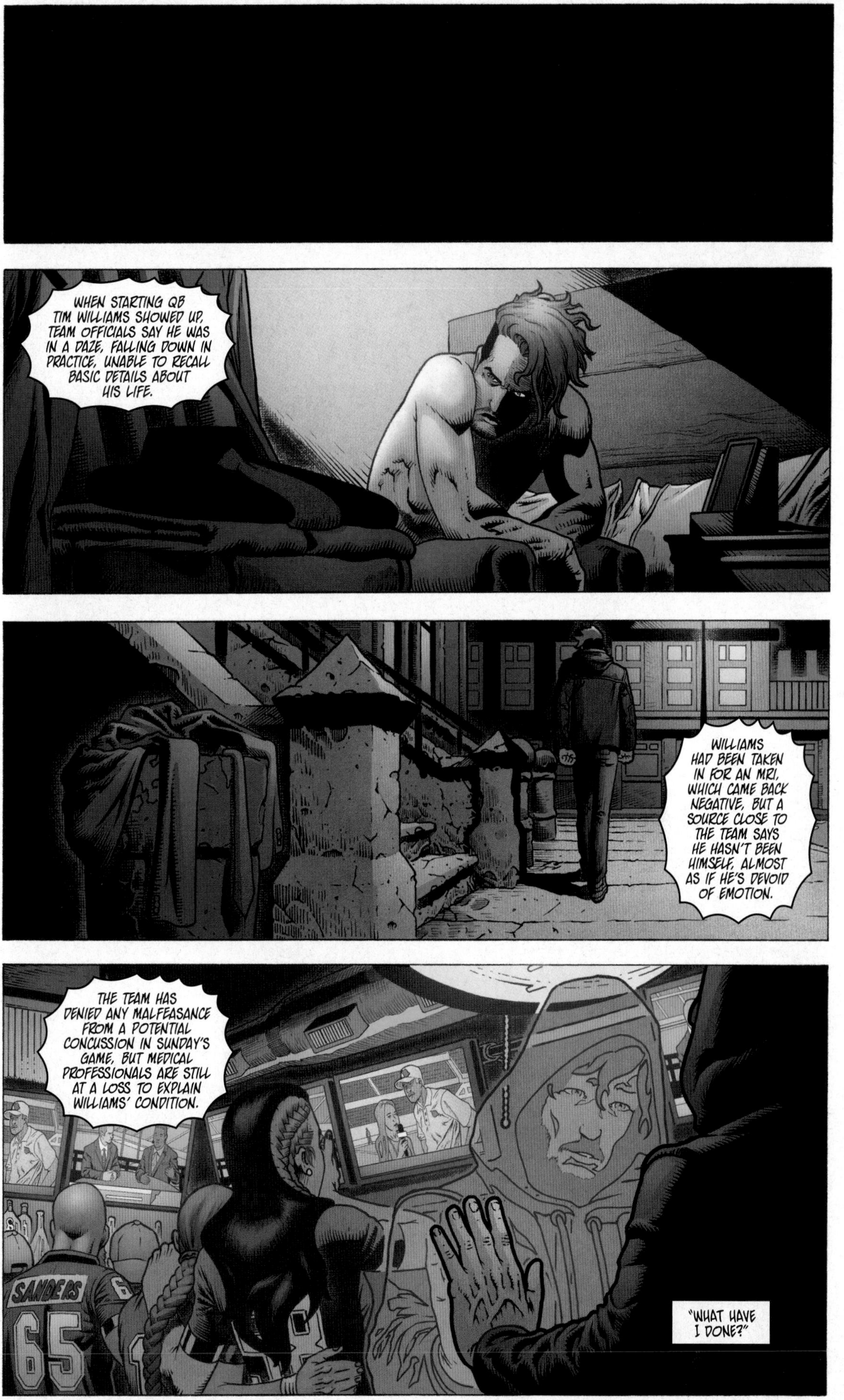
WHEN STARTING QB TIM WILLIAMS SHOWED UP, TEAM OFFICIALS SAY HE WAS IN A DAZE, FALLING DOWN IN PRACTICE, UNABLE TO RECALL BASIC DETAILS ABOUT HIS LIFE.
WILLIAMS HAD BEEN TAKEN IN FOR AN MRI, WHICH CAME BACK NEGATIVE, BUT A SOURCE CLOSE TO THE TEAM SAYS HE HASN'T BEEN HIMSELF, ALMOST AS IF HE'S DEVOID OF EMOTION.
THE TEAM HAS DENIED ANY MALFEASANCE FROM A POTENTIAL CONCUSSION IN SUNDAY'S GAME, BUT MEDICAL PROFESSIONALS ARE STILL AT A LOSS TO EXPLAIN WILLIAMS' CONDITION.
SANDERS 65
"WHAT HAVE I DONE?"

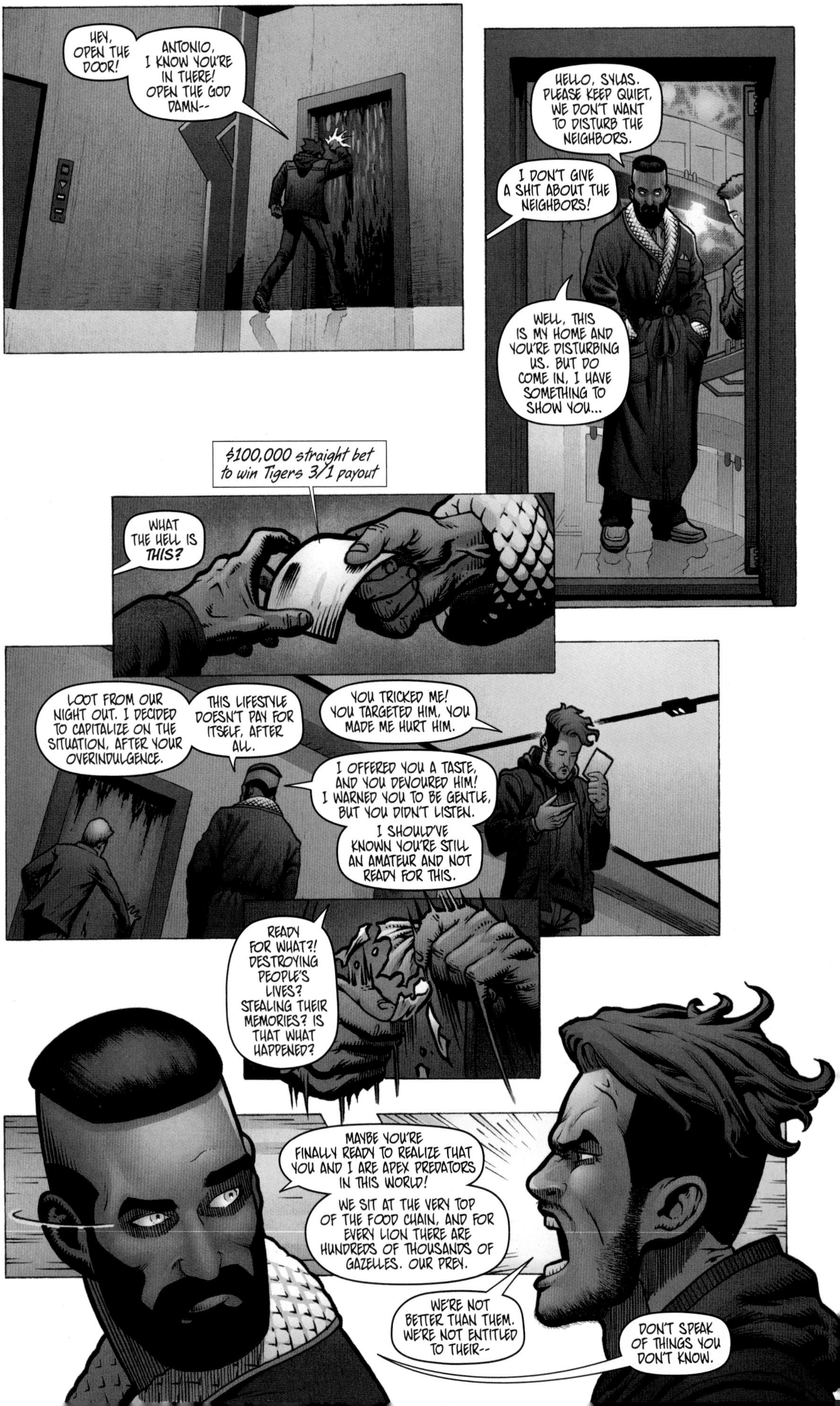
HEY, OPEN THE DOOR!
ANTONIO, I KNOW YOU'RE IN THERE! OPEN THE GOD DAMN--
HELLO, SYLAS. PLEASE KEEP QUIET, WE DON'T WANT TO DISTURB THE NEIGHBORS.
I DON'T GIVE A SHIT ABOUT THE NEIGHBORS!
WELL, THIS IS MY HOME AND YOU'RE DISTURBING US. BUT DO COME IN, I HAVE SOMETHING TO SHOW YOU...
$100,000 straight bet to win Tigers 3/1 payout
WHAT THE HELL IS THIS?
LOOT FROM OUR NIGHT OUT. I DECIDED TO CAPITALIZE ON THE SITUATION, AFTER YOUR OVERINDULGENCE.
THIS LIFESTYLE DOESN'T PAY FOR ITSELF, AFTER ALL.
YOU TRICKED ME! YOU TARGETED HIM, YOU MADE ME HURT HIM.
I OFFERED YOU A TASTE, AND YOU DEVOURED HIM! I WARNED YOU TO BE GENTLE, BUT YOU DIDN'T LISTEN.
I SHOULD'VE KNOWN YOU'RE STILL AN AMATEUR AND NOT READY FOR THIS.
READY FOR WHAT?! DESTROYING PEOPLE'S LIVES? STEALING THEIR MEMORIES? IS THAT WHAT HAPPENED?
MAYBE YOU'RE FINALLY READY TO REALIZE THAT YOU AND I ARE APEX PREDATORS IN THIS WORLD!
WE SIT AT THE VERY TOP OF THE FOOD CHAIN, AND FOR EVERY LION THERE ARE HUNDREDS OF THOUSANDS OF GAZELLES. OUR PREY.
WE'RE NOT BETTER THAN THEM. WE'RE NOT ENTITLED TO THEIR--
DON'T SPEAK OF THINGS YOU DON'T KNOW.

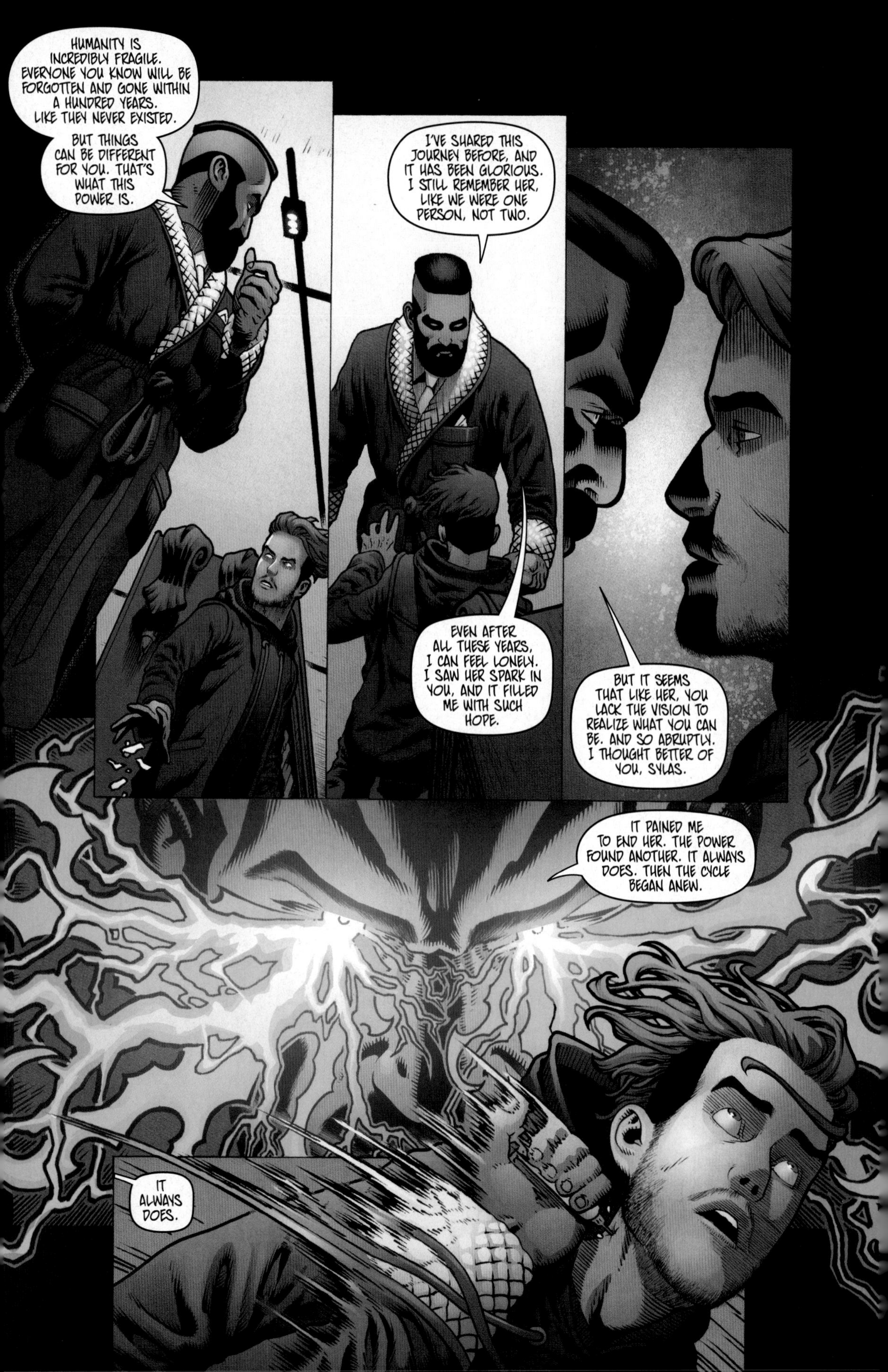
HUMANITY IS INCREDIBLY FRAGILE. EVERYONE YOU KNOW WILL BE FORGOTTEN AND GONE WITHIN A HUNDRED YEARS. LIKE THEY NEVER EXISTED.
BUT THINGS CAN BE DIFFERENT FOR YOU. THAT'S WHAT THIS POWER IS.
I'VE SHARED THIS JOURNEY BEFORE, AND IT HAS BEEN GLORIOUS. I STILL REMEMBER HER, LIKE WE WERE ONE PERSON, NOT TWO.
EVEN AFTER ALL THESE YEARS, I CAN FEEL LONELY. I SAW HER SPARK IN YOU, AND IT FILLED ME WITH SUCH HOPE.
BUT IT SEEMS THAT LIKE HER, YOU LACK THE VISION TO REALIZE WHAT YOU CAN BE. AND SO ABRUPTLY. I THOUGHT BETTER OF YOU, SYLAS.
IT PAINED ME TO END HER. THE POWER FOUND ANOTHER. IT ALWAYS DOES. THEN THE CYCLE BEGAN ANEW.
IT ALWAYS DOES.

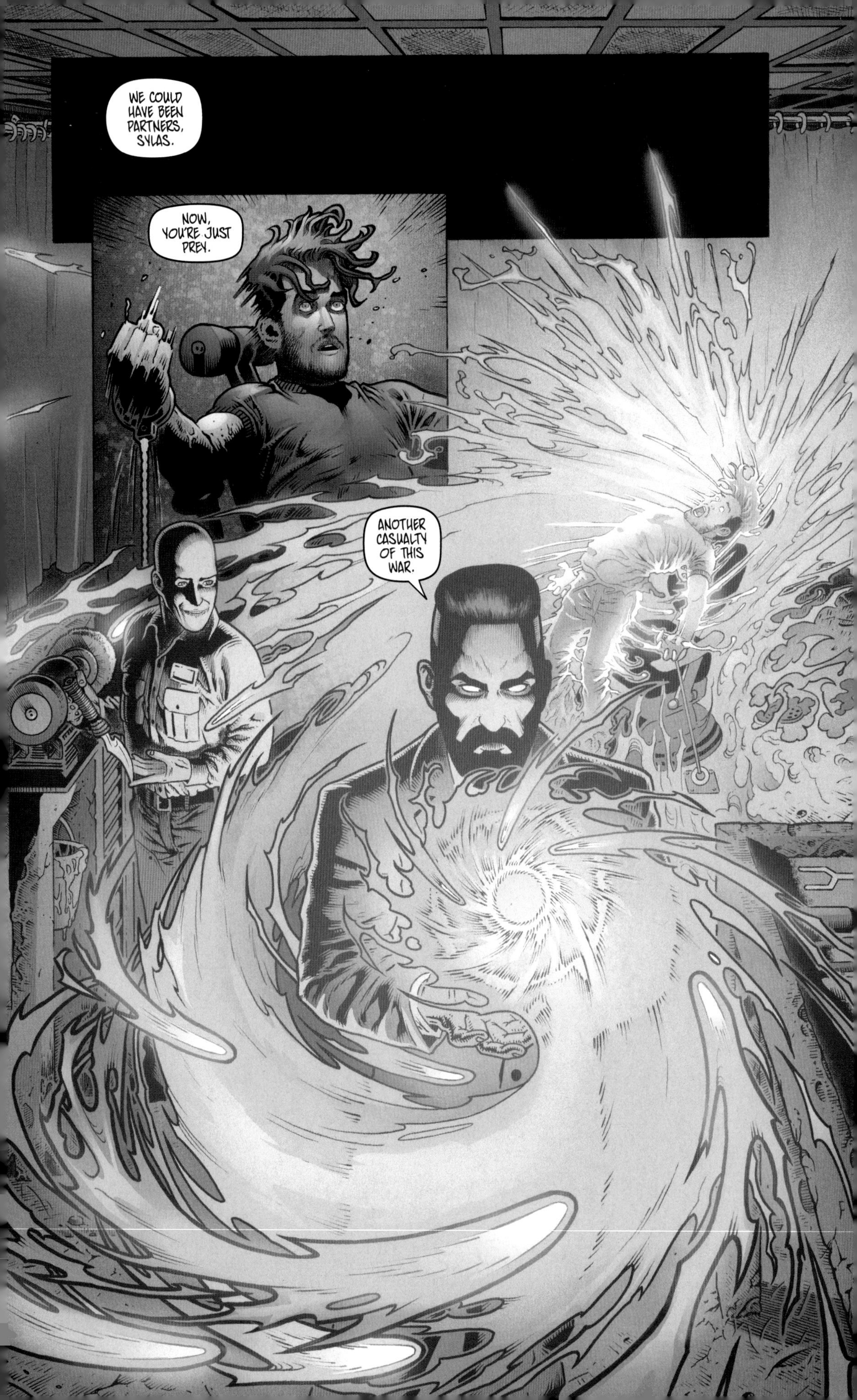
WE COULD HAVE BEEN PARTNERS, SYLAS.
NOW, YOU'RE JUST PREY.
ANOTHER CASUALTY OF THIS WAR.

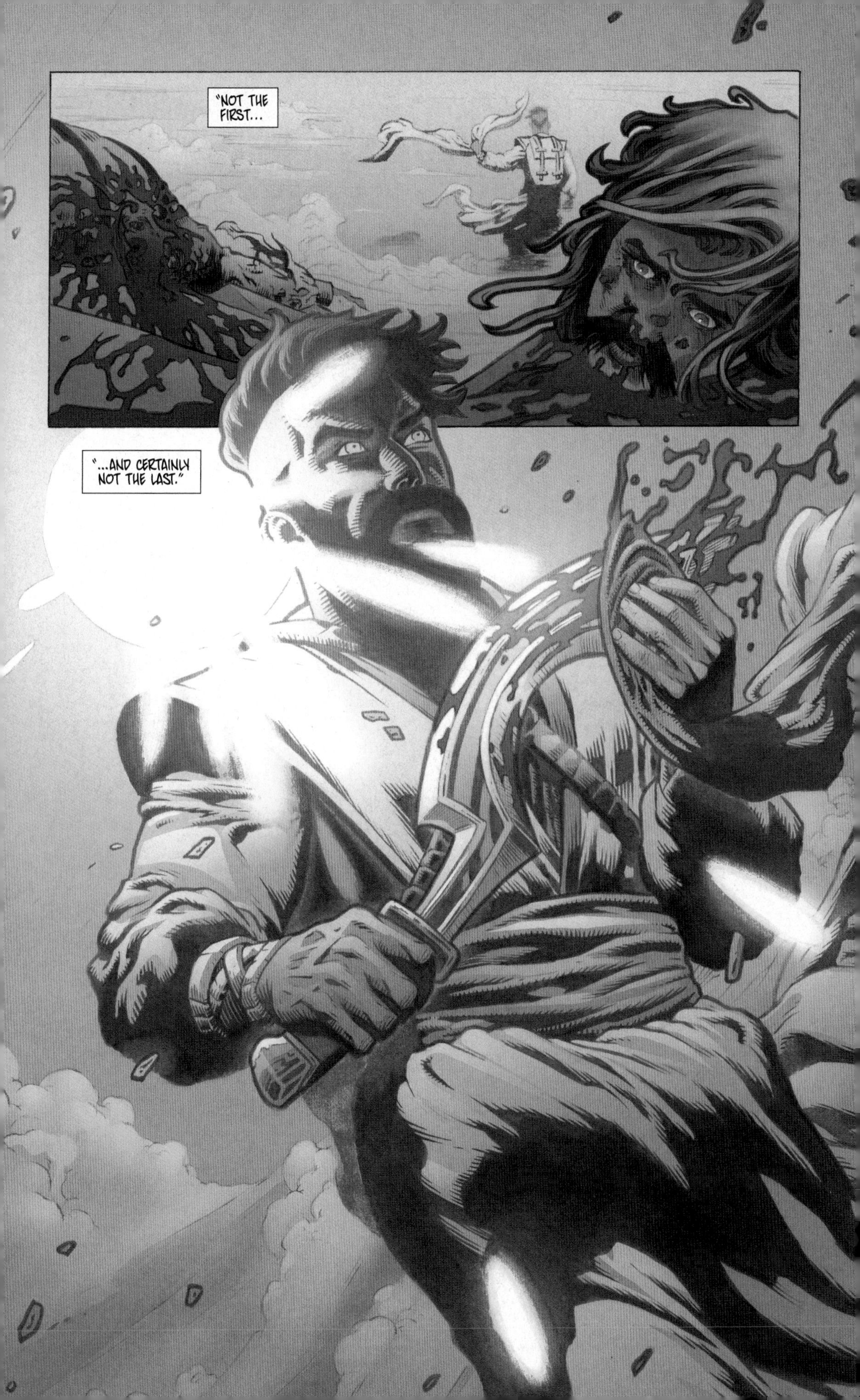
"NOT THE FIRST...
"...AND CERTAINLY NOT THE LAST."

CHAPTER THREE

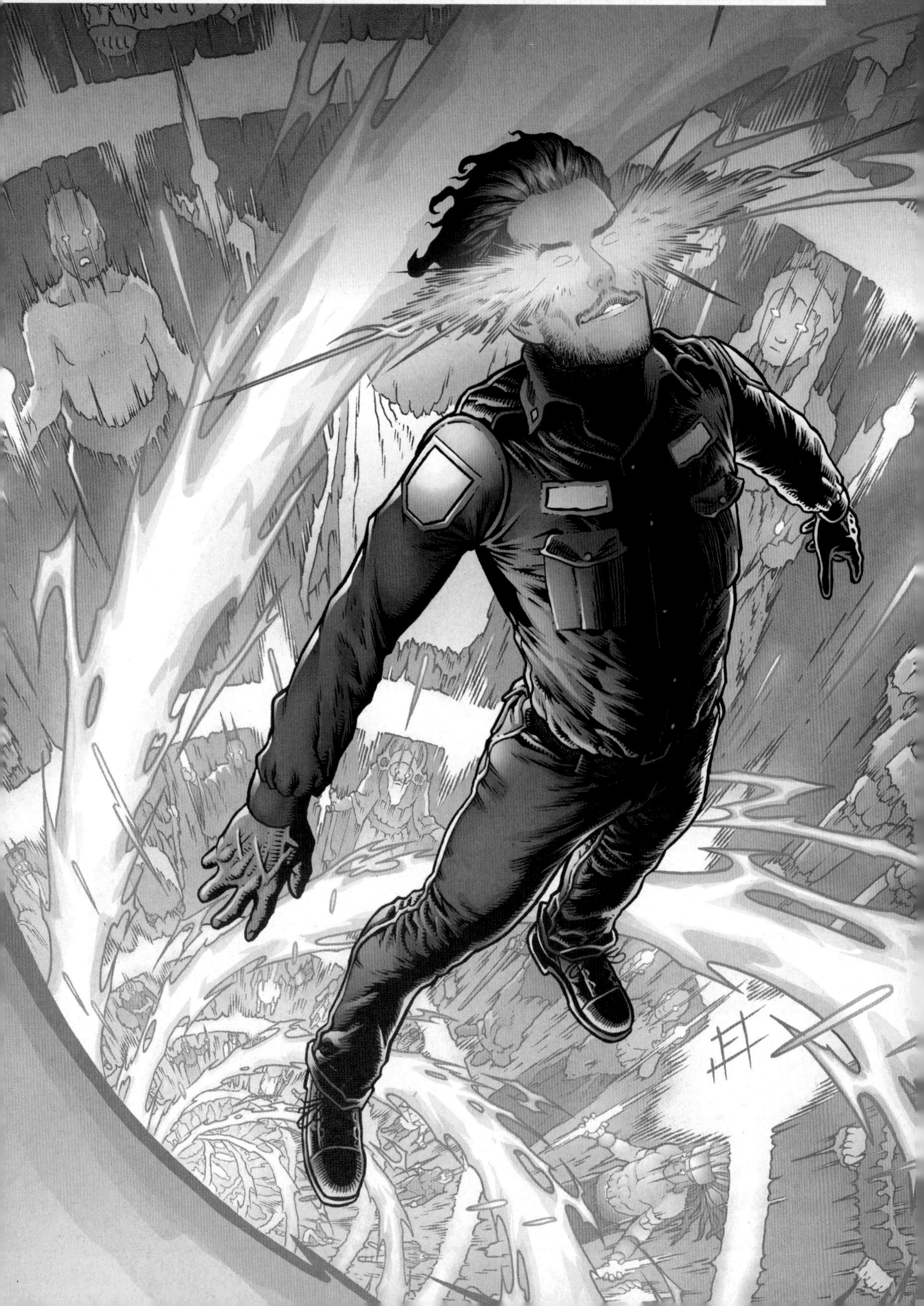

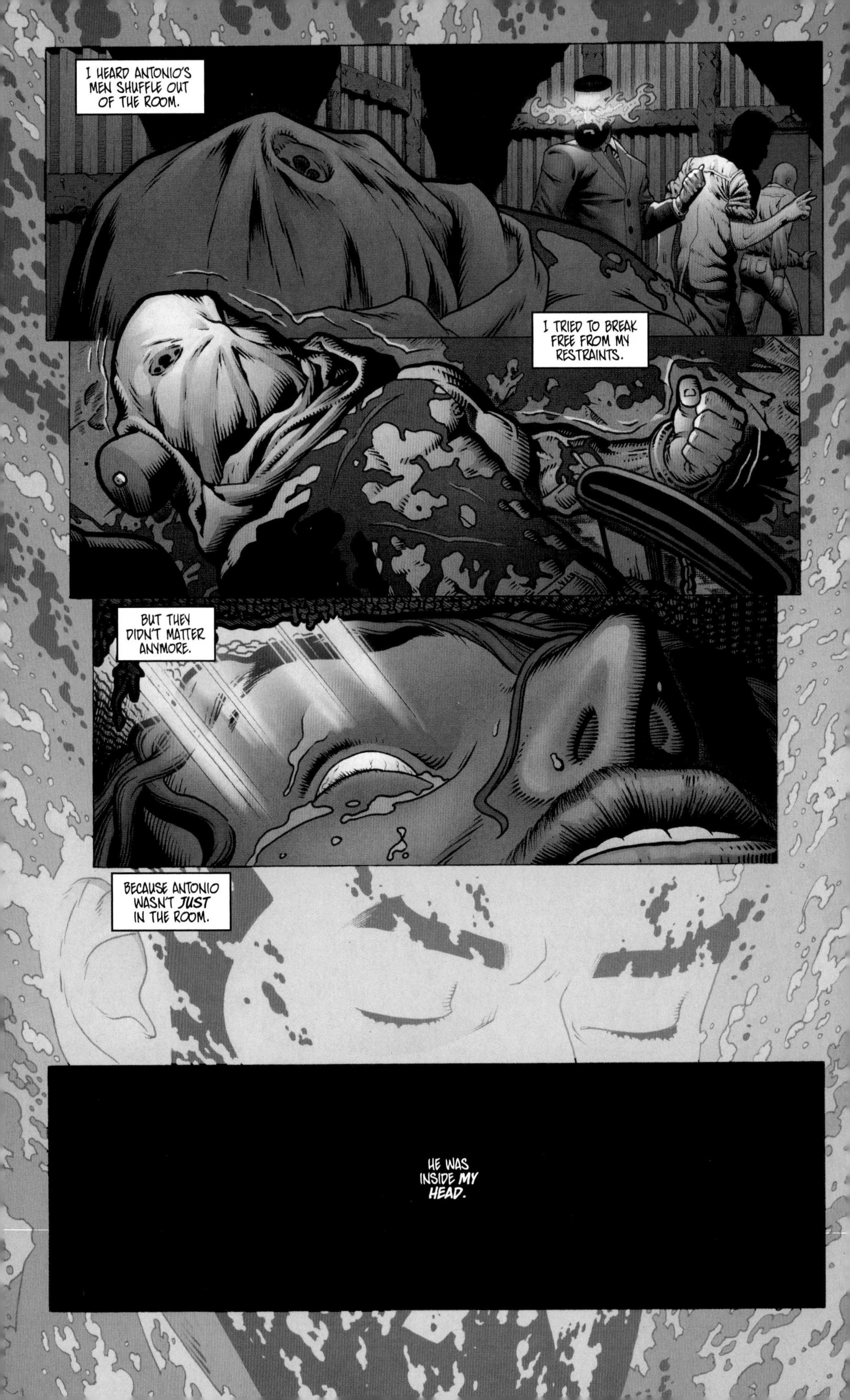

I HEARD ANTONIO'S MEN SHUFFLE OUT OF THE ROOM.
I TRIED TO BREAK FREE FROM MY RESTRAINTS.
BUT THEY DIDN'T MATTER ANYMORE.
BECAUSE ANTONIO WASN'T *JUST* IN THE ROOM.
HE WAS INSIDE ***MY HEAD.***

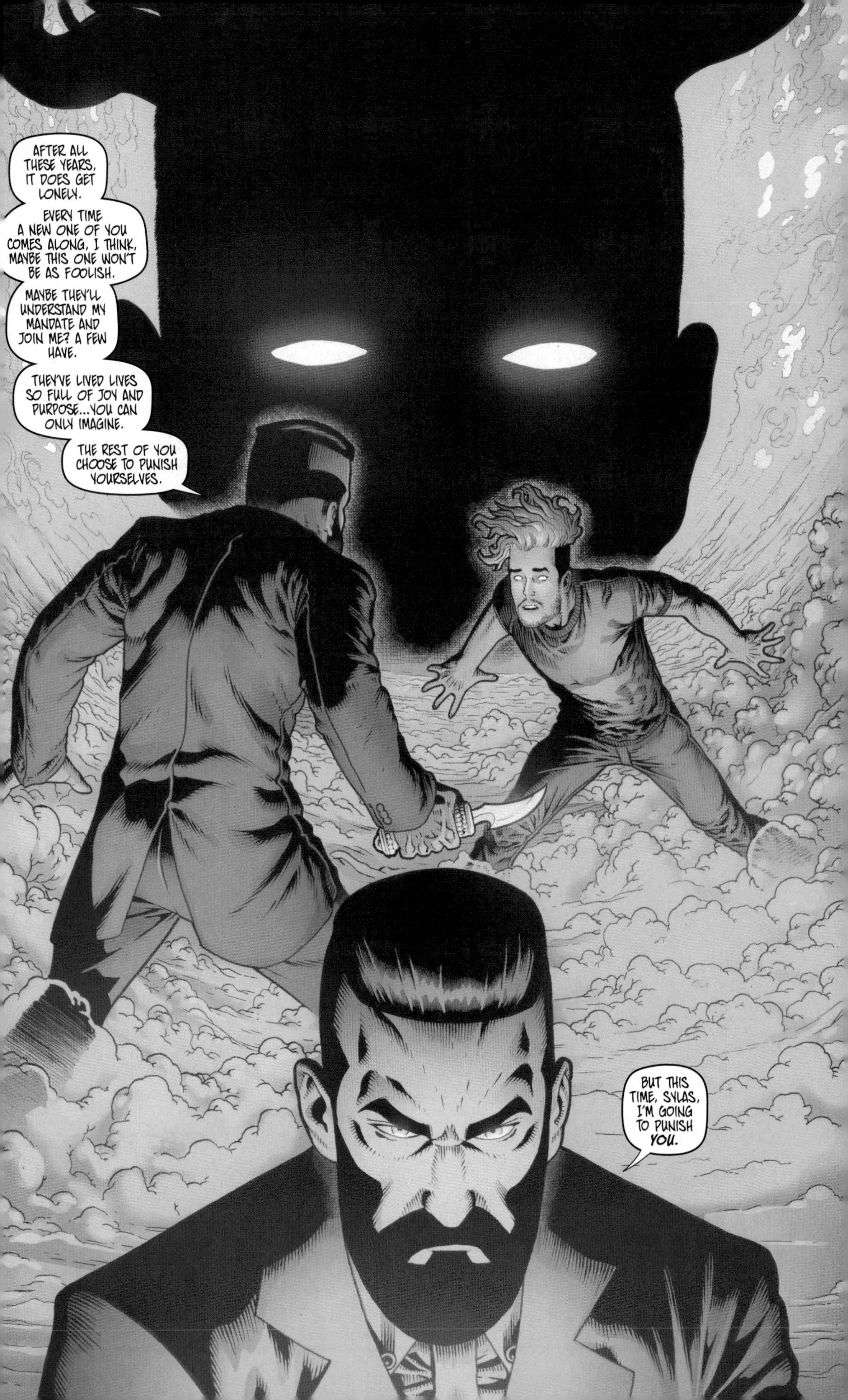
AFTER ALL THESE YEARS, IT DOES GET LONELY.
EVERY TIME A NEW ONE OF YOU COMES ALONG, I THINK, MAYBE THIS ONE WON'T BE AS FOOLISH.
MAYBE THEY'LL UNDERSTAND MY MANDATE AND JOIN ME? A FEW HAVE.
THEY'VE LIVED LIVES SO FULL OF JOY AND PURPOSE...YOU CAN ONLY IMAGINE.
THE REST OF YOU CHOOSE TO PUNISH YOURSELVES.
BUT THIS TIME, SYLAS, I'M GOING TO PUNISH *YOU*.

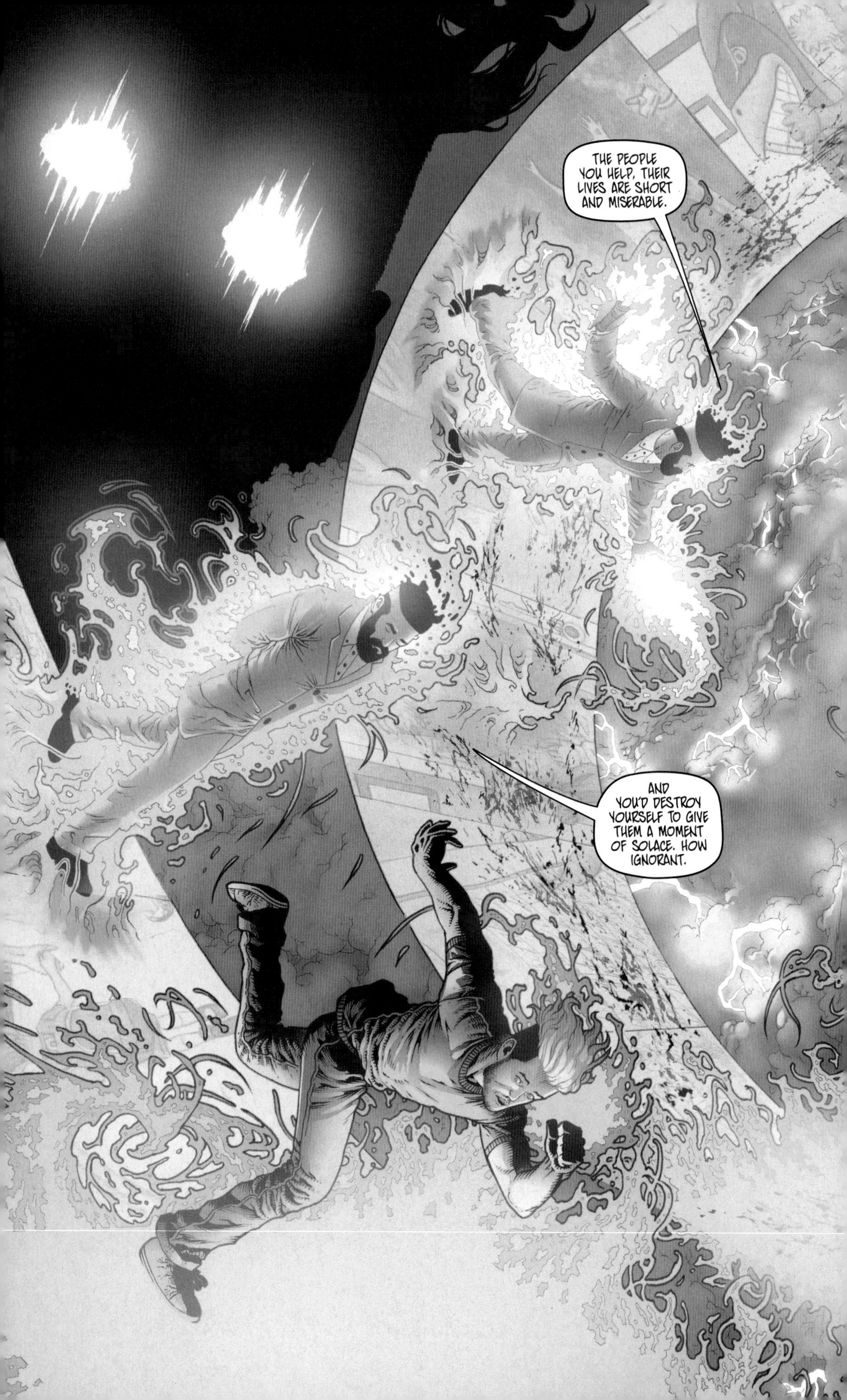
THE PEOPLE YOU HELP, THEIR LIVES ARE SHORT AND MISERABLE.
AND YOU'D DESTROY YOURSELF TO GIVE THEM A MOMENT OF SOLACE. HOW IGNORANT.

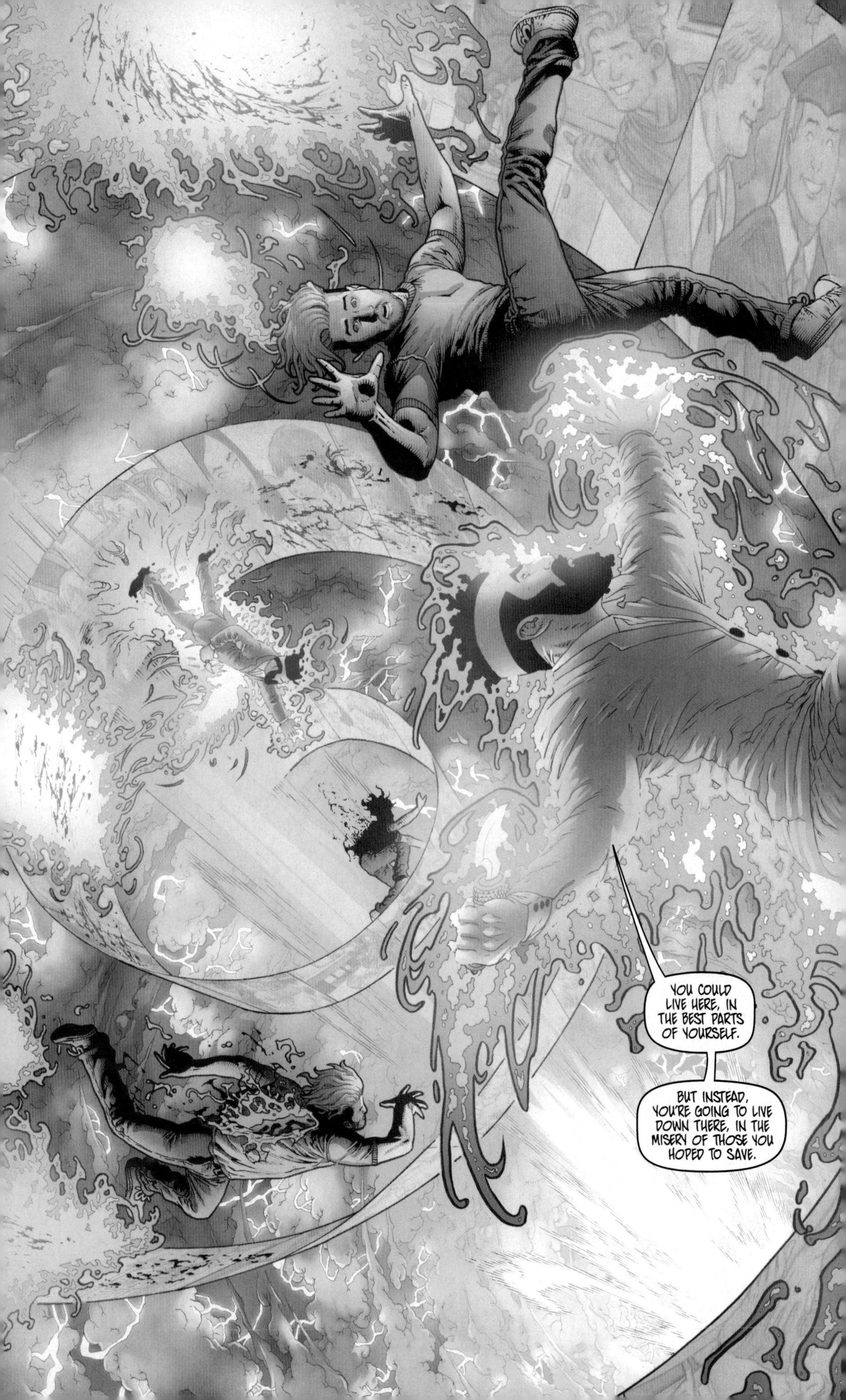
YOU COULD LIVE HERE, IN THE BEST PARTS OF YOURSELF.
BUT INSTEAD, YOU'RE GOING TO LIVE DOWN THERE, IN THE MISERY OF THOSE YOU HOPED TO SAVE.

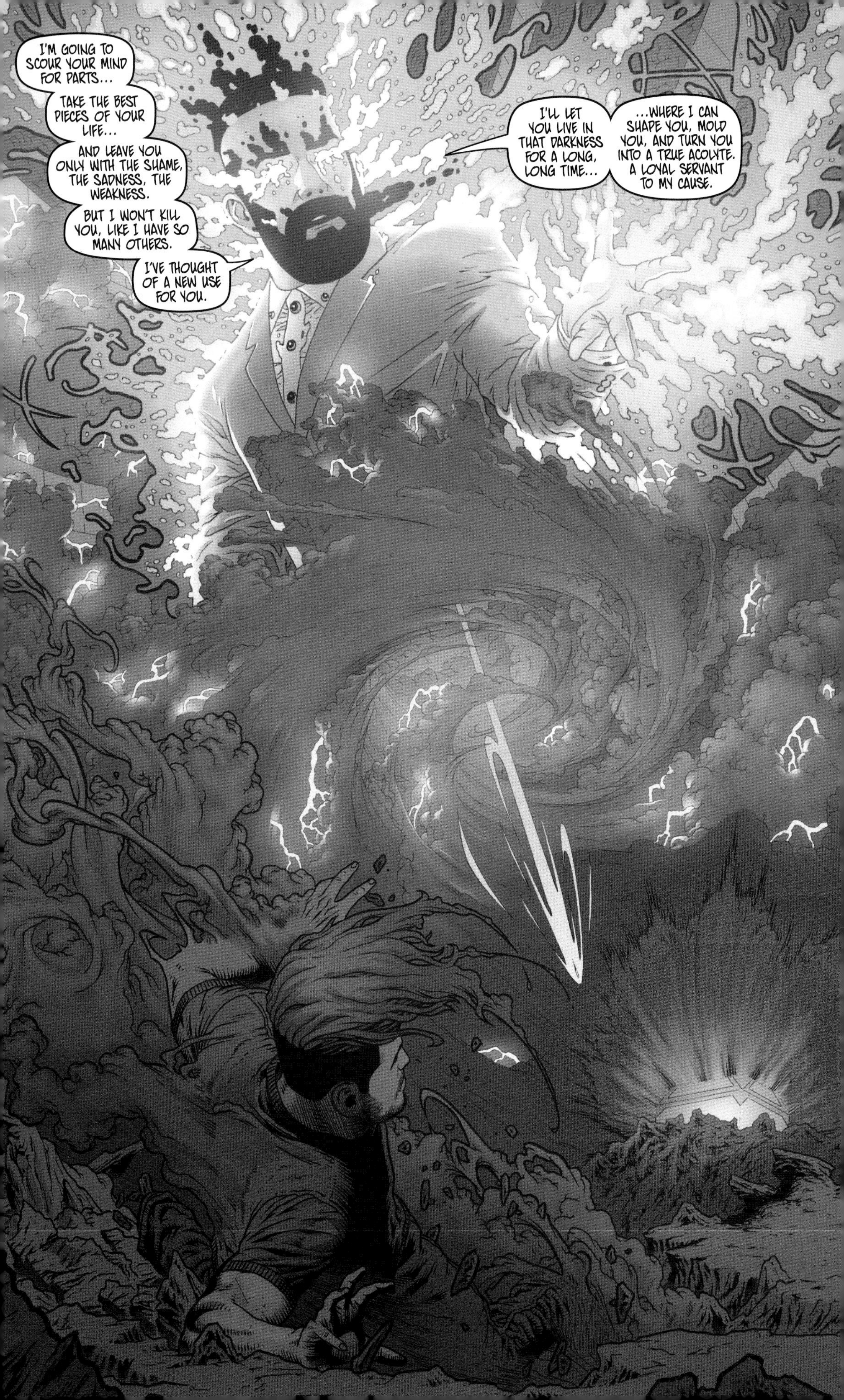
I'M GOING TO SCOUR YOUR MIND FOR PARTS...
TAKE THE BEST PIECES OF YOUR LIFE...
AND LEAVE YOU ONLY WITH THE SHAME, THE SADNESS, THE WEAKNESS.
BUT I WON'T KILL YOU, LIKE I HAVE SO MANY OTHERS.
I'VE THOUGHT OF A NEW USE FOR YOU.
I'LL LET YOU LIVE IN THAT DARKNESS FOR A LONG, LONG TIME...
...WHERE I CAN SHAPE YOU, MOLD YOU, AND TURN YOU INTO A TRUE ACOLYTE. A LOYAL SERVANT TO MY CAUSE.

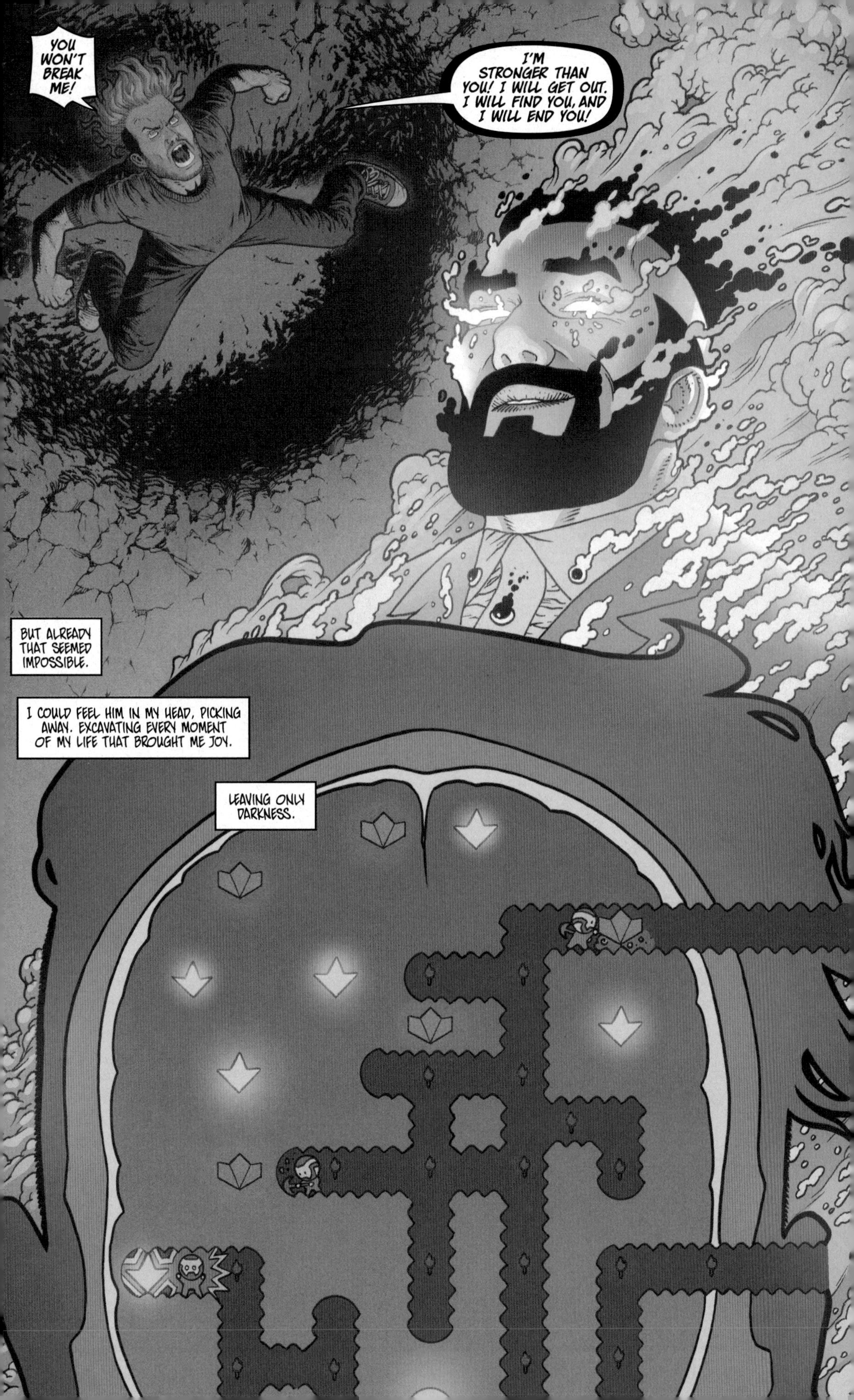
YOU WON'T BREAK ME!
I'M STRONGER THAN YOU! I WILL GET OUT. I WILL FIND YOU, AND I WILL END YOU!
BUT ALREADY THAT SEEMED IMPOSSIBLE.
I COULD FEEL HIM IN MY HEAD, PICKING AWAY. EXCAVATING EVERY MOMENT OF MY LIFE THAT BROUGHT ME JOY.
LEAVING ONLY DARKNESS.

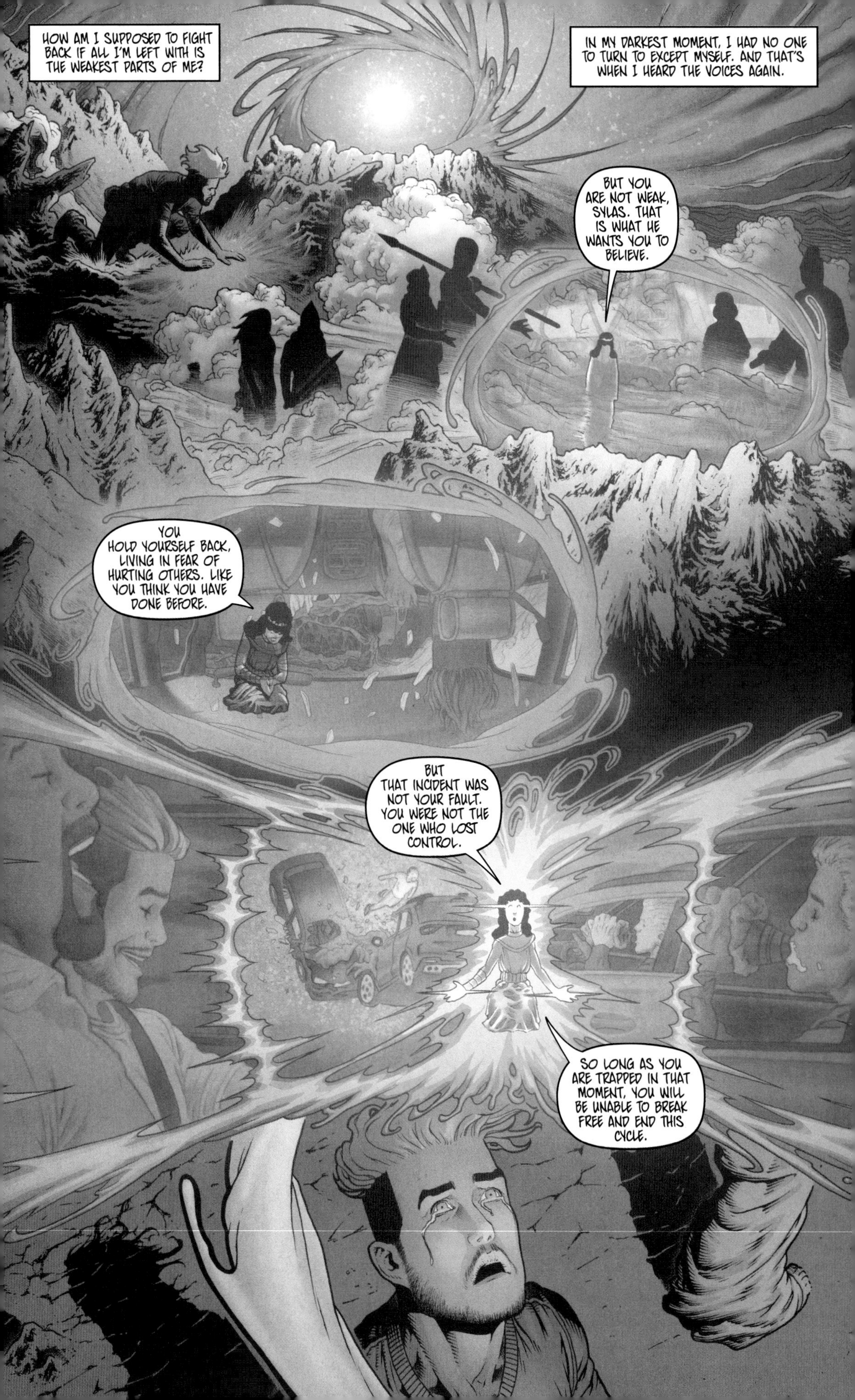
HOW AM I SUPPOSED TO FIGHT BACK IF ALL I'M LEFT WITH IS THE WEAKEST PARTS OF ME?
IN MY DARKEST MOMENT, I HAD NO ONE TO TURN TO EXCEPT MYSELF. AND THAT'S WHEN I HEARD THE VOICES AGAIN.
BUT YOU ARE NOT WEAK, SYLAS. THAT IS WHAT HE WANTS YOU TO BELIEVE.
YOU HOLD YOURSELF BACK, LIVING IN FEAR OF HURTING OTHERS. LIKE YOU THINK YOU HAVE DONE BEFORE.
BUT THAT INCIDENT WAS NOT YOUR FAULT. YOU WERE NOT THE ONE WHO LOST CONTROL.
SO LONG AS YOU ARE TRAPPED IN THAT MOMENT, YOU WILL BE UNABLE TO BREAK FREE AND END THIS CYCLE.

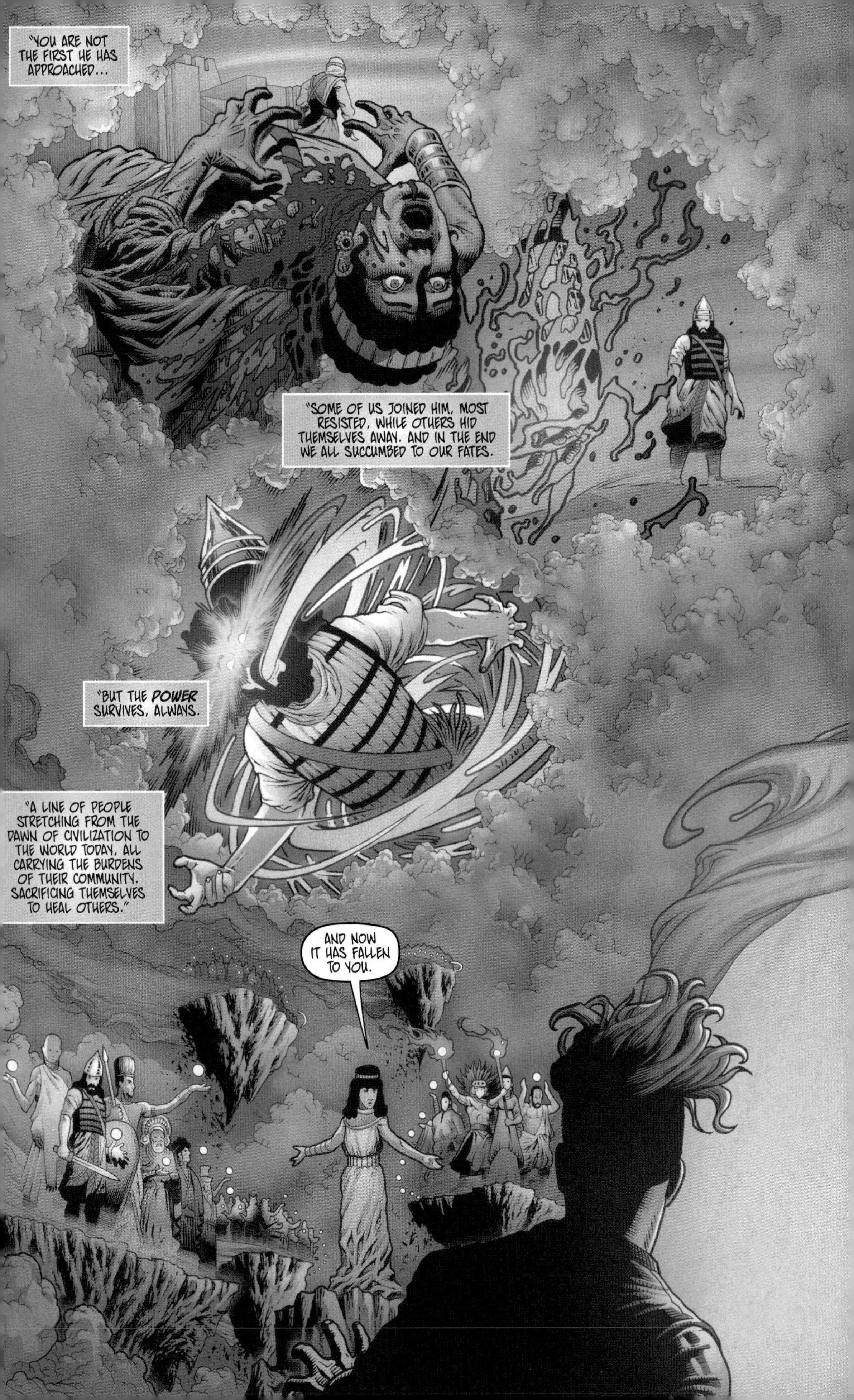
"YOU ARE NOT THE FIRST HE HAS APPROACHED...
"SOME OF US JOINED HIM, MOST RESISTED, WHILE OTHERS HID THEMSELVES AWAY. AND IN THE END WE ALL SUCCUMBED TO OUR FATES.
"BUT THE POWER SURVIVES, ALWAYS.
"A LINE OF PEOPLE STRETCHING FROM THE DAWN OF CIVILIZATION TO THE WORLD TODAY, ALL CARRYING THE BURDENS OF THEIR COMMUNITY. SACRIFICING THEMSELVES TO HEAL OTHERS."
AND NOW IT HAS FALLEN TO YOU.

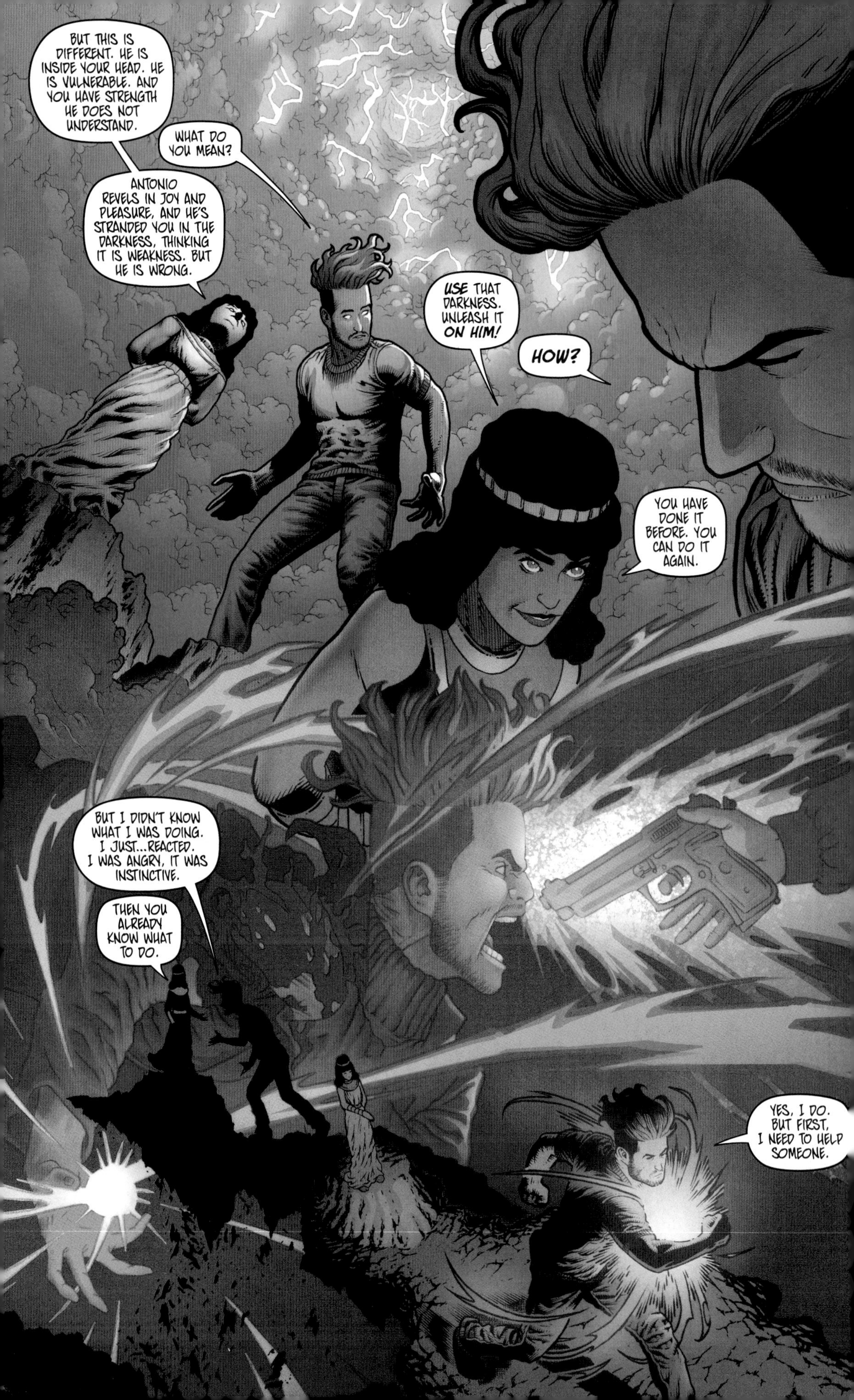
BUT THIS IS DIFFERENT. HE IS INSIDE YOUR HEAD. HE IS VULNERABLE. AND YOU HAVE STRENGTH HE DOES NOT UNDERSTAND.
WHAT DO YOU MEAN?
ANTONIO REVELS IN JOY AND PLEASURE, AND HE'S STRANDED YOU IN THE DARKNESS, THINKING IT IS WEAKNESS. BUT HE IS WRONG.
USE THAT DARKNESS. UNLEASH IT ON HIM!
HOW?
YOU HAVE DONE IT BEFORE. YOU CAN DO IT AGAIN.
BUT I DIDN'T KNOW WHAT I WAS DOING. I JUST...REACTED. I WAS ANGRY, IT WAS INSTINCTIVE.
THEN YOU ALREADY KNOW WHAT TO DO.
YES, I DO. BUT FIRST, I NEED TO HELP SOMEONE.

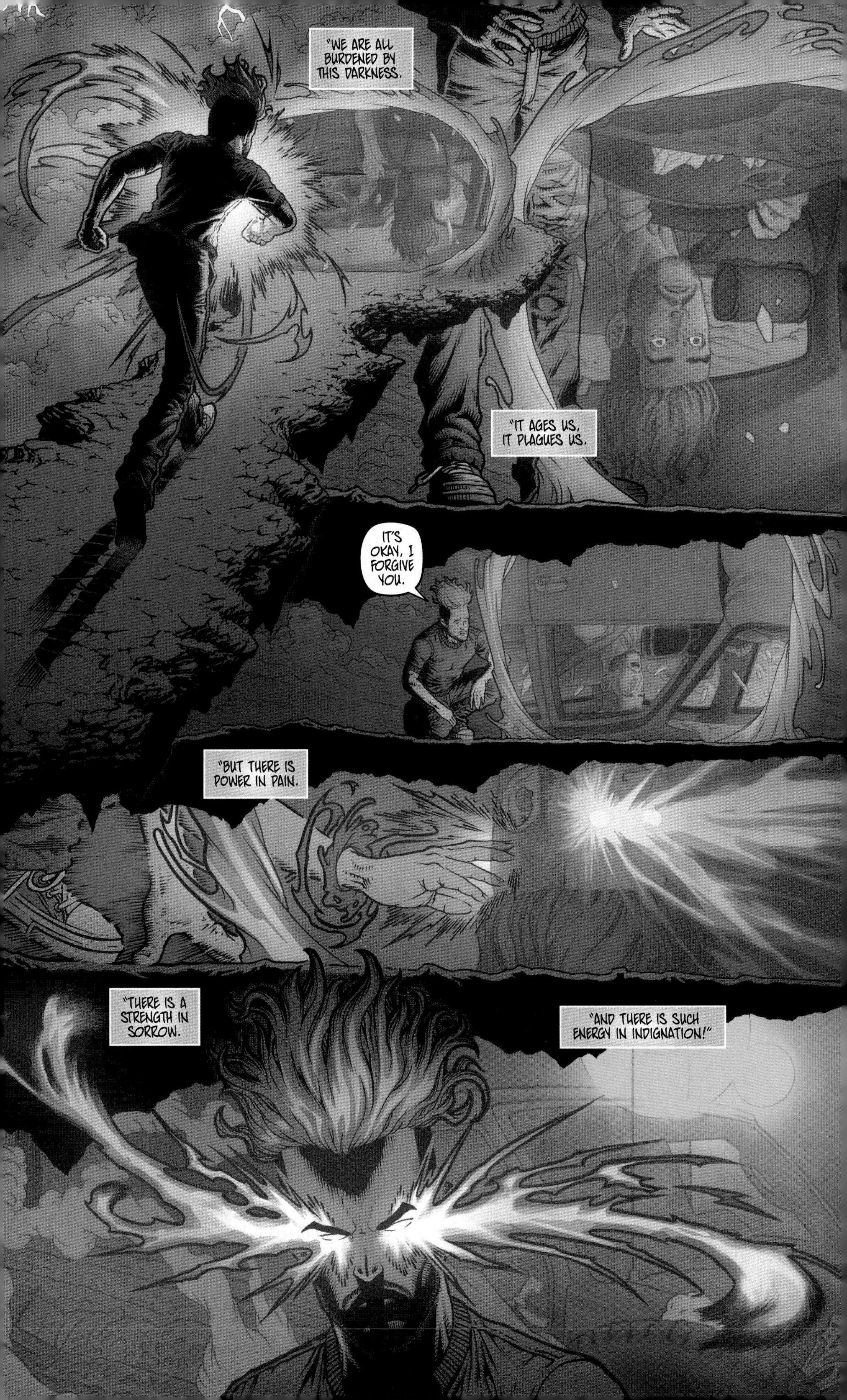
"WE ARE ALL BURDENED BY THIS DARKNESS.
"IT AGES US, IT PLAGUES US.
IT'S OKAY, I FORGIVE YOU.
"BUT THERE IS POWER IN PAIN.
"THERE IS A STRENGTH IN SORROW.
"AND THERE IS SUCH ENERGY IN INDIGNATION!"

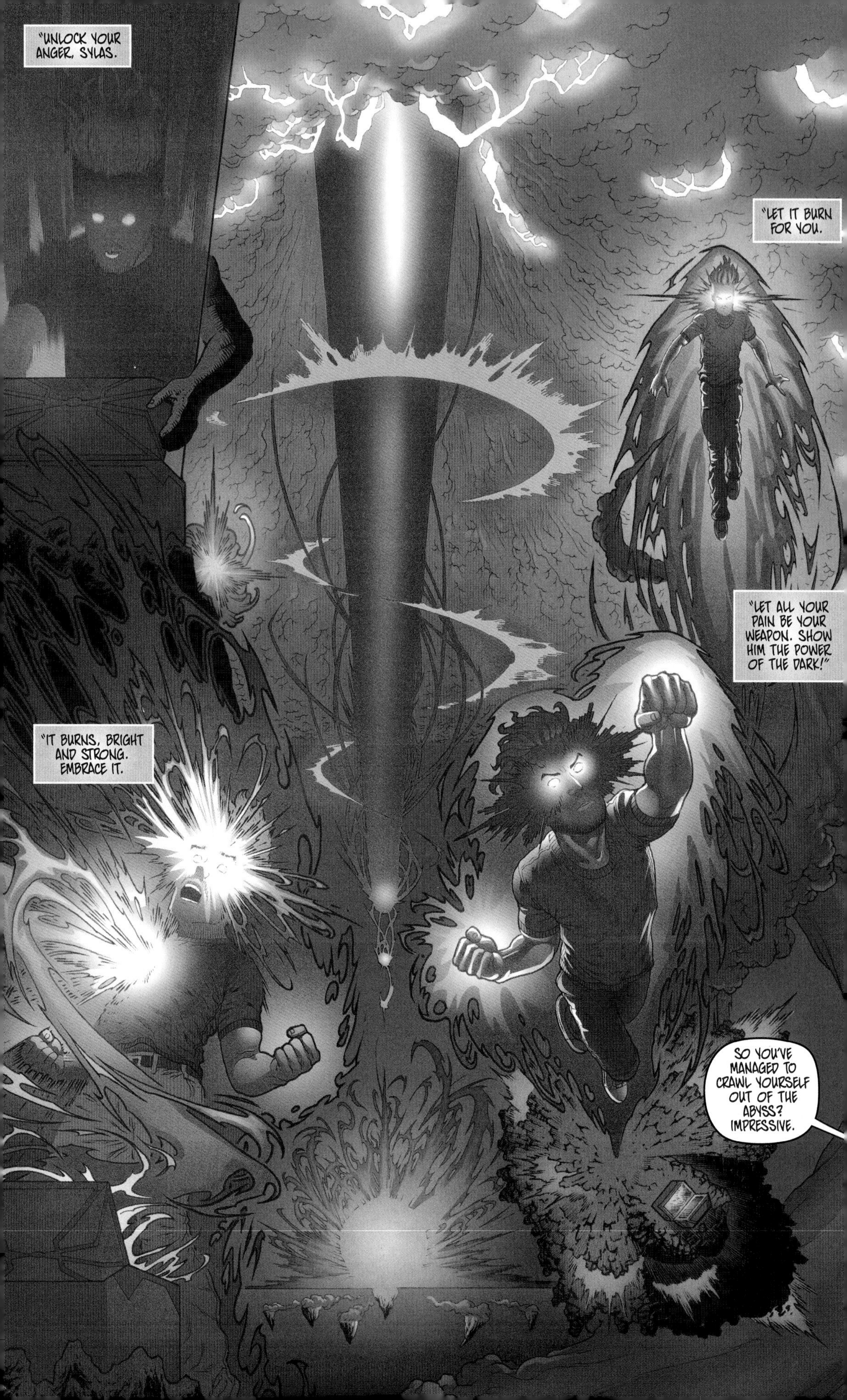
"UNLOCK YOUR ANGER, SYLAS.
"LET IT BURN FOR YOU.
"LET ALL YOUR PAIN BE YOUR WEAPON. SHOW HIM THE POWER OF THE DARK!"
"IT BURNS, BRIGHT AND STRONG. EMBRACE IT.
SO YOU'VE MANAGED TO CRAWL YOURSELF OUT OF THE ABYSS? IMPRESSIVE.

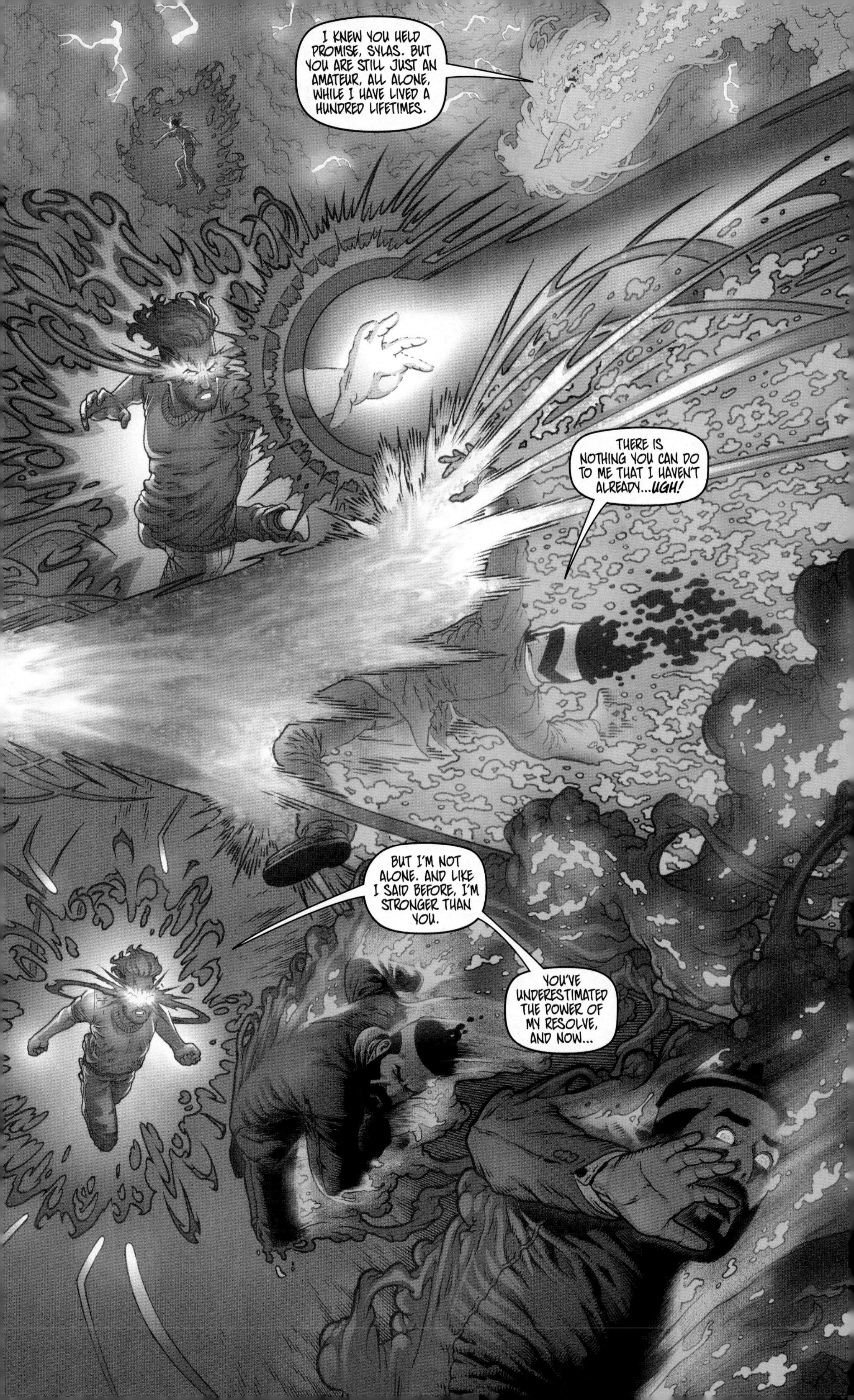
I KNEW YOU HELD PROMISE, SYLAS. BUT YOU ARE STILL JUST AN AMATEUR, ALL ALONE, WHILE I HAVE LIVED A HUNDRED LIFETIMES.
THERE IS NOTHING YOU CAN DO TO ME THAT I HAVEN'T ALREADY...UGH!
BUT I'M NOT ALONE. AND LIKE I SAID BEFORE, I'M STRONGER THAN YOU.
YOU'VE UNDERESTIMATED THE POWER OF MY RESOLVE, AND NOW...

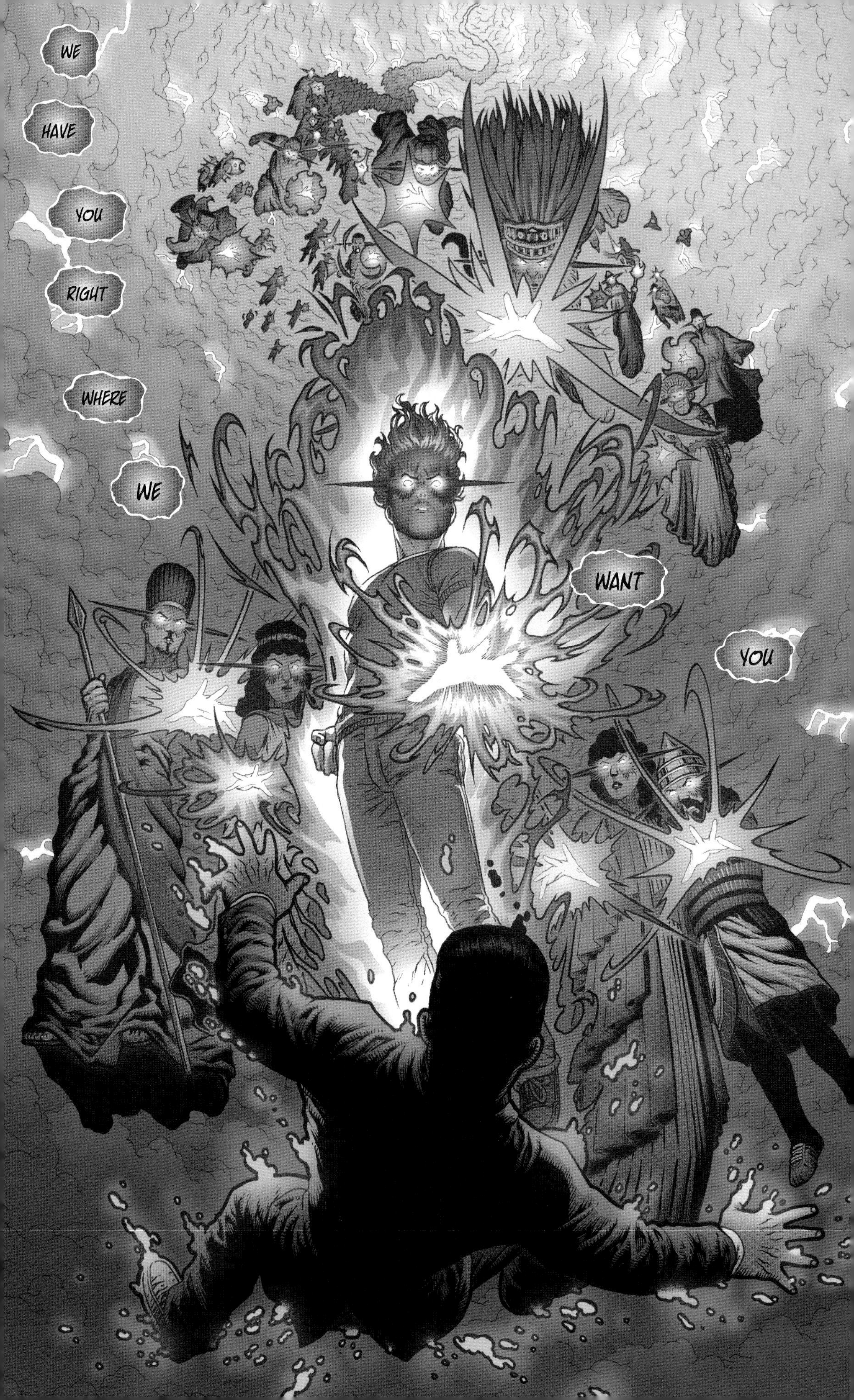
WE
HAVE
YOU
RIGHT
WHERE
WE
WANT
YOU

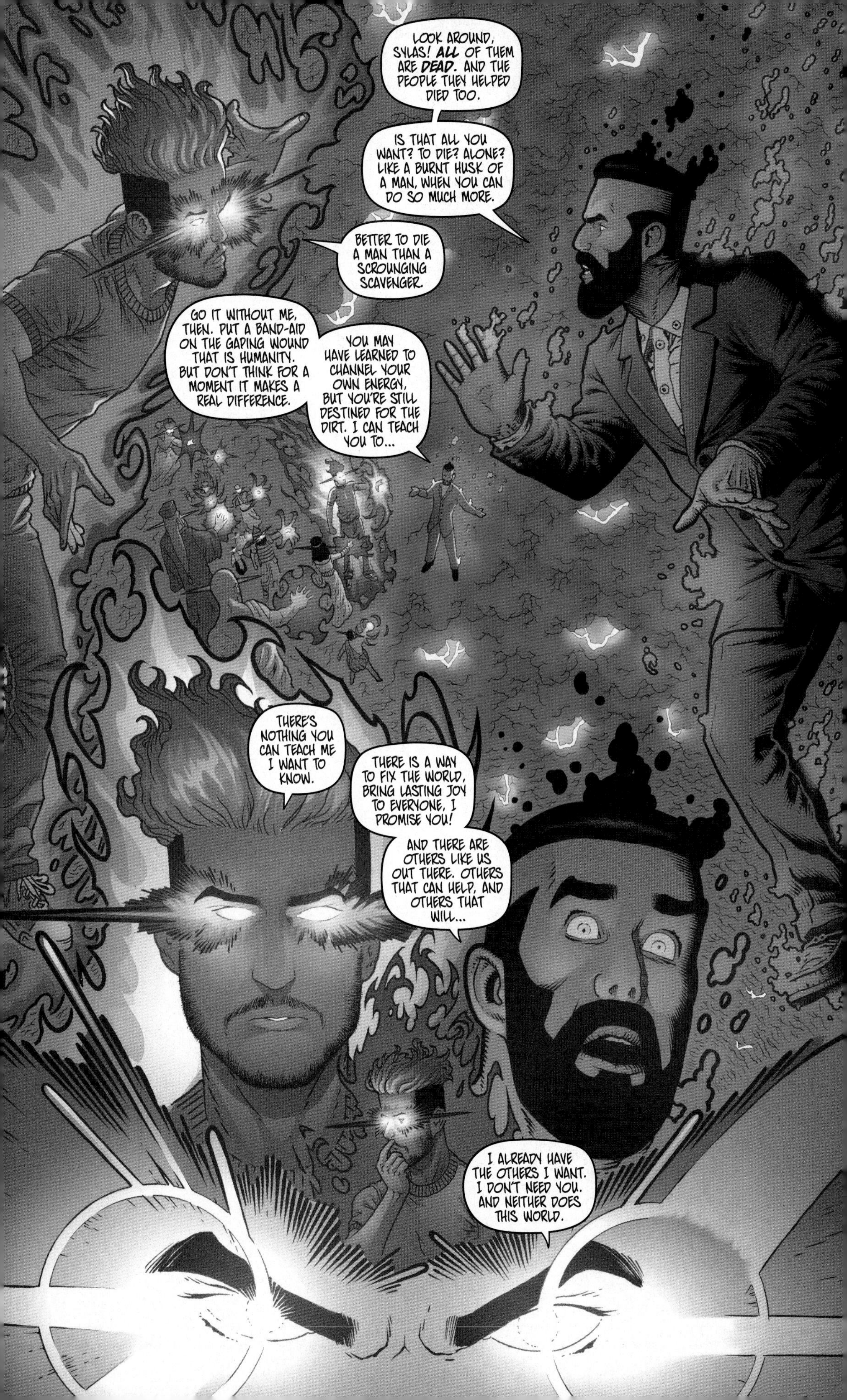
LOOK AROUND, SYLAS! ALL OF THEM ARE DEAD. AND THE PEOPLE THEY HELPED DIED TOO.
IS THAT ALL YOU WANT? TO DIE? ALONE? LIKE A BURNT HUSK OF A MAN, WHEN YOU CAN DO SO MUCH MORE.
BETTER TO DIE A MAN THAN A SCROUNGING SCAVENGER.
GO IT WITHOUT ME, THEN. PUT A BAND-AID ON THE GAPING WOUND THAT IS HUMANITY. BUT DON'T THINK FOR A MOMENT IT MAKES A REAL DIFFERENCE.
YOU MAY HAVE LEARNED TO CHANNEL YOUR OWN ENERGY, BUT YOU'RE STILL DESTINED FOR THE DIRT. I CAN TEACH YOU TO...
THERE'S NOTHING YOU CAN TEACH ME I WANT TO KNOW.
THERE IS A WAY TO FIX THE WORLD, BRING LASTING JOY TO EVERYONE, I PROMISE YOU!
AND THERE ARE OTHERS LIKE US OUT THERE. OTHERS THAT CAN HELP, AND OTHERS THAT WILL...
I ALREADY HAVE THE OTHERS I WANT. I DON'T NEED YOU. AND NEITHER DOES THIS WORLD.

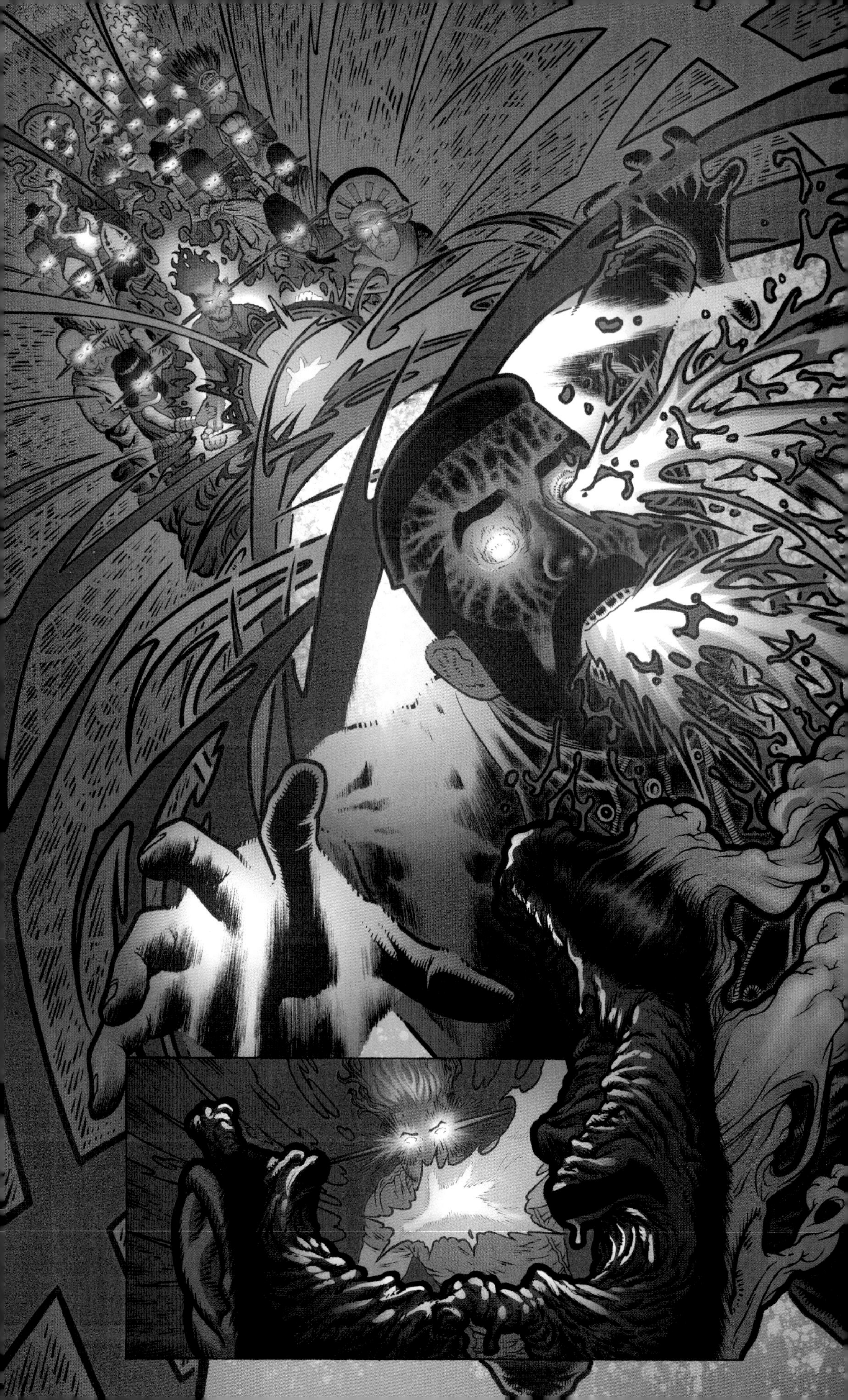

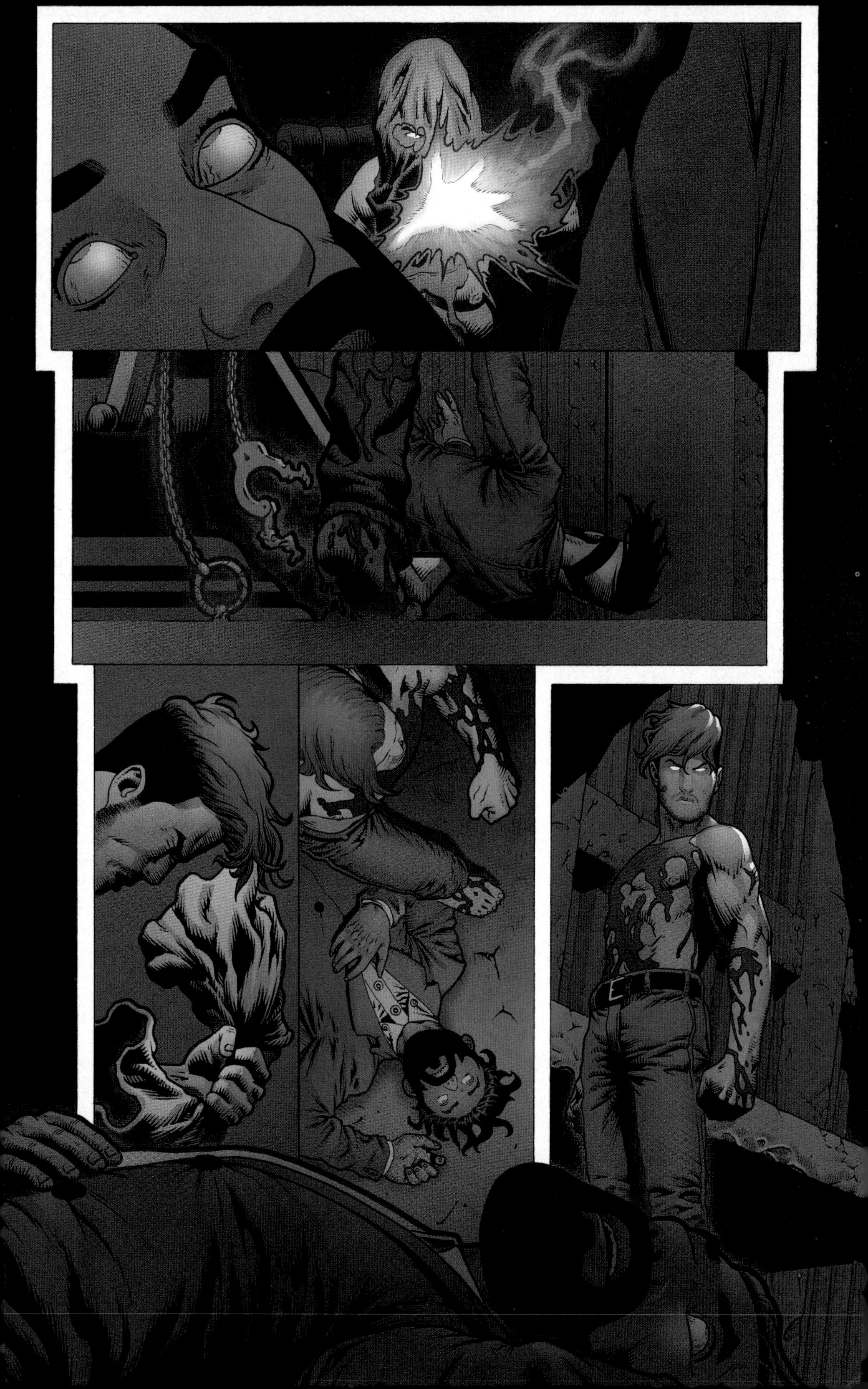

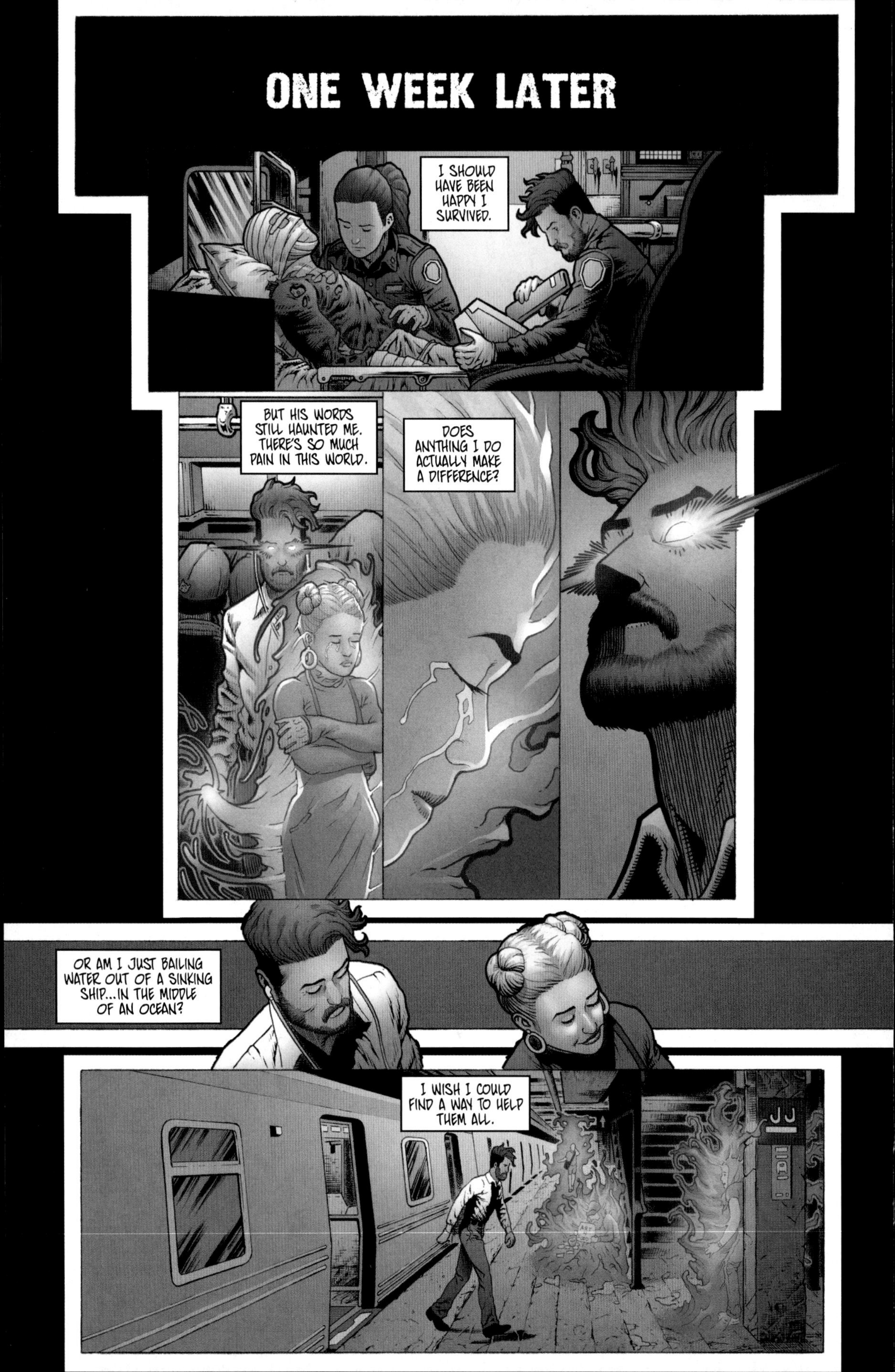
ONE WEEK LATER
I SHOULD HAVE BEEN HAPPY I SURVIVED.
BUT HIS WORDS STILL HAUNTED ME. THERE'S SO MUCH PAIN IN THIS WORLD.
DOES ANYTHING I DO ACTUALLY MAKE A DIFFERENCE?
OR AM I JUST BAILING WATER OUT OF A SINKING SHIP...IN THE MIDDLE OF AN OCEAN?
I WISH I COULD FIND A WAY TO HELP THEM ALL.
JJ

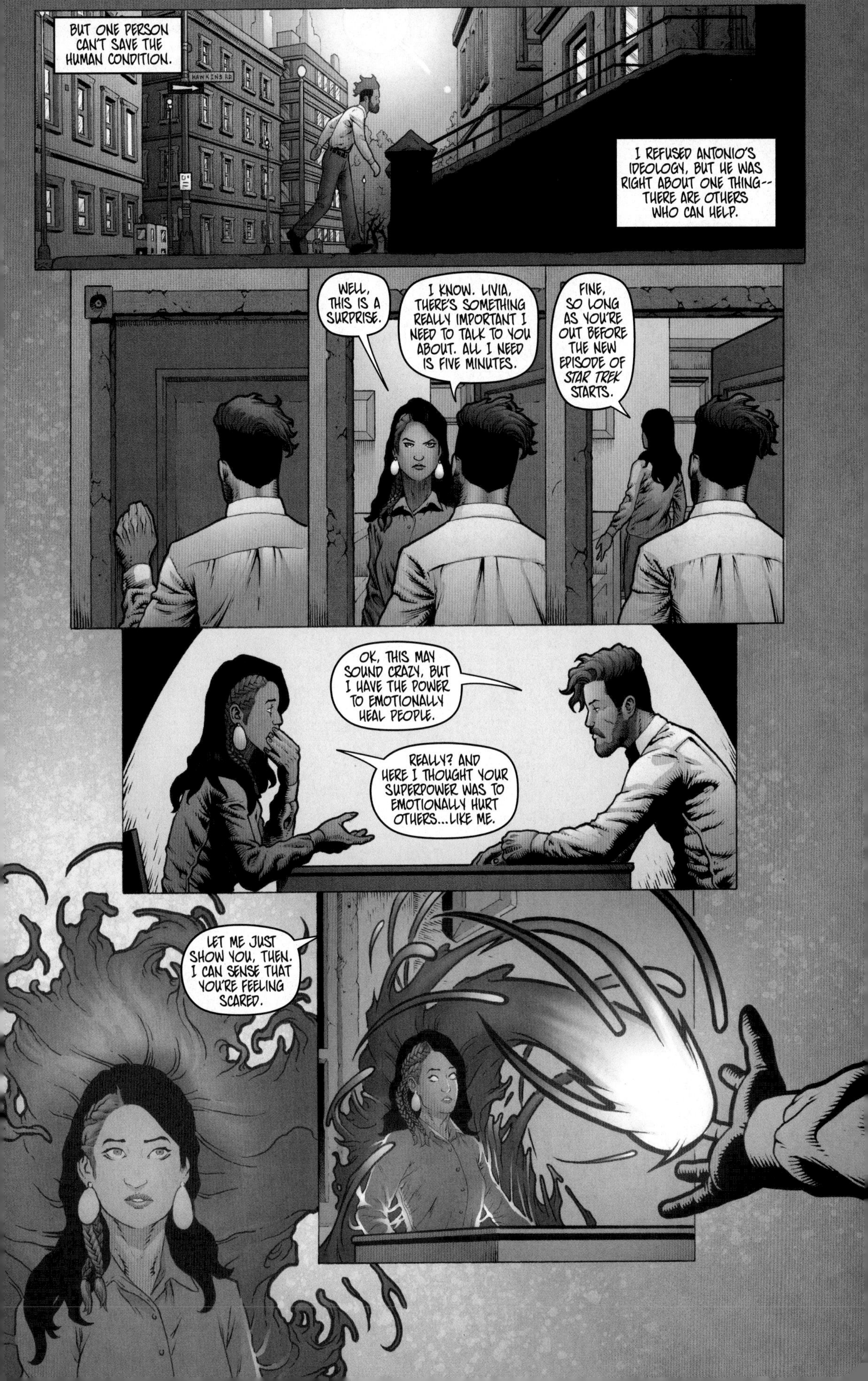

BUT ONE PERSON CAN'T SAVE THE HUMAN CONDITION.
HAWKINS RD
I REFUSED ANTONIO'S IDEOLOGY, BUT HE WAS RIGHT ABOUT ONE THING-- THERE ARE OTHERS WHO CAN HELP.
WELL, THIS IS A SURPRISE.
I KNOW. LIVIA, THERE'S SOMETHING REALLY IMPORTANT I NEED TO TALK TO YOU ABOUT. ALL I NEED IS FIVE MINUTES.
FINE, SO LONG AS YOU'RE OUT BEFORE THE NEW EPISODE OF *STAR TREK* STARTS.
OK, THIS MAY SOUND CRAZY, BUT I HAVE THE POWER TO EMOTIONALLY HEAL PEOPLE.
REALLY? AND HERE I THOUGHT YOUR SUPERPOWER WAS TO EMOTIONALLY HURT OTHERS...LIKE ME.
LET ME JUST SHOW YOU, THEN. I CAN SENSE THAT YOU'RE FEELING SCARED.

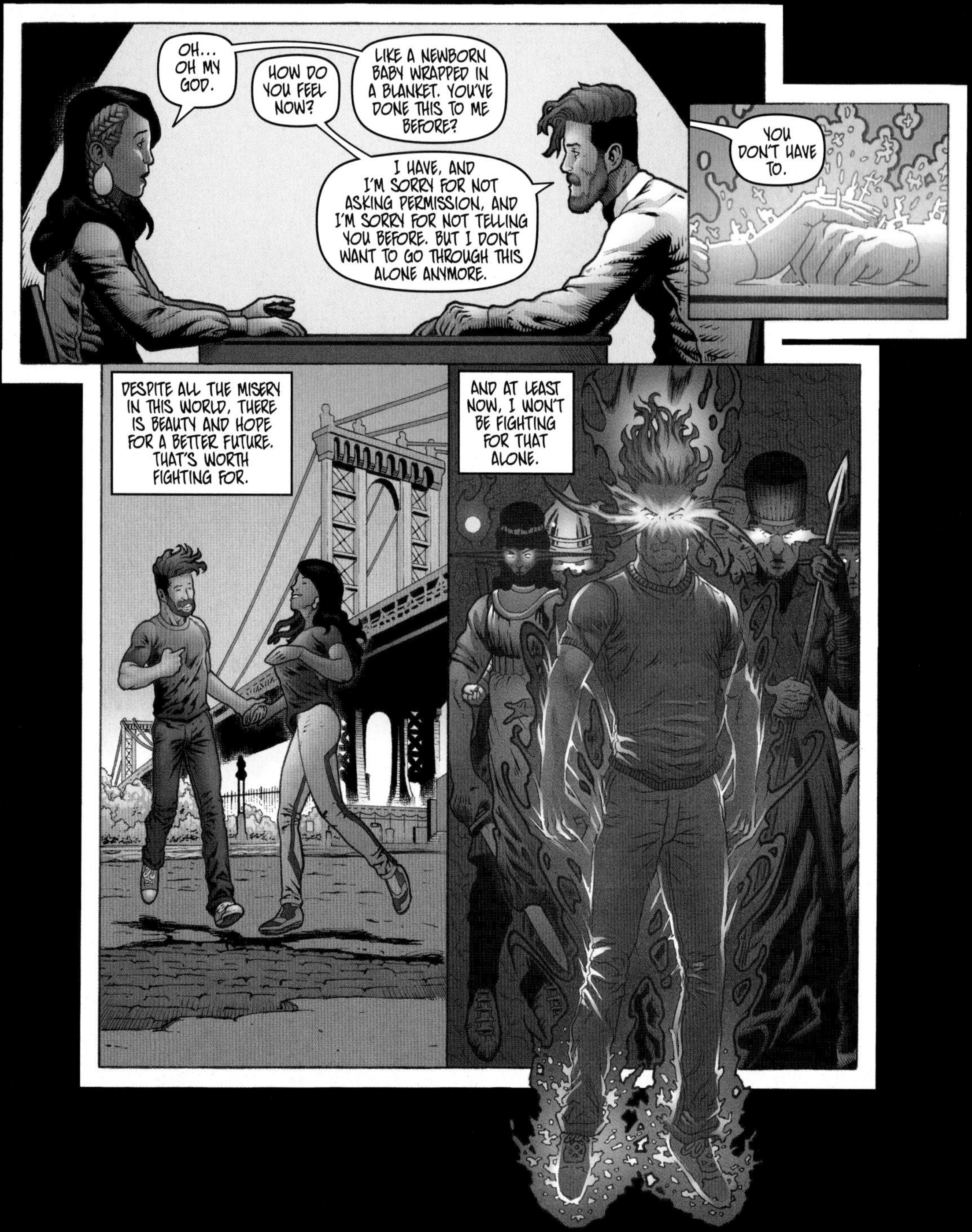
OH... OH MY GOD.
LIKE A NEWBORN BABY WRAPPED IN A BLANKET. YOU'VE DONE THIS TO ME BEFORE?
HOW DO YOU FEEL NOW?
I HAVE, AND I'M SORRY FOR NOT ASKING PERMISSION, AND I'M SORRY FOR NOT TELLING YOU BEFORE. BUT I DON'T WANT TO GO THROUGH THIS ALONE ANYMORE.
YOU DON'T HAVE TO.
DESPITE ALL THE MISERY IN THIS WORLD, THERE IS BEAUTY AND HOPE FOR A BETTER FUTURE. THAT'S WORTH FIGHTING FOR.
AND AT LEAST NOW, I WON'T BE FIGHTING FOR THAT ALONE.

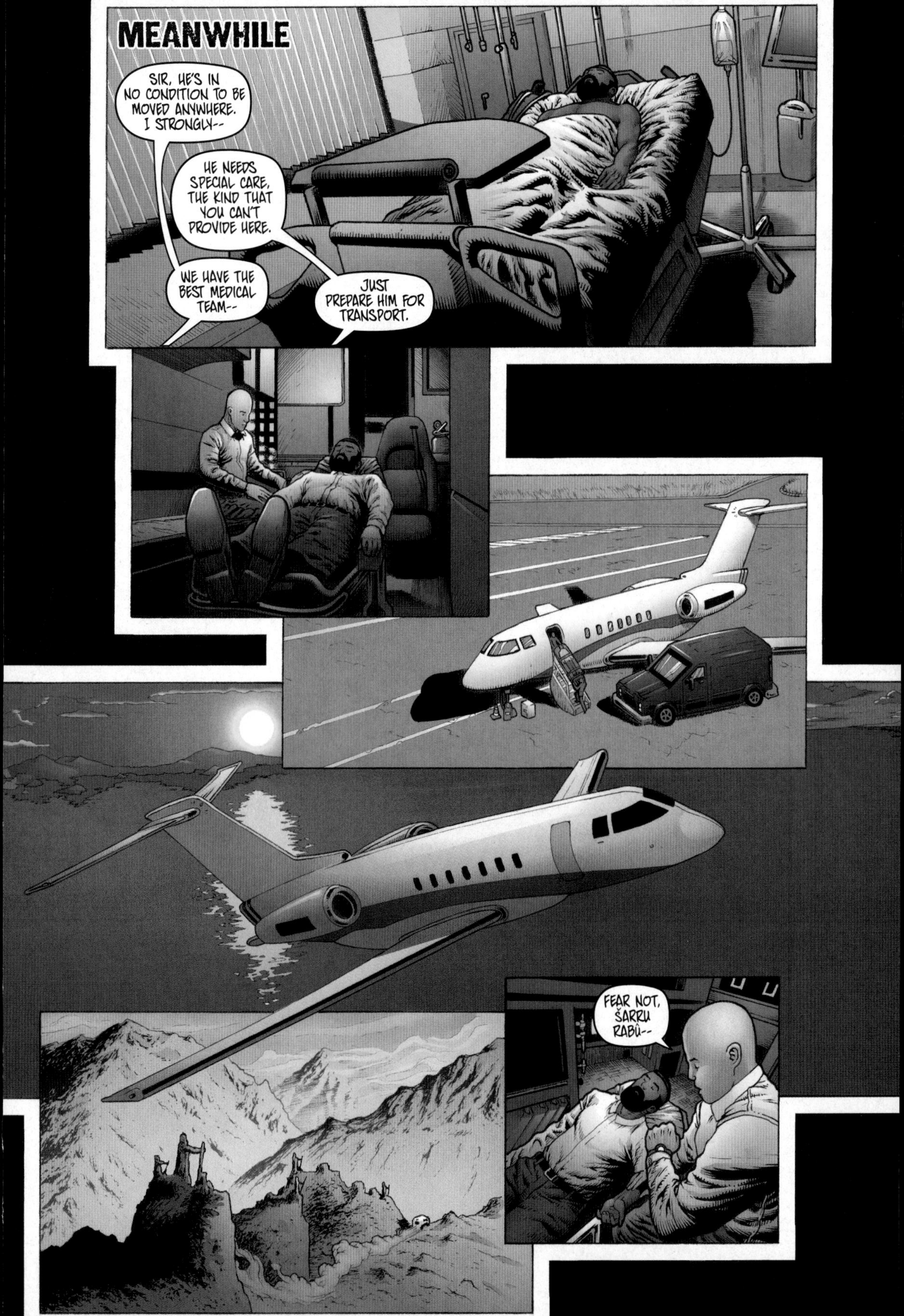
MEANWHILE
SIR, HE'S IN NO CONDITION TO BE MOVED ANYWHERE. I STRONGLY--
HE NEEDS SPECIAL CARE, THE KIND THAT YOU CAN'T PROVIDE HERE.
WE HAVE THE BEST MEDICAL TEAM--
JUST PREPARE HIM FOR TRANSPORT.
FEAR NOT, ŠARRU RABÛ--

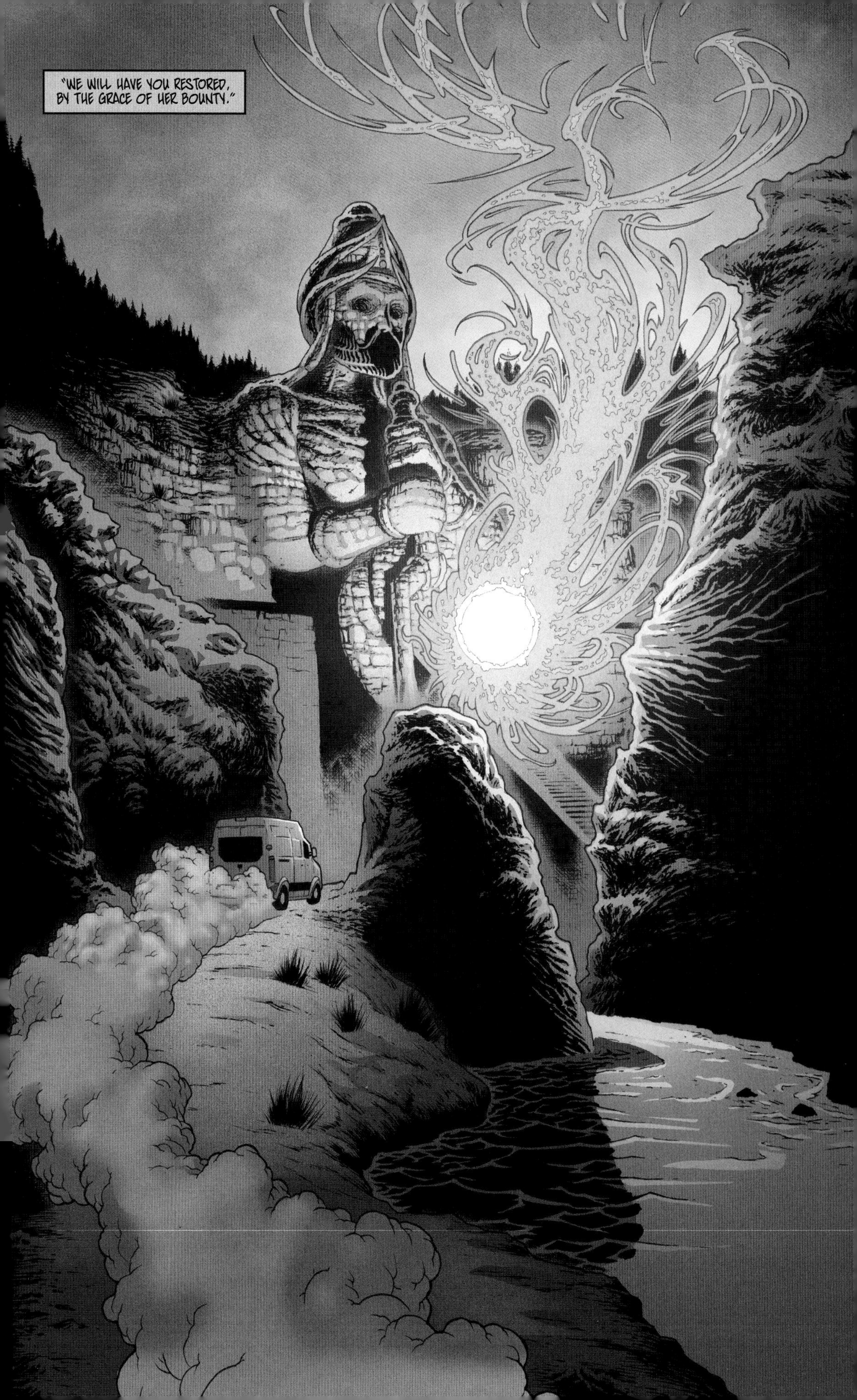
"WE WILL HAVE YOU RESTORED, BY THE GRACE OF HER BOUNTY."

MEET THE TEAM

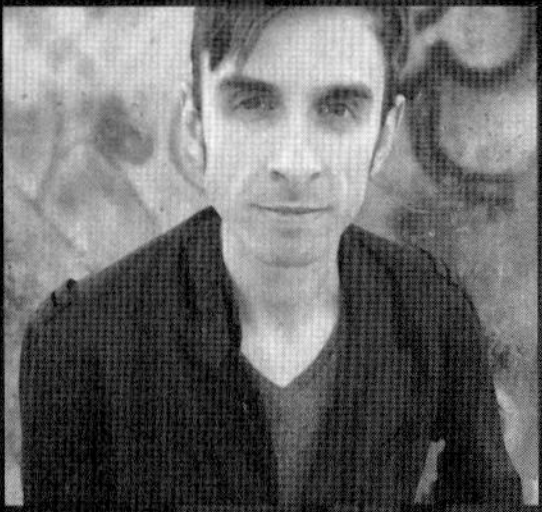

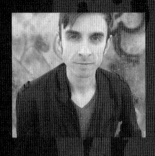

PATRICK MEANEY

Patrick is a writer and filmmaker. He directed a series of acclaimed documentaries about some of the biggest names and events in comics history, including *Grant Morrison: Talking With Gods, The Image Revolution, Neil Gaiman: Dream Dangerously* and Chris Claremont's *X-Men*, as well as the horror film *House of Demons*, distributed by Sony Pictures Home Entertainment. On the comic book page, he wrote Last Born for Black Mask Studios, and contributed to the *Occupy Comics* anthology.

MOHSEN ASHRAF

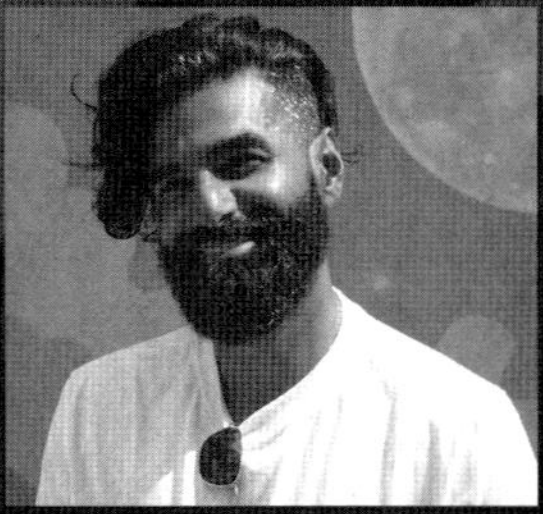

Mohsen is a writer and Silicon Valley executive with a passion for storytelling. He recently completed his first novel in a new mythic fantasy series entitled *Pantheon*, and is incredibly excited to now announce his first comic series, SYPHON. Prior to this, he worked on several entrepreneurial ventures and was an investment banker in New York City. Although a San Francisco Bay Area native, Mohsen grew up overseas and continues to trek around the world with an intrepid sense of adventure.

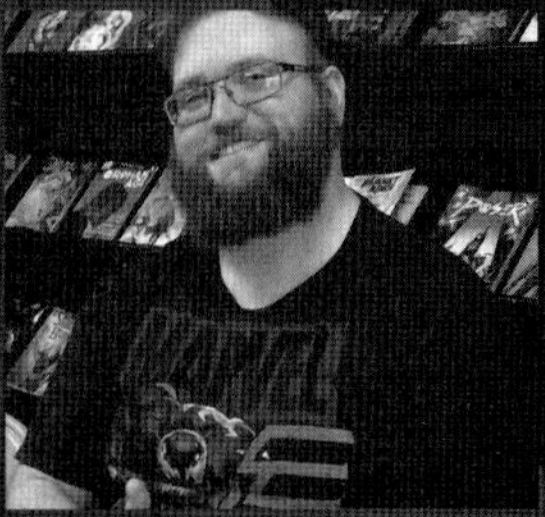

JEFF EDWARDS

Jeff is a professional comic book artist. He landed his first published project creating illustrations to be used in a series of articles written for Australia's pop-culture-driven magazine, *FilmInk*. He has since gone on to draw *GI JOE, Transformers, Warlock 5*, and *TMNT*.

JOHN KALISZ

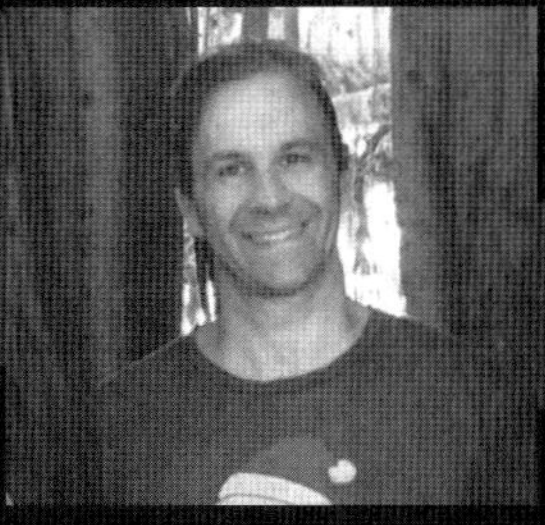

John has been coloring comics for nearly thirty years, working on *Avengers, Zatanna*, and everything in between!

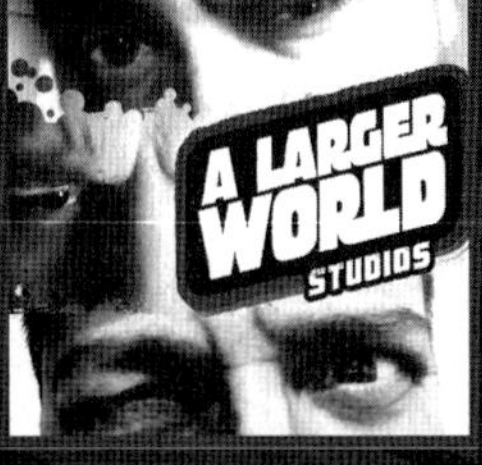
A LARGER WORLD
STUDIOS

TROY PETERI

Troy and Dave Lanphear are collectively known as A Larger World Studios. They've lettered everything from *The Avengers, Iron Man, Wolverine, Amazing Spider-Man* and *X-Men* to more recent titles such as *Witchblade, Cyberforce*, and *Batman/Wonder Woman: The Brave & The Bold*. They can be reached at studio@alargerworld.com for your lettering and design needs. (Hooray, commerce!)

COVER GALLERY

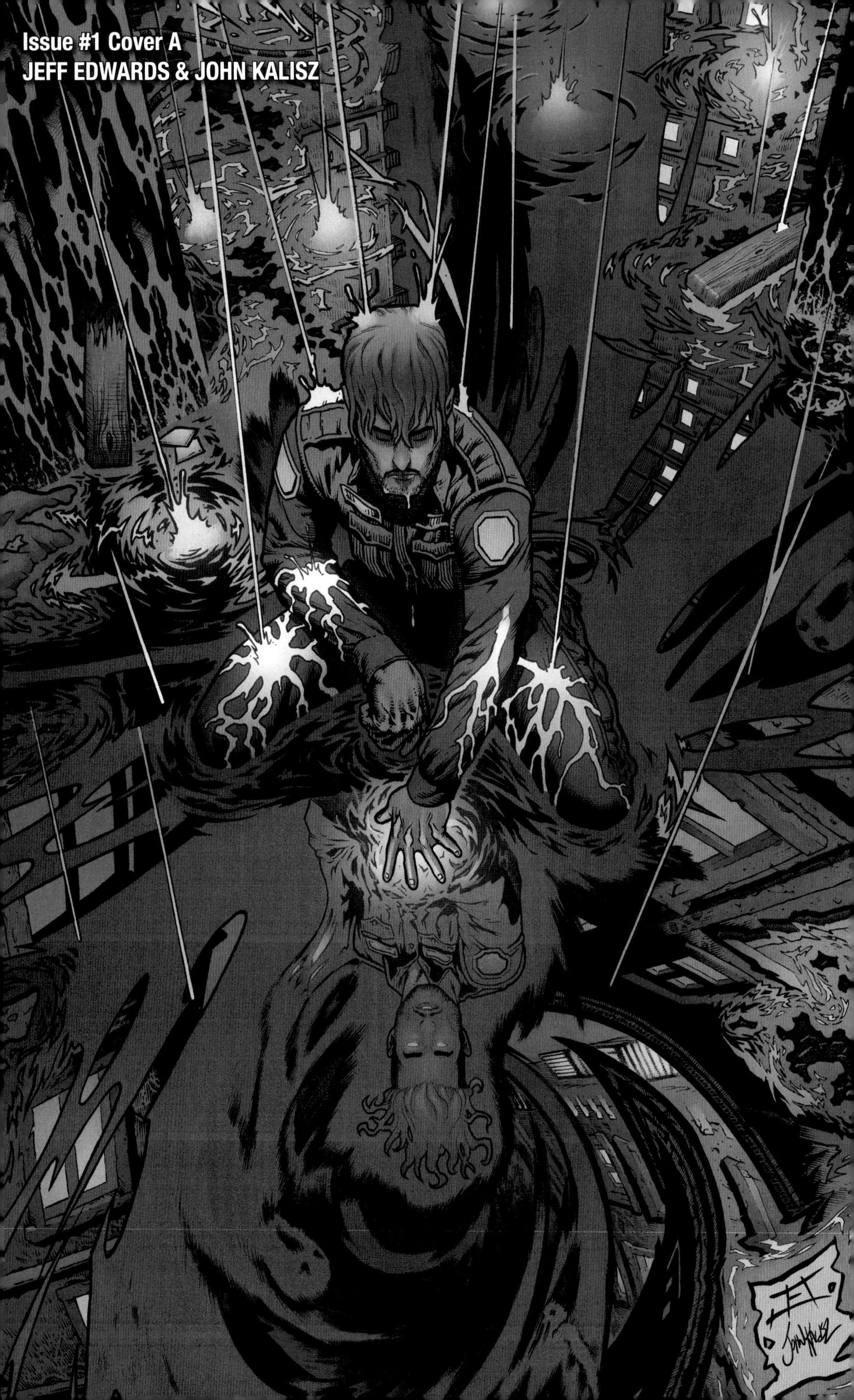

Issue #1 Cover A
JEFF EDWARDS & JOHN KALISZ

Issue #1 Frankie's Comics Variant
JOHN GALLAGHER

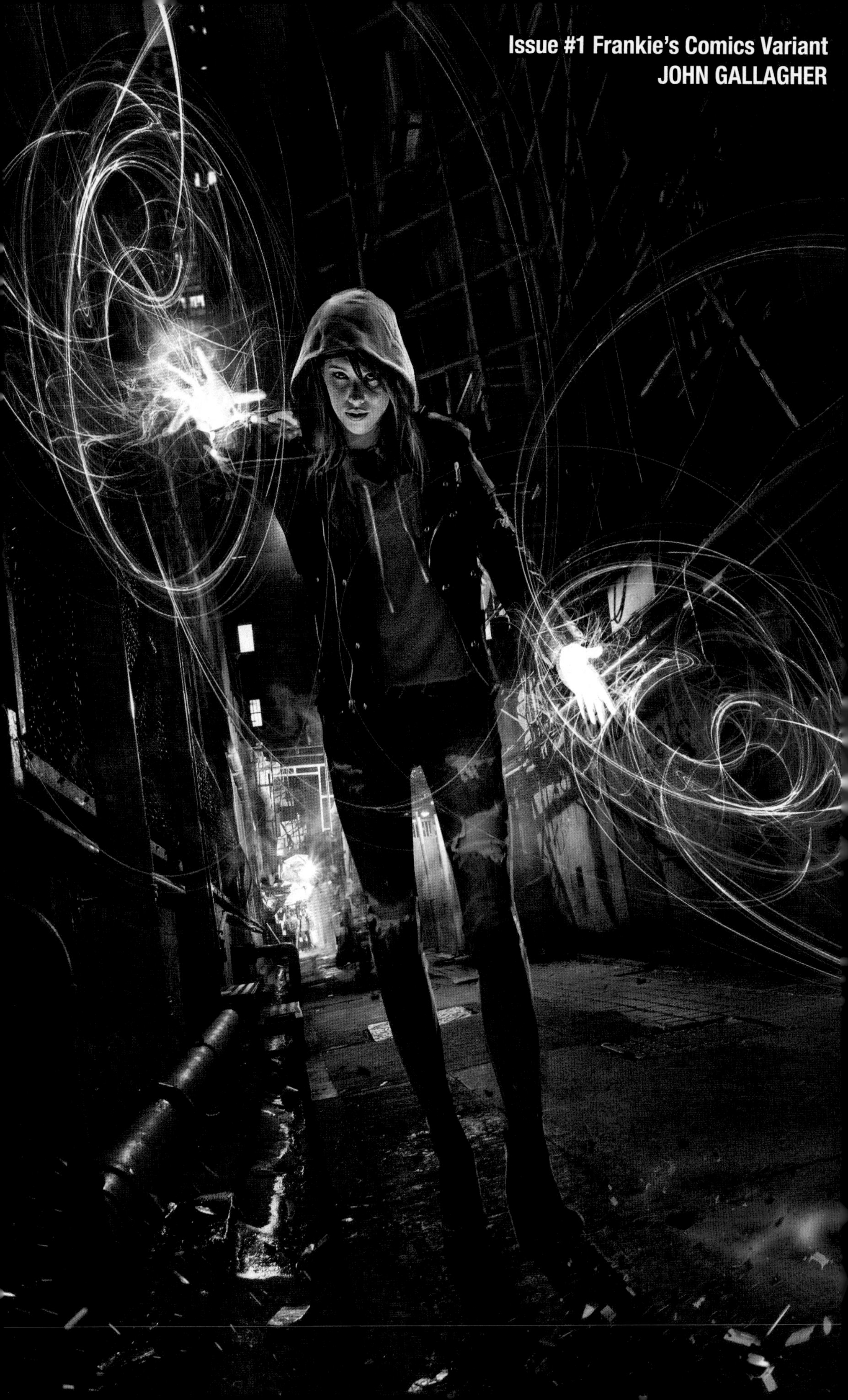

Issue #1 One Stop Comic Shop Variant
STEVE KURTH & BRIAN REBER

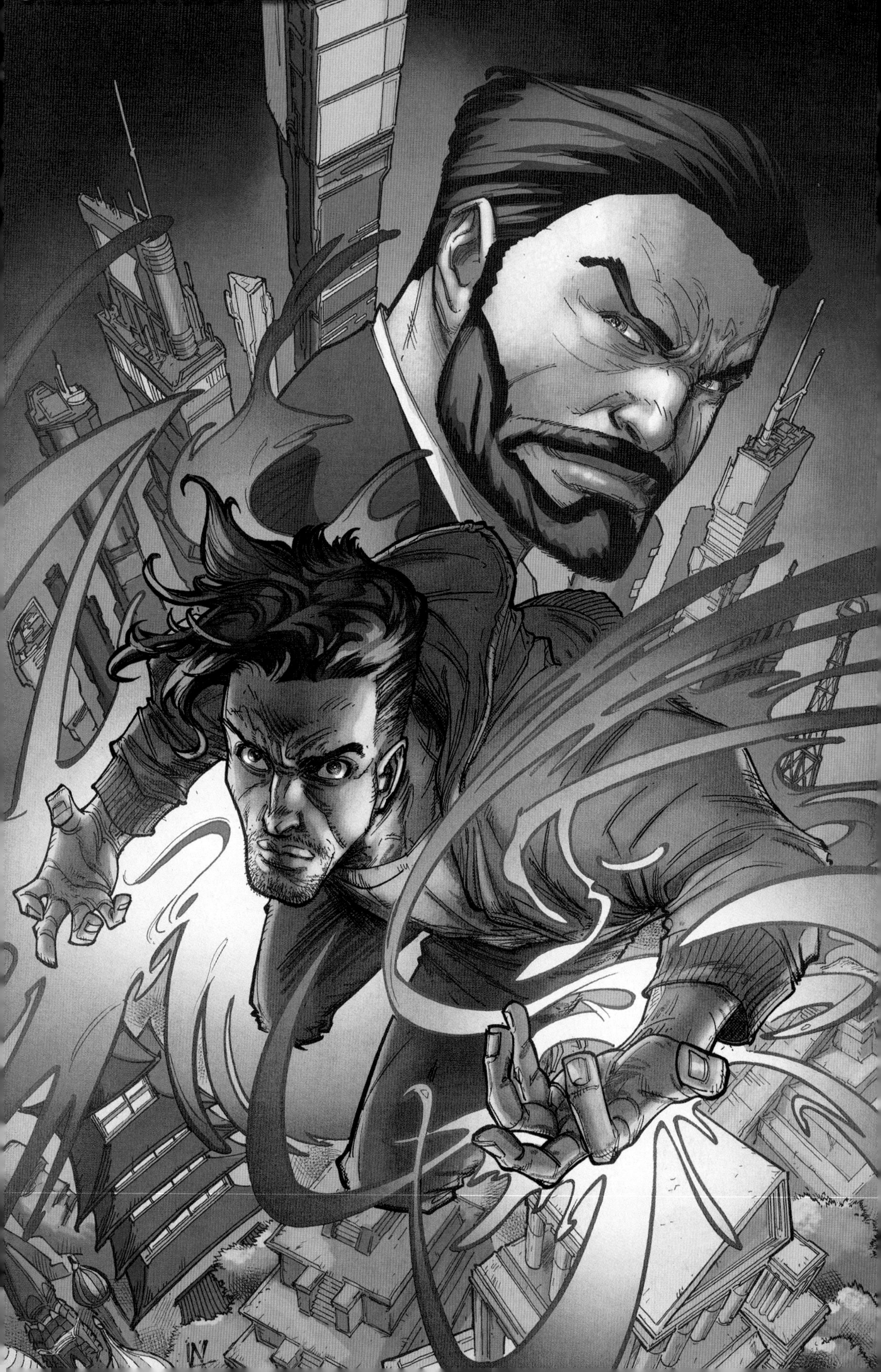

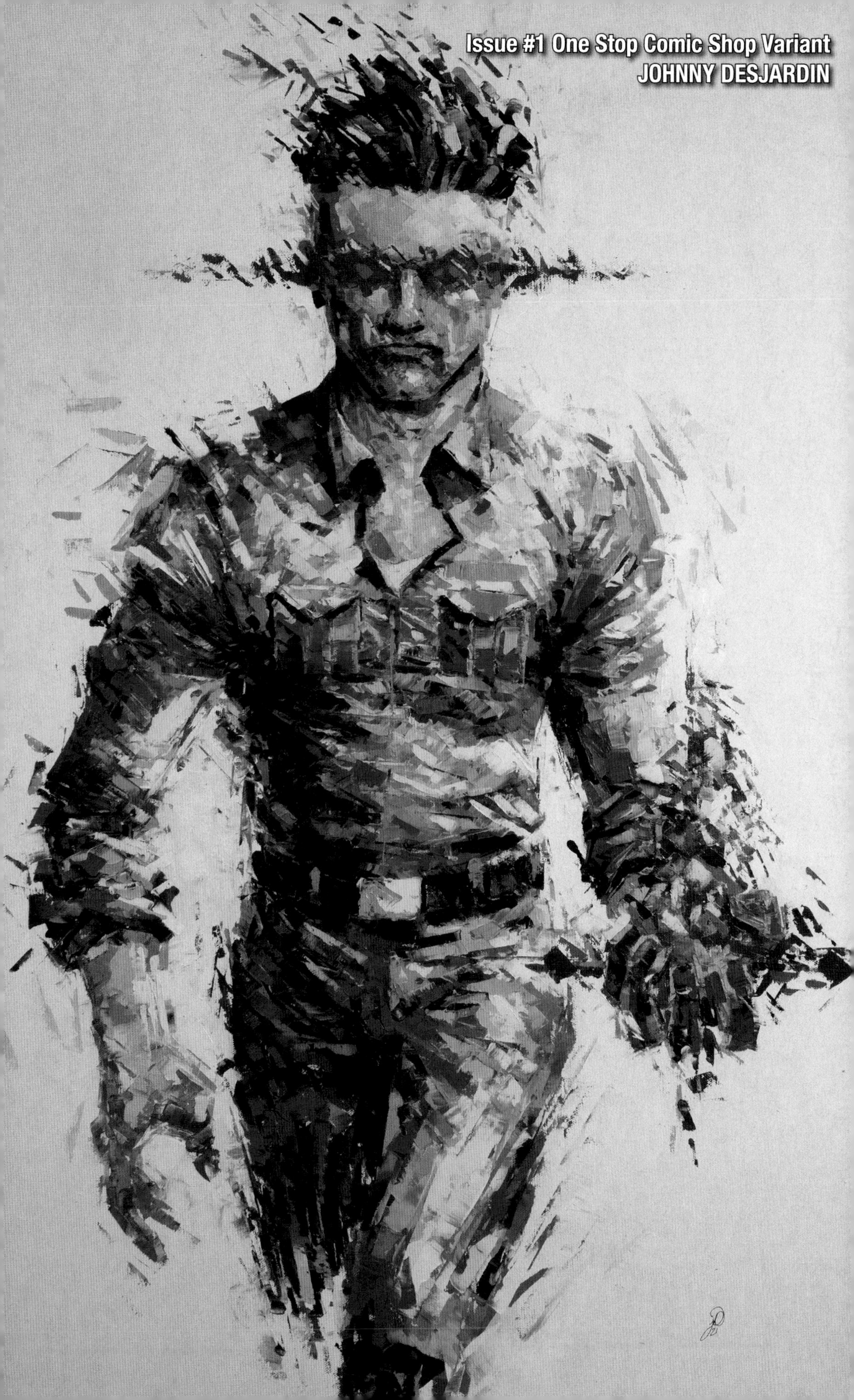

Issue #1 One Stop Comic Shop Variant
JOHNNY DESJARDIN

Issue #1 The Comic Book Dealer Variant
STEVE KURTH & BRIAN REBER

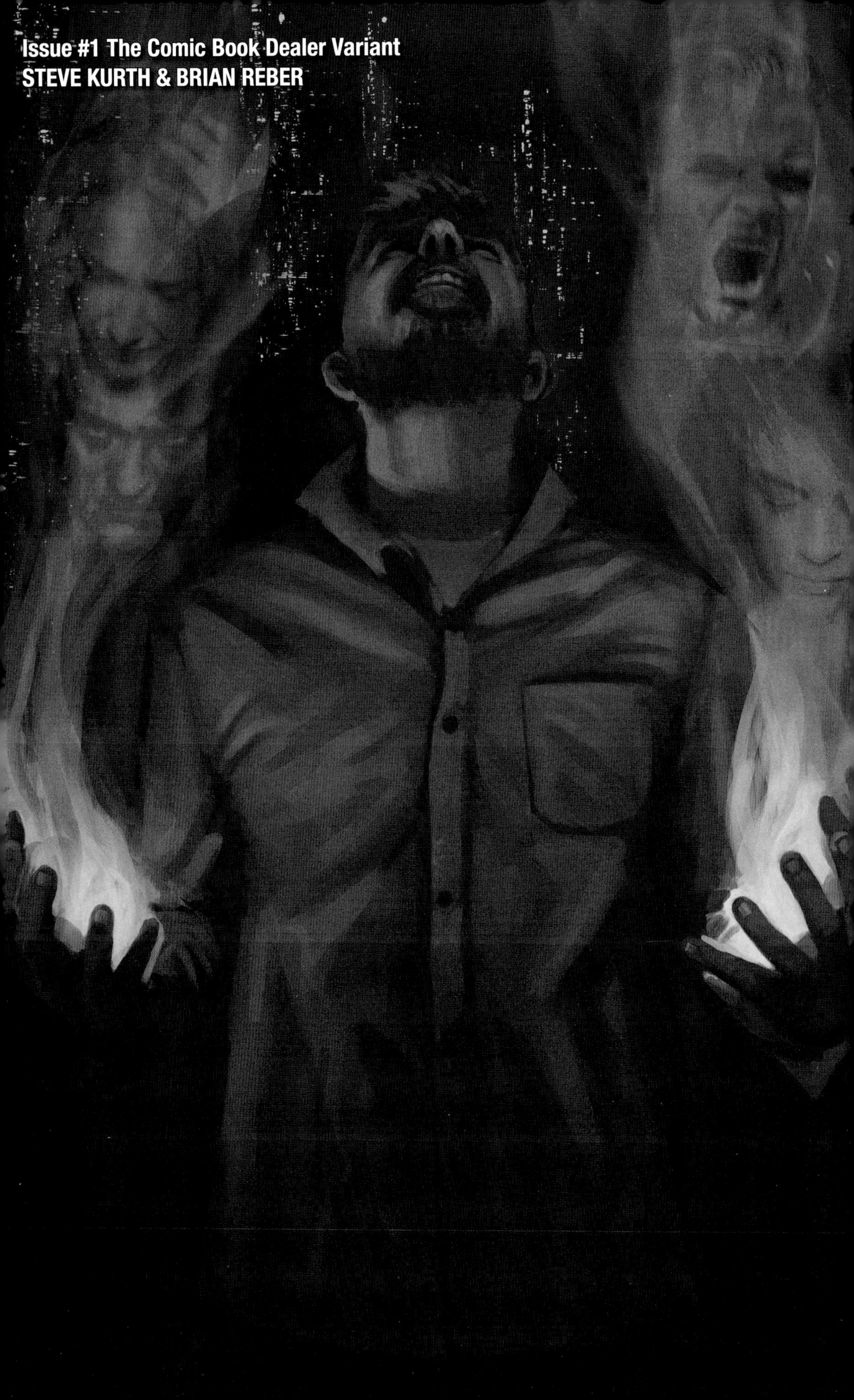

Issue #2 Cover
JEFF EDWARDS & JOHN KALISZ

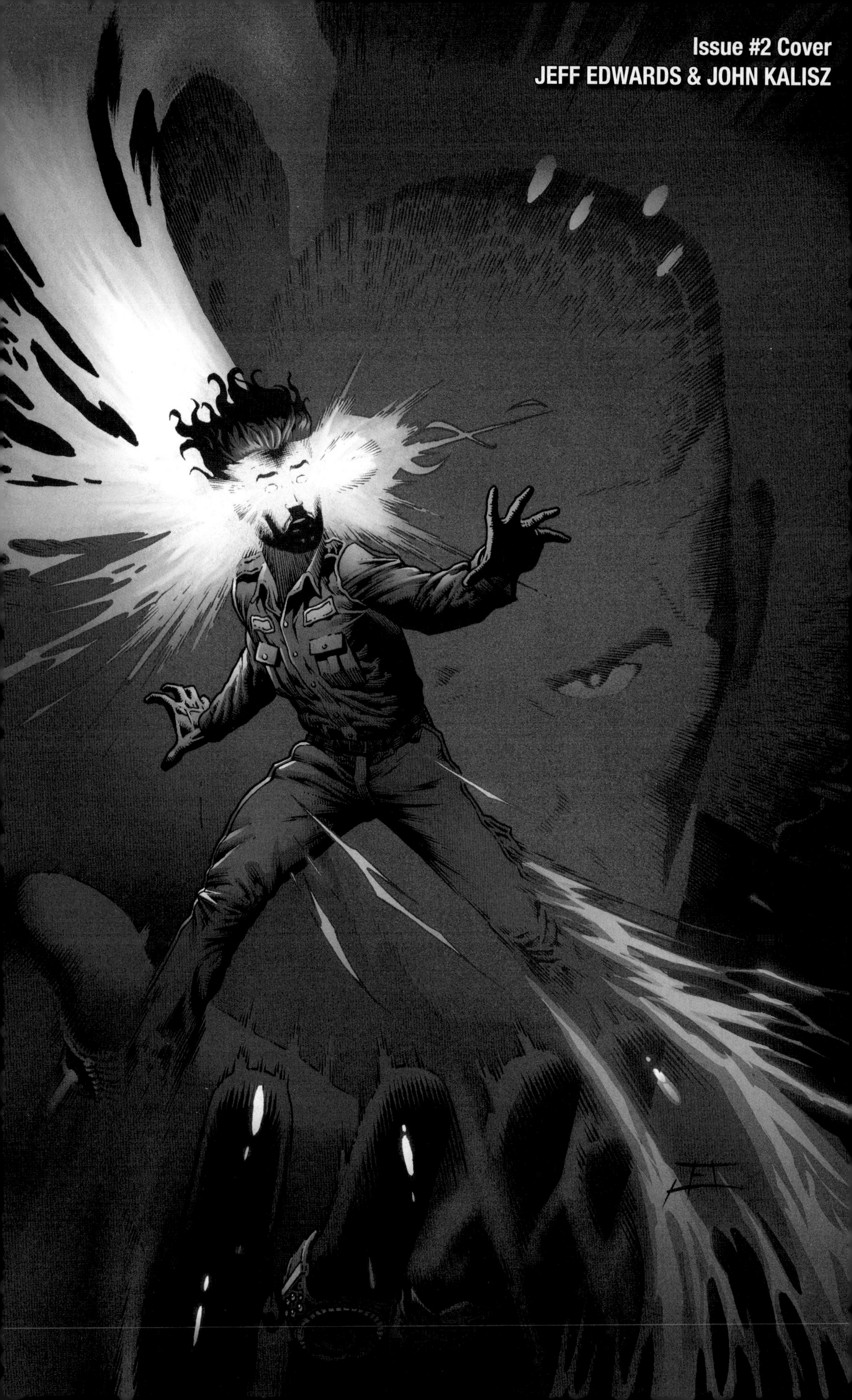

Issue #3 Cover A
JEFF EDWARDS & JOHN KALISZ

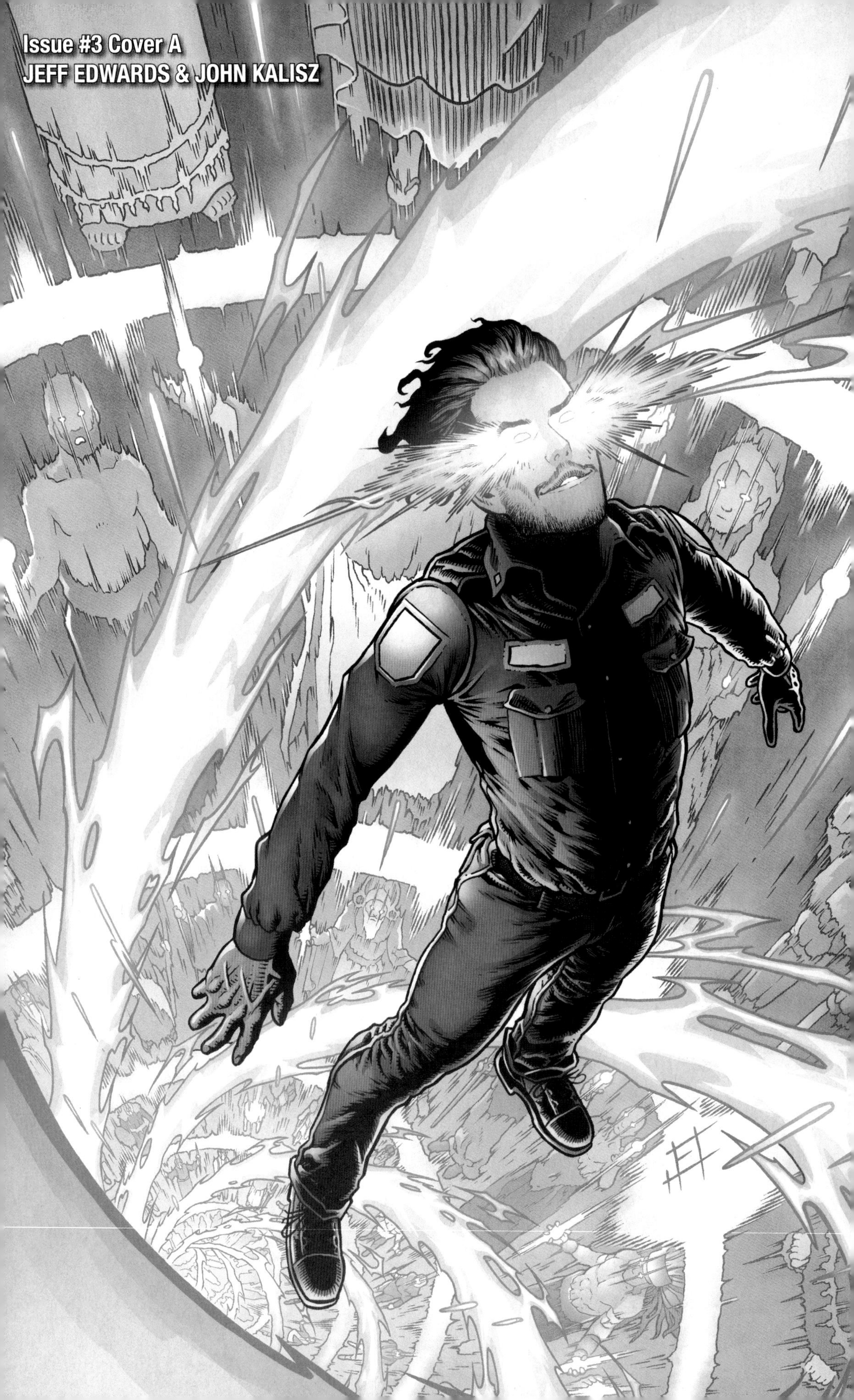

Issue #3 Cover B
Steve Cleff

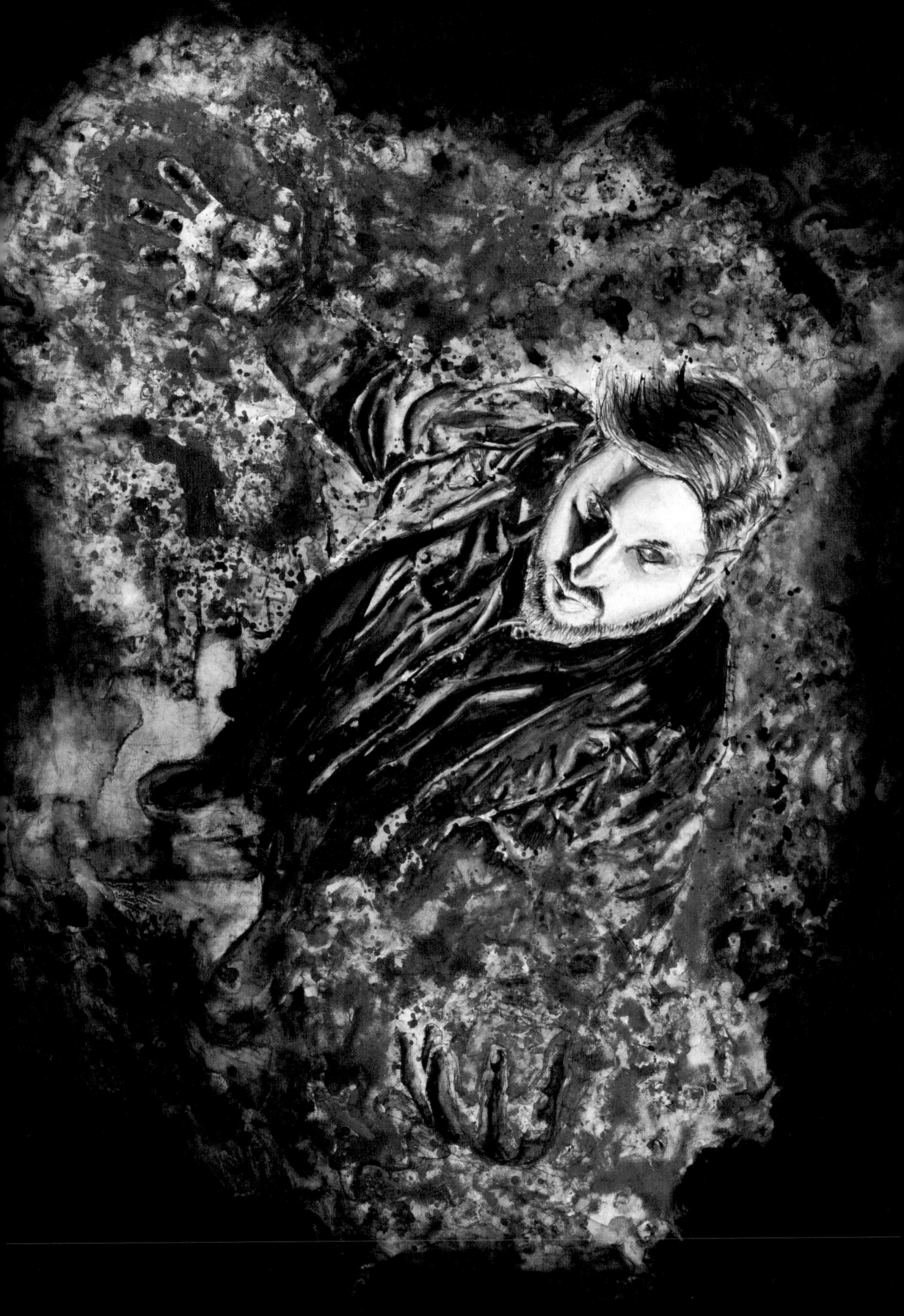

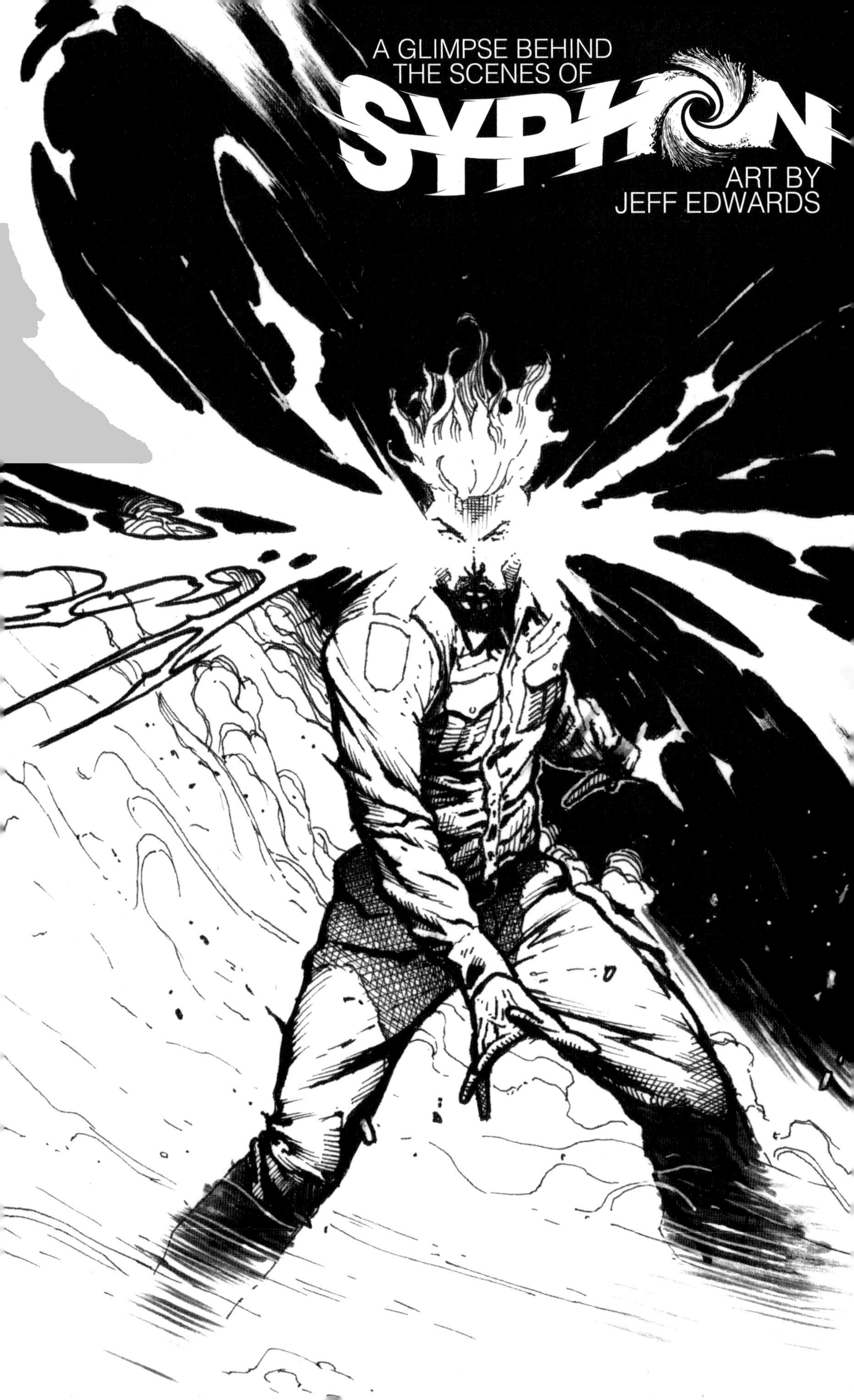
A GLIMPSE BEHIND
THE SCENES OF
SYPHON
ART BY
JEFF EDWARDS

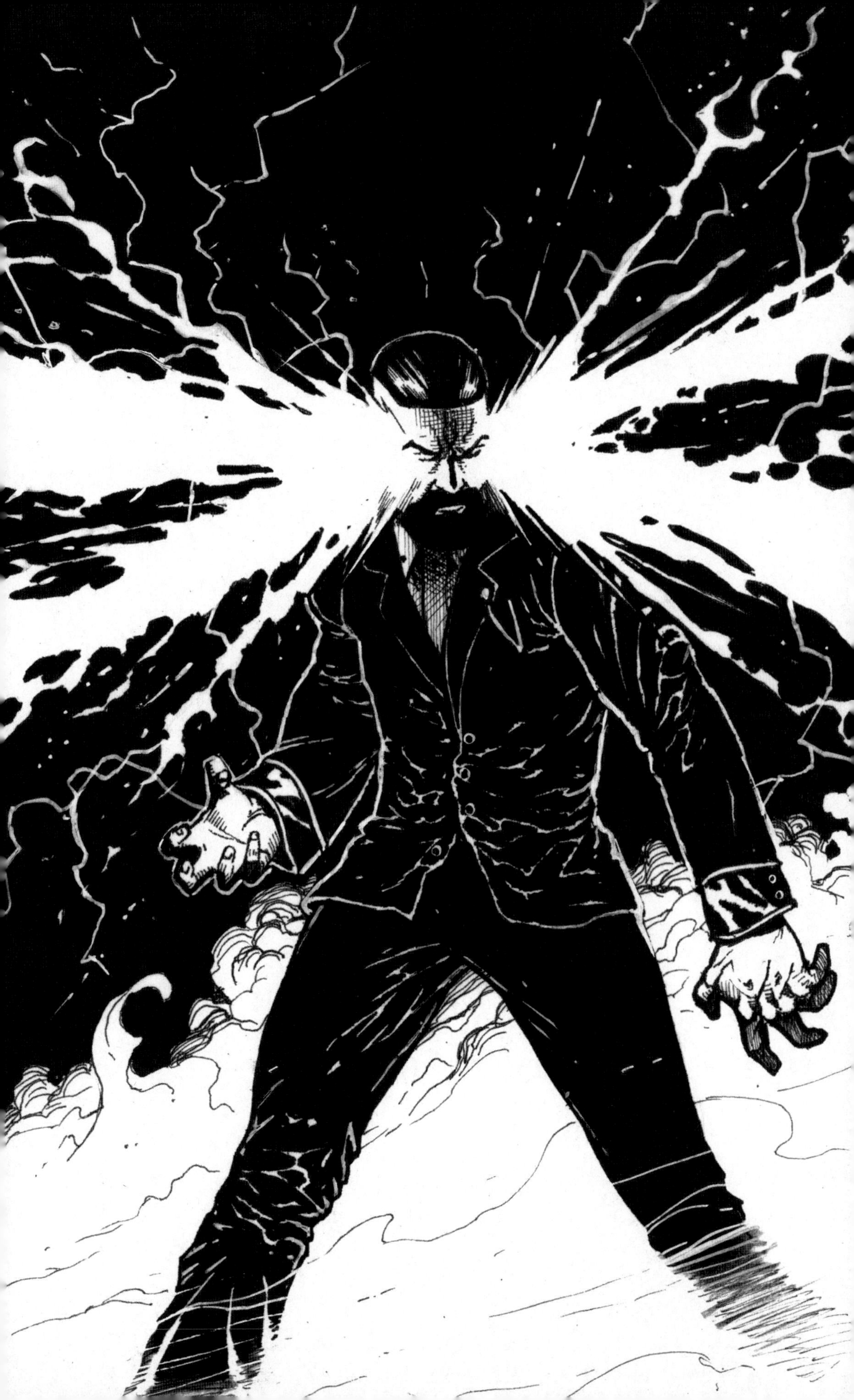

Syphon
Issue 1

PAGE 1:
Panel 1:

Open with KATHARINE, an Asian woman with grey hair, is walking down a crowded New York street. She appears old, but is wearing dark jeans and a tight leather jacket that look like something a much younger person would wear.

In this panel, we see her from afar, at the entrance of an alley. It's night time, the alley is dingy, and not many people are on the streets behind her. She's staring intently at something that we can't quite see. But, there is a red glow rising up from just off the bottom of the panel.

The time is September in New York, it's not cold yet, but Fall is in the air.

Panel 2:
From above now, we see a bird's eye shot of Katharine walking down the alley, out of the light of the city into the darkness, towards something glowing red in the center of the alley. It seems to be a person, hunched over in pain. We can see fire escapes and things on the side of the building, and the overall sense should be of her moving out of safety and into a dangerous dark, like a moth drawn to the flame.

Katharine:
Hey, everything's going to be okay.

Panel 3:
Over her shoulder now, we see her walking towards the red glowing thing, and get a better sense of what it is. It's a homeless man hunched over in pain, clearly suffering. Katharine has her hand out.

Katharine:
My name's Katharine, I can help.

Panel 4:
Medium on Katharine now, we see wrinkles on her face, the grey in her hair, bags under her eyes. She seems stressed, but is still determined to press on. Just barely visible in the foreground, we see the Man standing up, the red energy rising up in the frame. Katharine seems quite compassionate, eager to help.

Katharine:
I know you're in pain.

Panel 5:
Close on her hand reaching out, we see the start of what looks like a red flame glowing out of it, the same as we saw on the Man who was standing up. I'm imagining this is a long thin panel.

Katharine:
Let me heal you.

Panel 6:
We're behind Katharine now. We can see the shadow cast on her back of a man approaching her from behind. She has her hand reached out towards the Man in the alley. He notices someone approaching behind her and looks terrified.

Man:
I'm sorry, lady.

Katharine:
What?

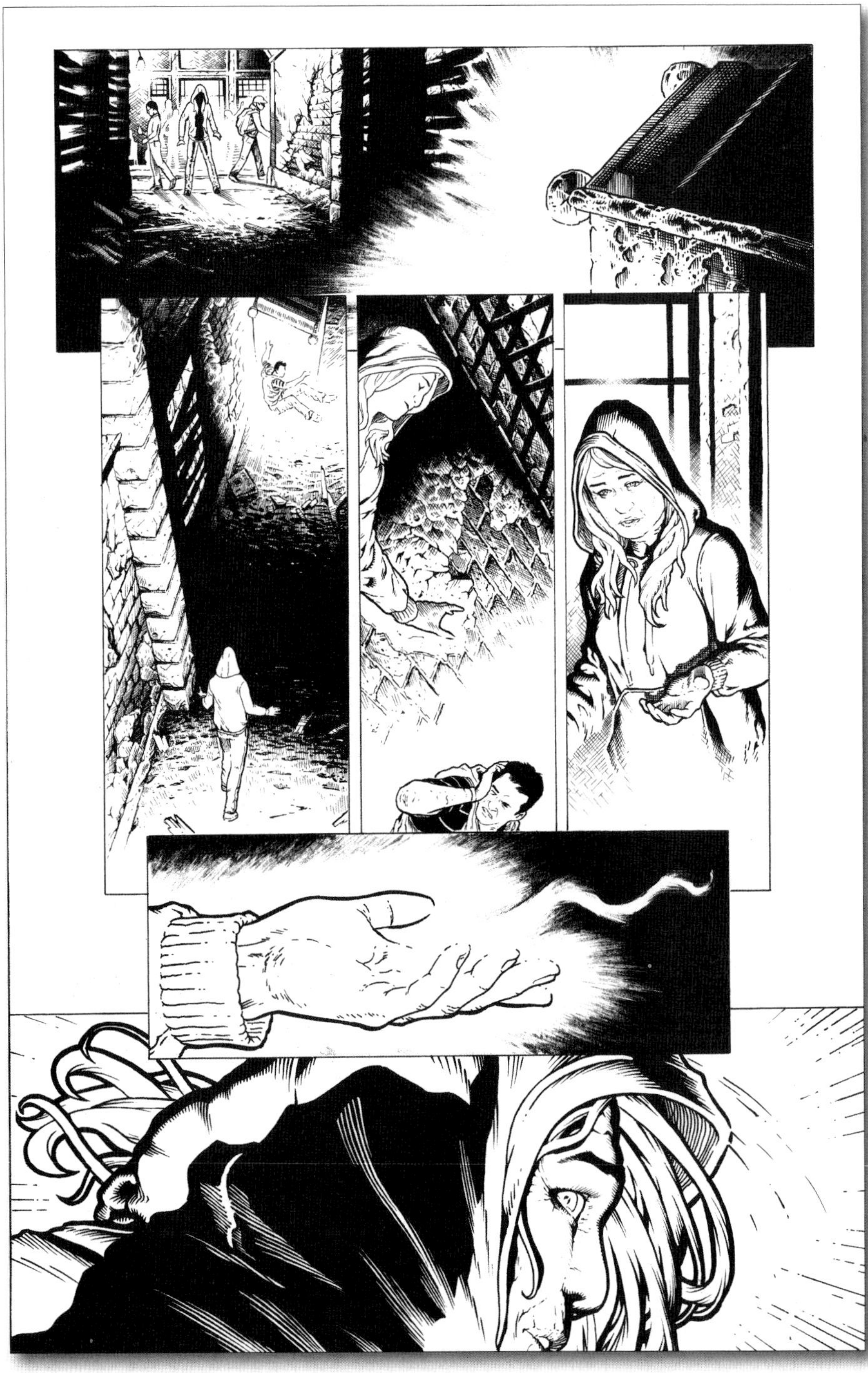

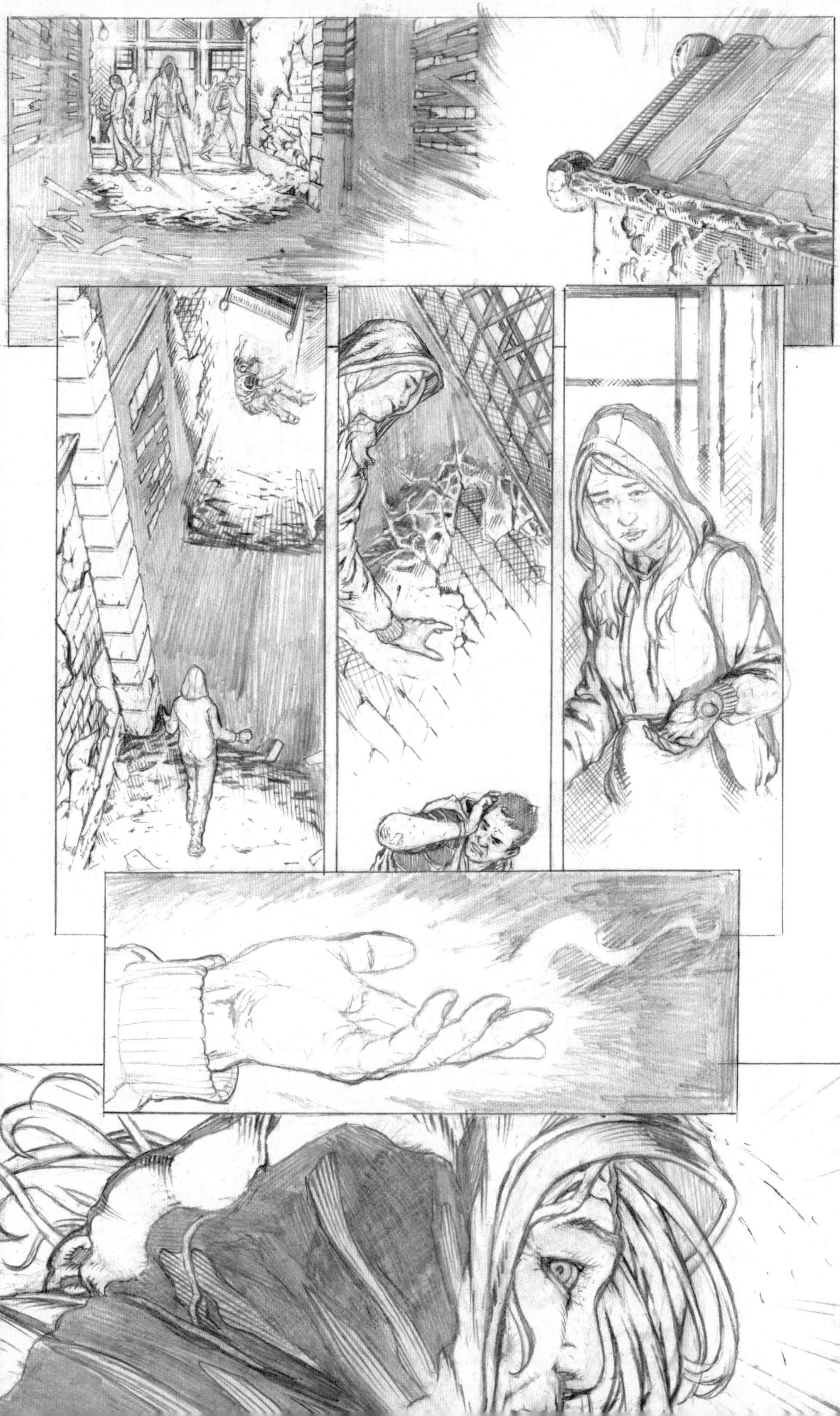

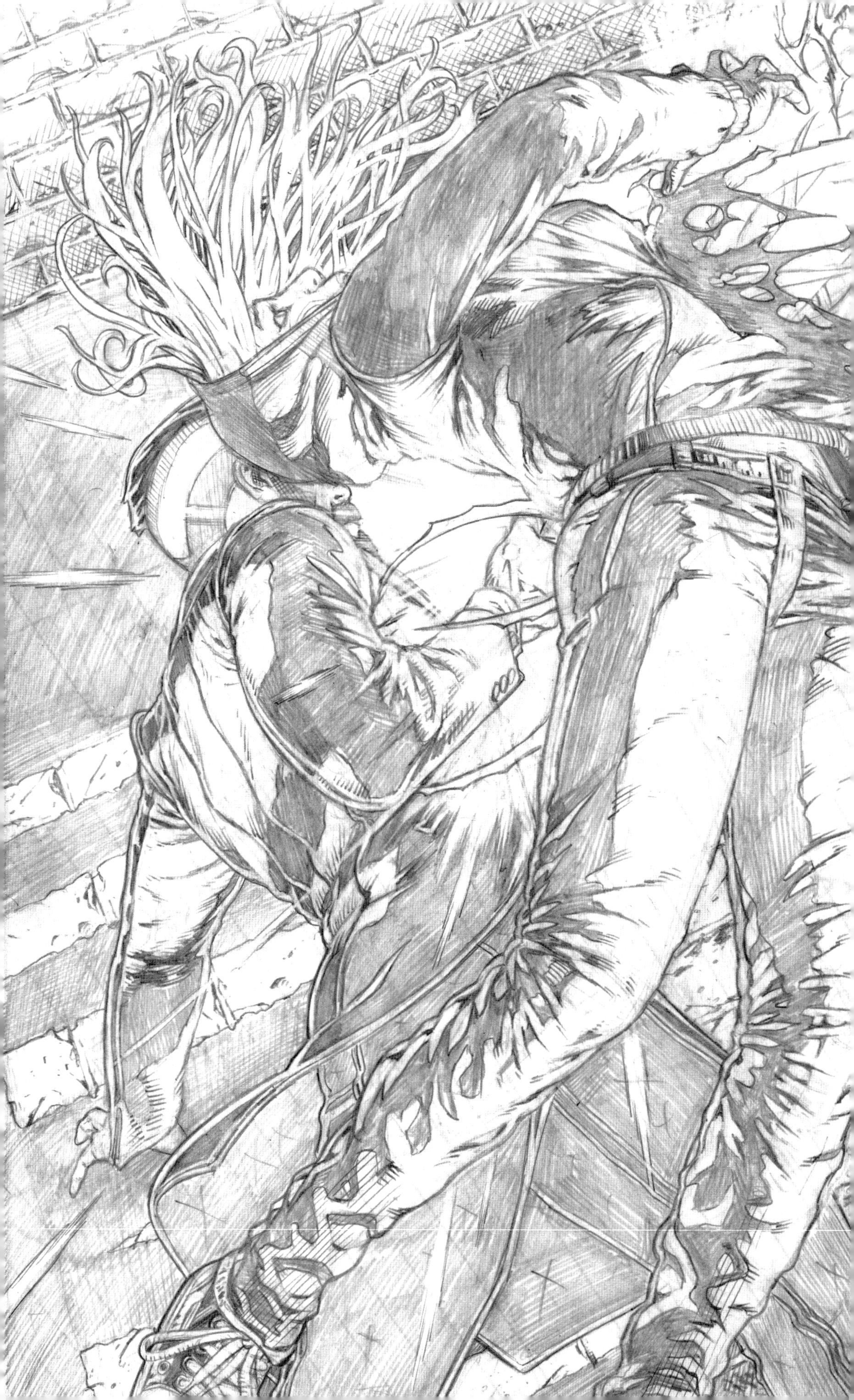

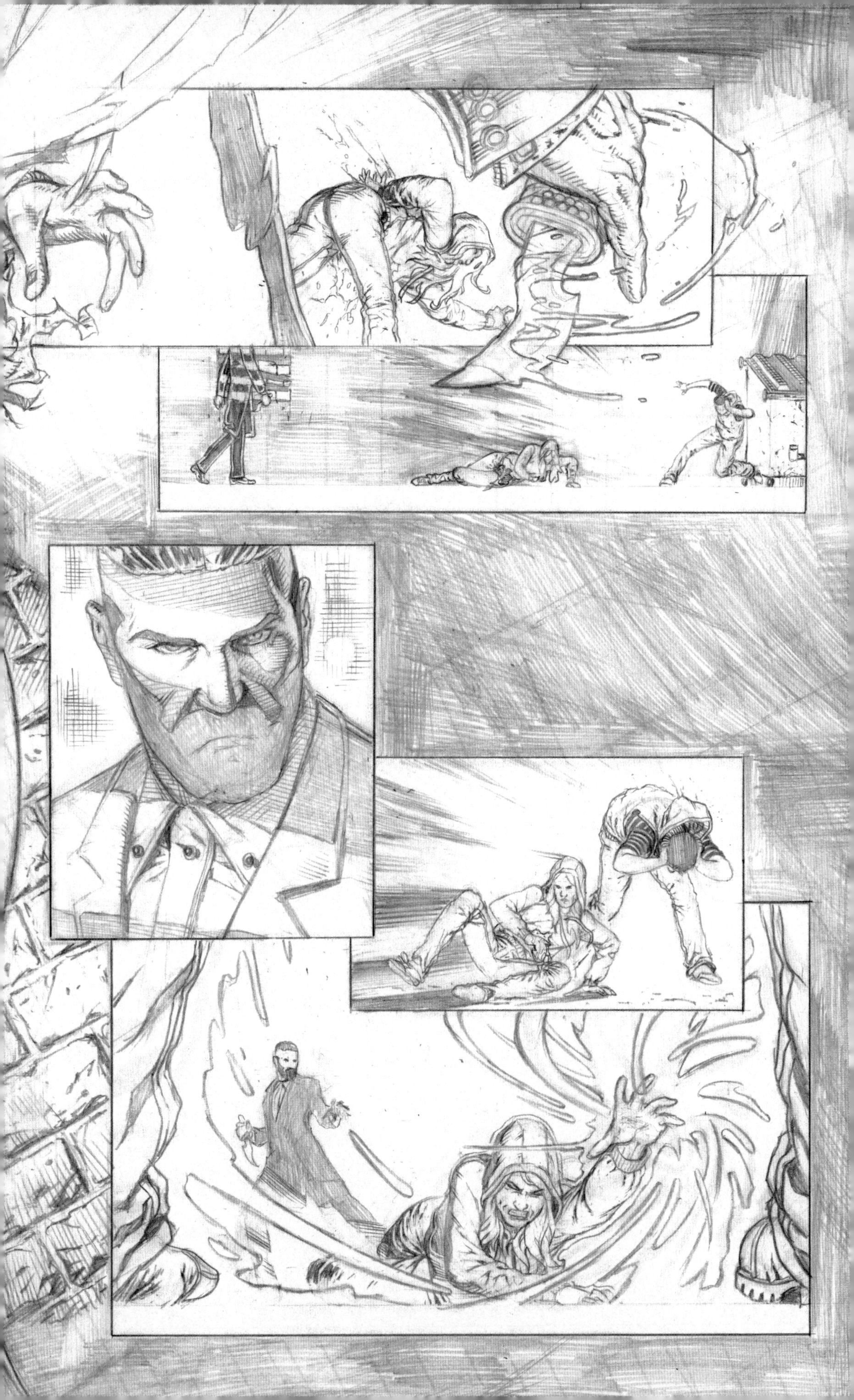

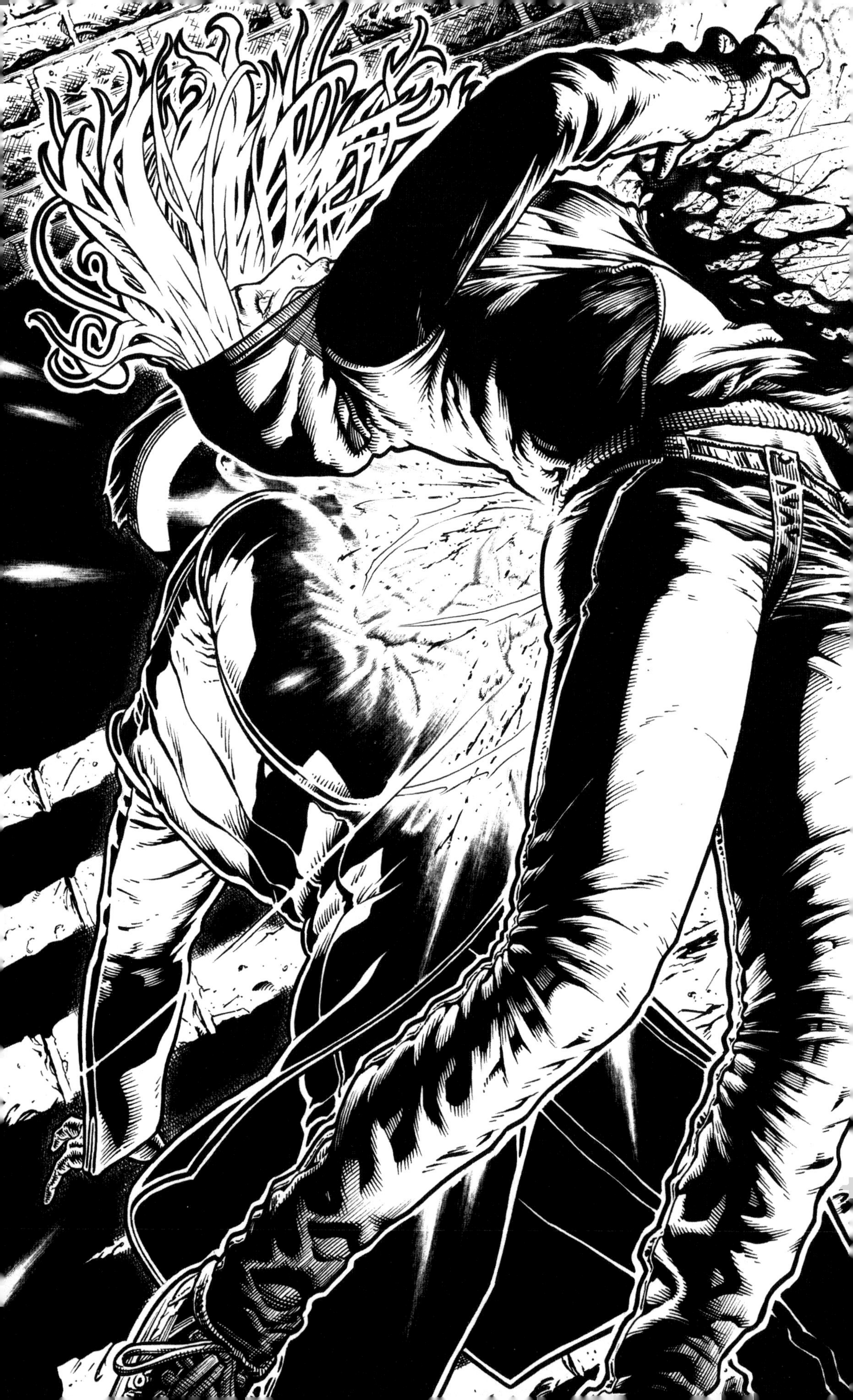

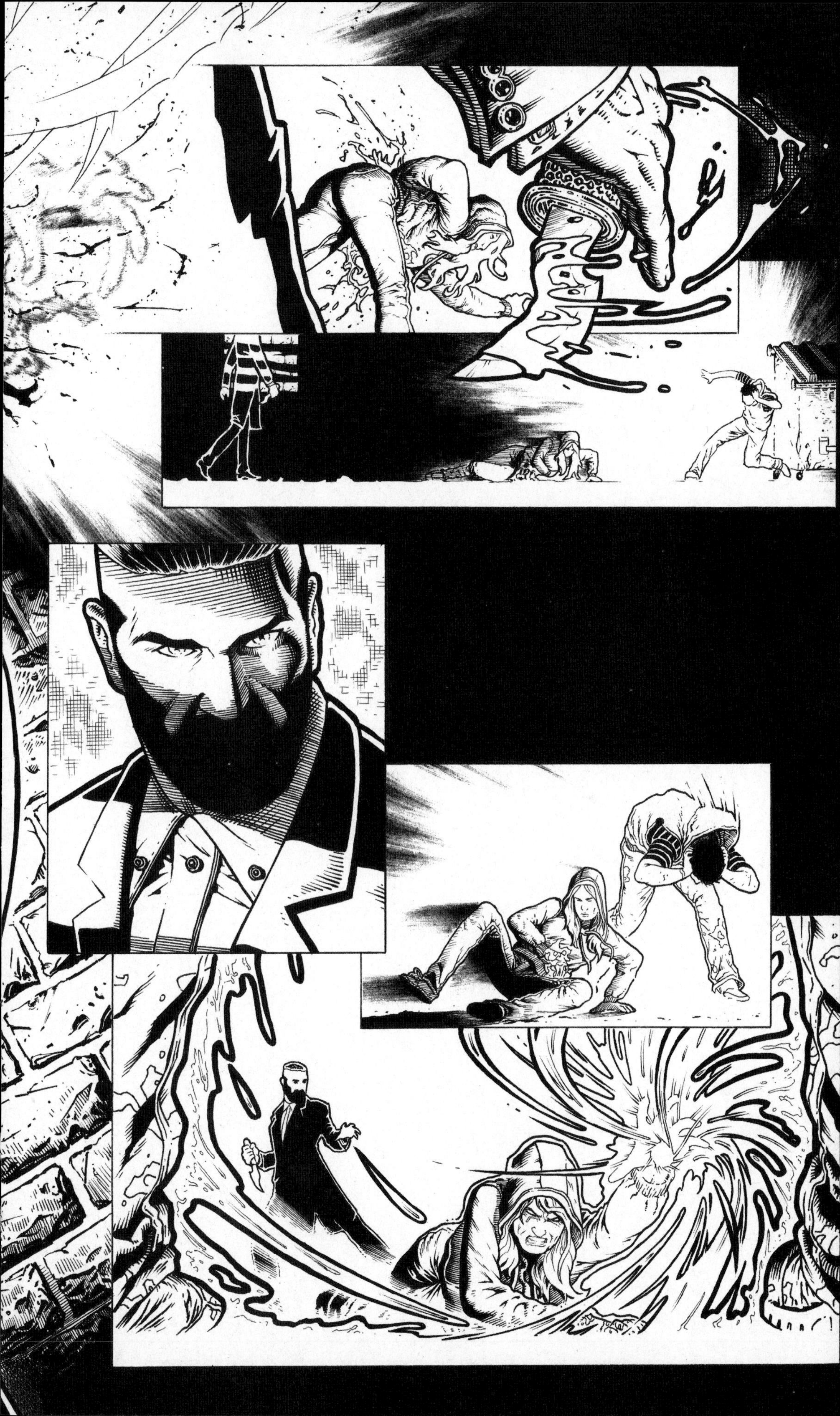

PAGE 2:
Panel 1:
Big splash page. Antonio has stabbed Katharine in the back. We can't quite see him, he's hidden behind her, but we can see her reaction. She's shocked by the pain, and her head is thrown back from the impact, as Antonio holds her body as she shudders, and then falls. We can already see blood pooling on the front of her shirt.

Antonio is hidden in the shadows, but we can see that he's wearing a long fancy coat, and can make out his silhouette behind her. He is quite taller than her, and it gives the impression of a force enveloping her.

She was absolutely defenseless, and the force has practically shoved her off her feet. We can tell that he has moved incredibly quickly and has great reflexes. The moment should feel big and grand, like this is the conclusion of an epic conflict.

One idea to make it feel big would be to do this as a two page splash, with all the action described above on the left side of the panel, and the panels for Page 3 overlaid on a background of the alley that's continuous from Page 2. Or we could just do it more normally and have the two pages separate.

Page 3:
Panel 1:
In the foreground, we see the Man gripping his knife. It's an ornate ritualistic knife that seems to be ancient and has Sumerian writing carved into it. The blade has blood dripping down the side of it.

Framed in the gap between the man's hand and the man's body, we see Katharine lying on the ground, bleeding out, and trying to get away from him.

Antonio:
Katharine, you should have listened to me.
I told you, compassion only makes you weak.

Panel 2:
Move to a wide profile shot showing the man advancing on her. She's creeping further into the alley, towards the homeless Man, who's still there, lying scared against a dumpster. We see the red glow on him still, while Antonio is in silhouette, light bouncing off the knife, but not illuminating his face fully yet.

He is wearing a beautiful wool jacket, and a nice suit, with a medallion around his neck. His hair seems impeccably styled, though we can't quite make out his face. This is not a homeless man, or someone who would normally be in an alley. It's clear this is a trap.

With keeping Antonio in silhouette most of the time, I'm imagining maybe play with a little Frank Miller Sin City style high contrast where all we see of him is his eyes or the knife or details of the suit, and then we can punctuate that with bits of color from the power.

Antonio:
I could have taught you so many things.
But you chose to betray me.

Panel 3:
Close on Antonio as he moves from the shadows. We can't quite make out his whole face, but there is disdain on it, and a strange blue glow hovers over his eyes. We can tell that he's wearing a suit and a nice coat over it.

Antonio:
All that power you hold, to waste it on people like him.
You don't deserve to be remembered.

Panel 4:
On Katharine, lying on the ground scooting back from Antonio. She is quite frightened, using one hand to help slide herself back and holding the other over the stab wound on her stomach. She's looking behind her at the Homeless Man, cowering in fear.

Antonio:
But I will carry you with me, like so many of the others.

Katharine:
You're a monster.

Panel 5:
Flip around so that Katharine is framed through the legs of the homeless MAN which have the glowing red energy around them. She is lying on her back, her head craned to look behind her. We see her face straining as the red energy moves from his leg into her hand. It's taking everything she has left, almost killing her, but something is keeping her alive.

Beyond them, we see Antonio still in silhouette, but through his body language, we can tell that he's alarmed by what's going on.

Katharine:
One day, one of us is gonna' stop you.
I'll do my best to make sure it's the next--

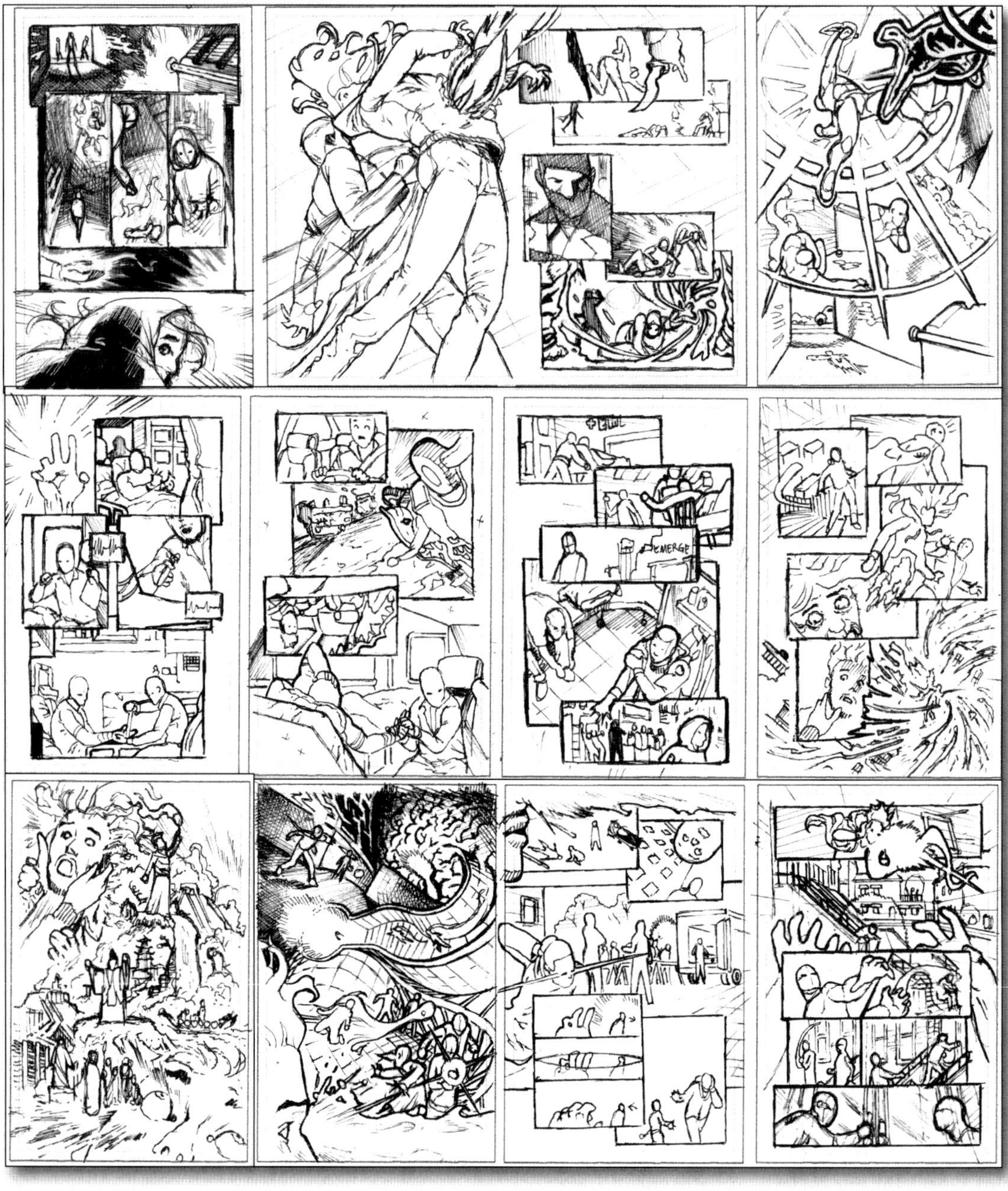

PAGE 4:

Panel 1:
A burst of red energy hits Antonio, knocking him back into the shadows. Maybe we see Katharine's hand in the foreground projecting it, or we could have it just be Antonio if that's cleaner. Antonio is surprised, and we get a nice contrast between the red of the blast and the dark of the alley. It's almost like the red energy is pushing him back into the darkness.

Perhaps do a JH Williams style design element where we see the power itself forming the border of the panel below it, or even use it as a frame for all the panels on the page, like have the power shooting up from the center of the bottom of the page, and hitting Antonio at the top where panel 1 would be, then have the other panels overlaid on top of it. Whatever you think is best.

Either way, let's have a little gap with some energy between panels 1 and 2 that implies a moment where Antonio has been hit hard and in panel 2 is getting his composure back together.

Panel 2:
We're looking over Antonio's head. He's been knocked back and is lying on the ground, but is craning his head up to look down the alley. There's some blood on the ground, but no sign of Katharine or the Homeless Man.

Antonio (Caption):
Tricky, tricky...She hid her skills from me.

Panel 3:
Antonio winces in pain as he pulls out his phone and makes a call.

Antonio:
But nothing to worry about. You can pick me up now.

Panel 3:
Bird's eye shot looking down at the alley. Antonio has gotten up and is walking towards the street as a fancy Town Car pulls up.

Driver (Caption):
I'm sorry sir, I didn't see where she went.

Panel 4:
From deep in the alley, mirroring the first panel of page 1, we see the car driving away. A small pool of blood is visible in the foreground.

Antonio (Caption):
Check the morgue records. We'll be seeing her soon.
And then it begins again. Perhaps our next subject will be more accommodating.

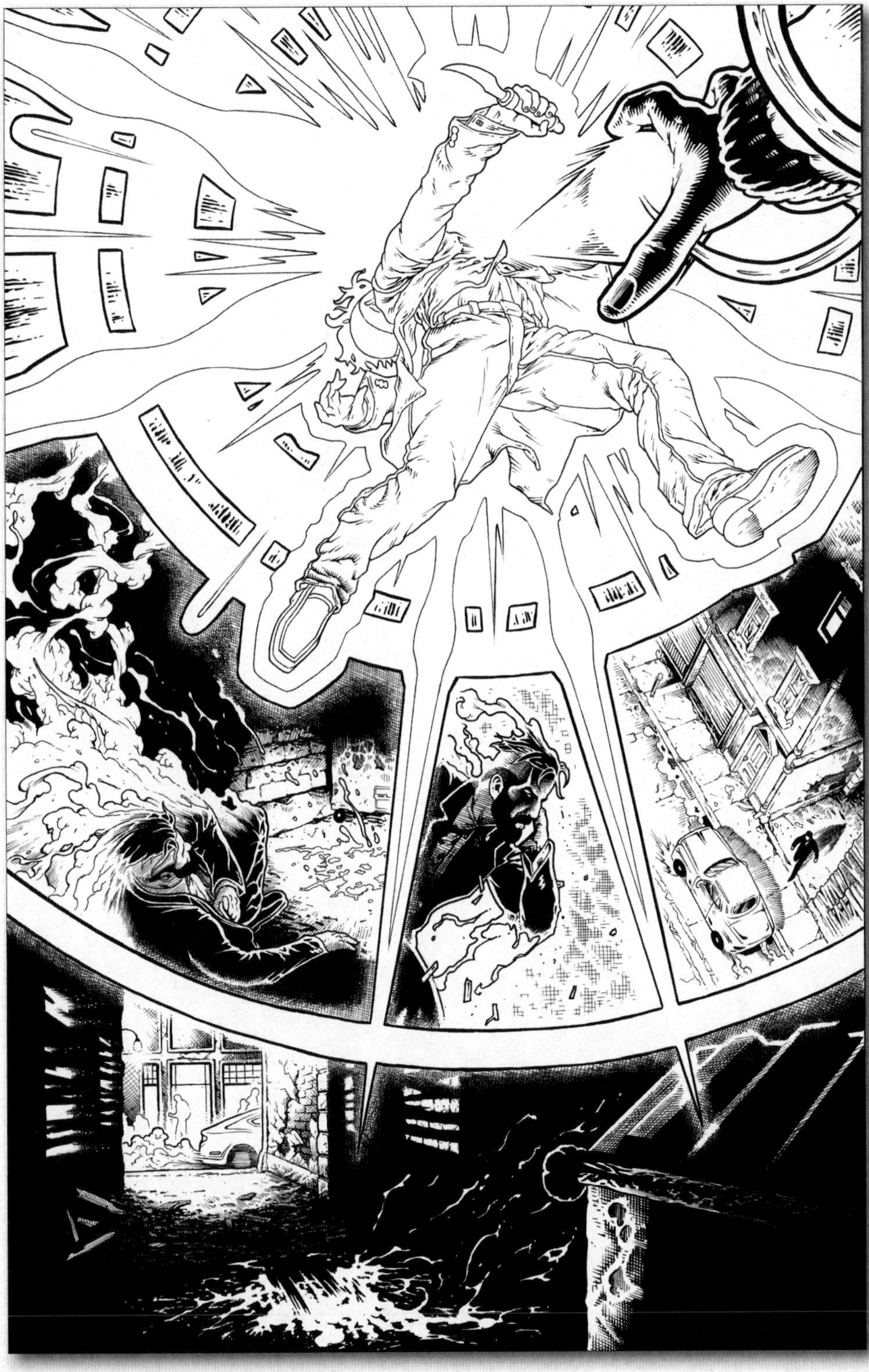

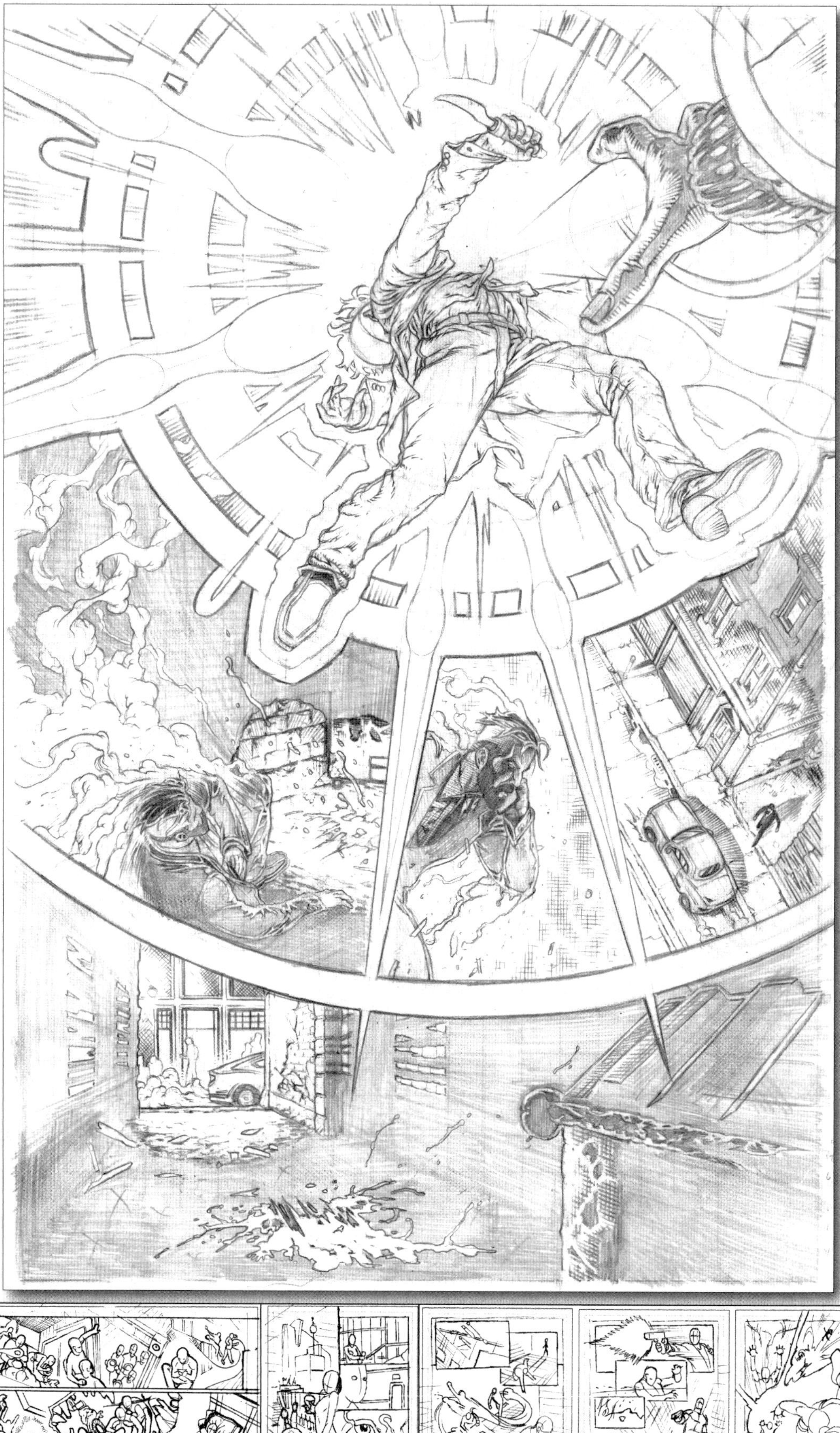

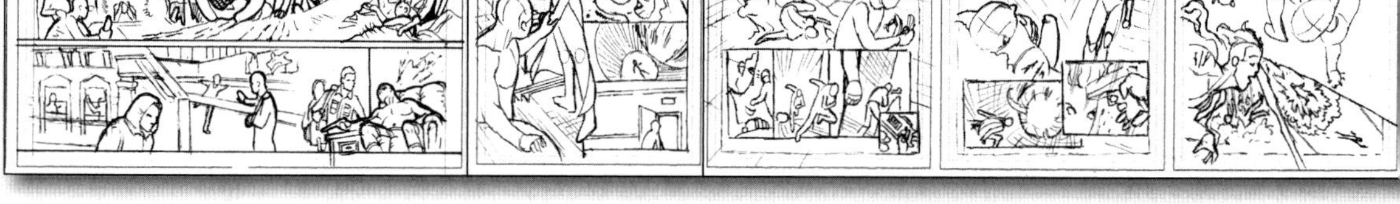

Syphon 7 5

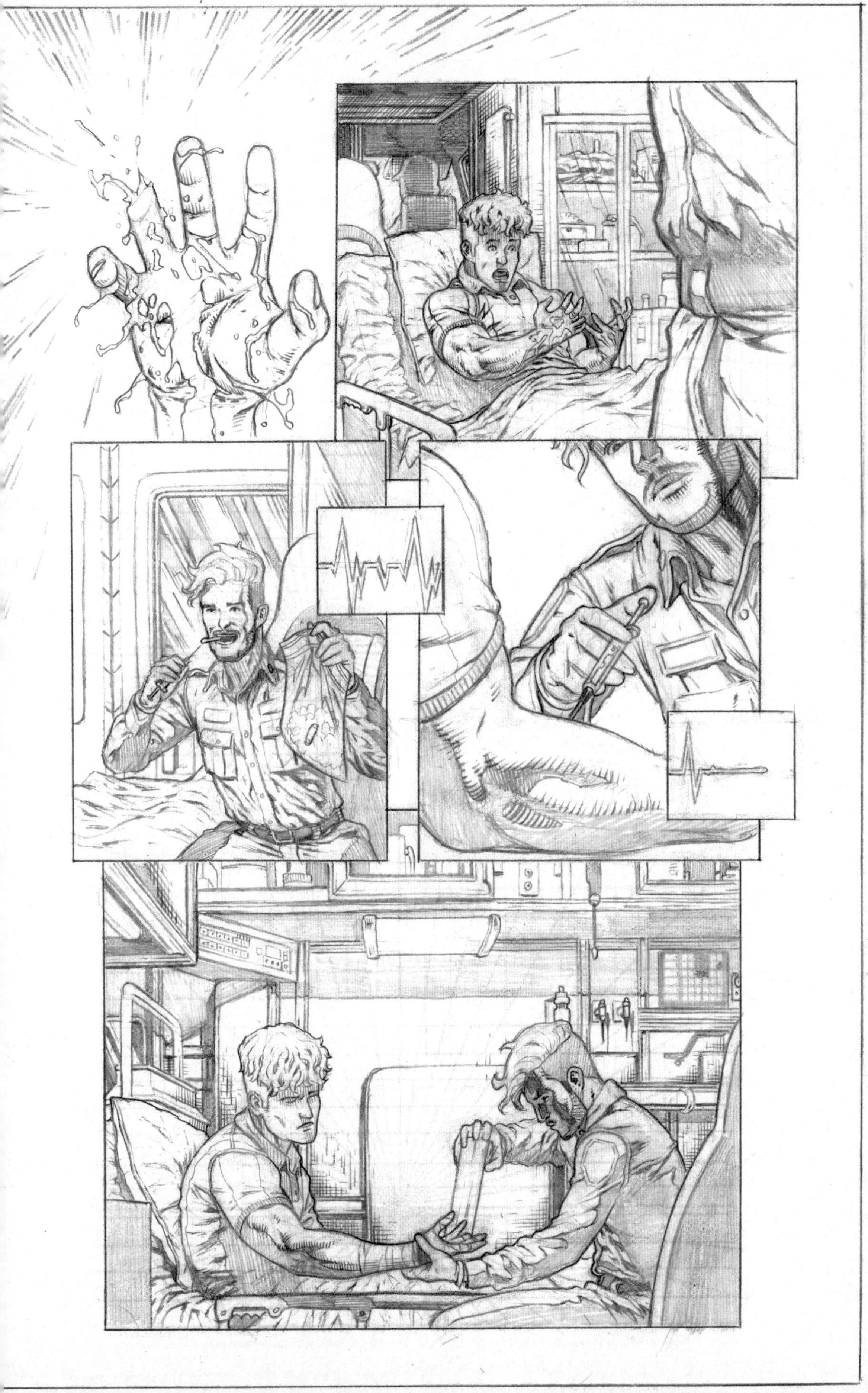

Syphon 1 6

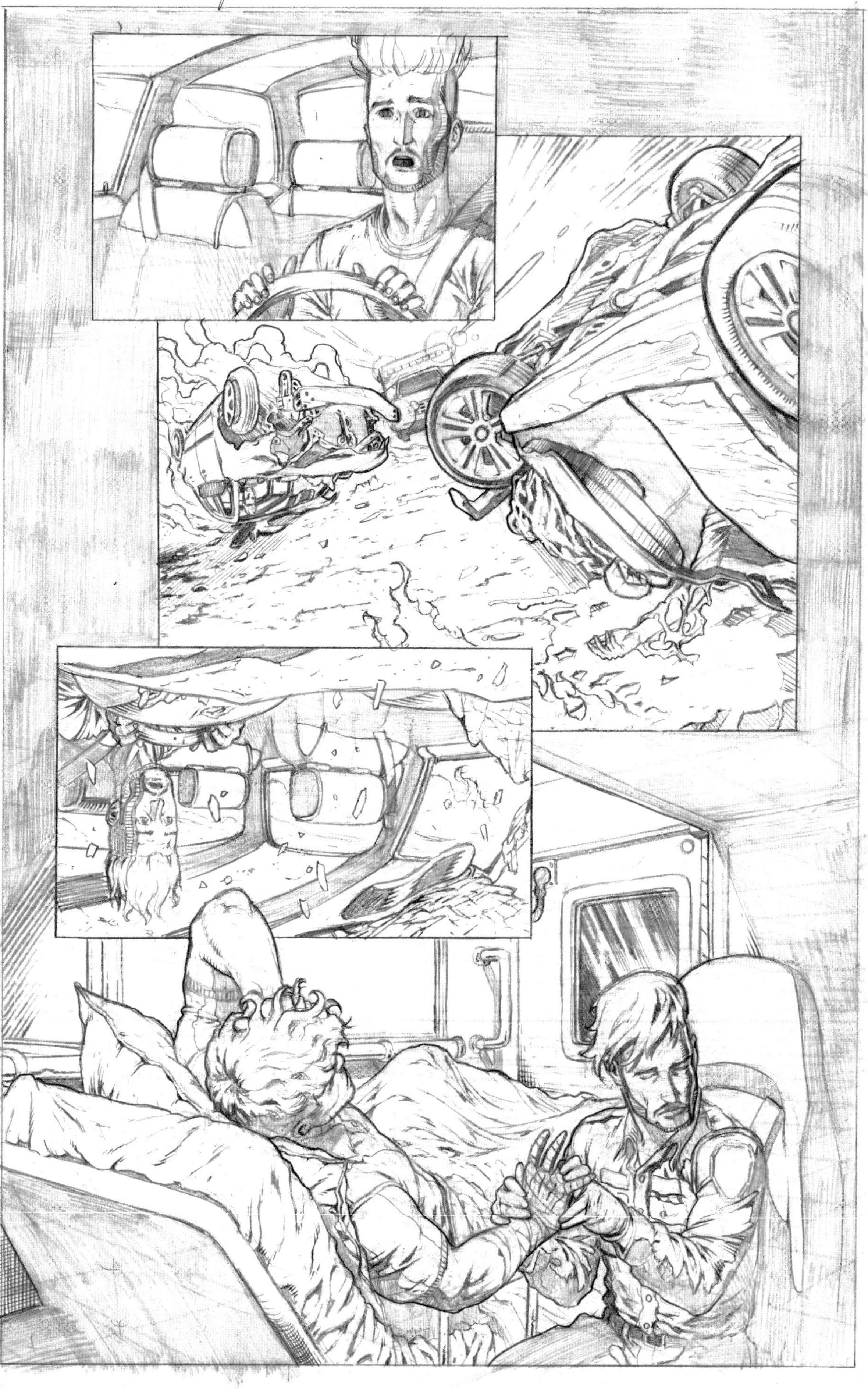

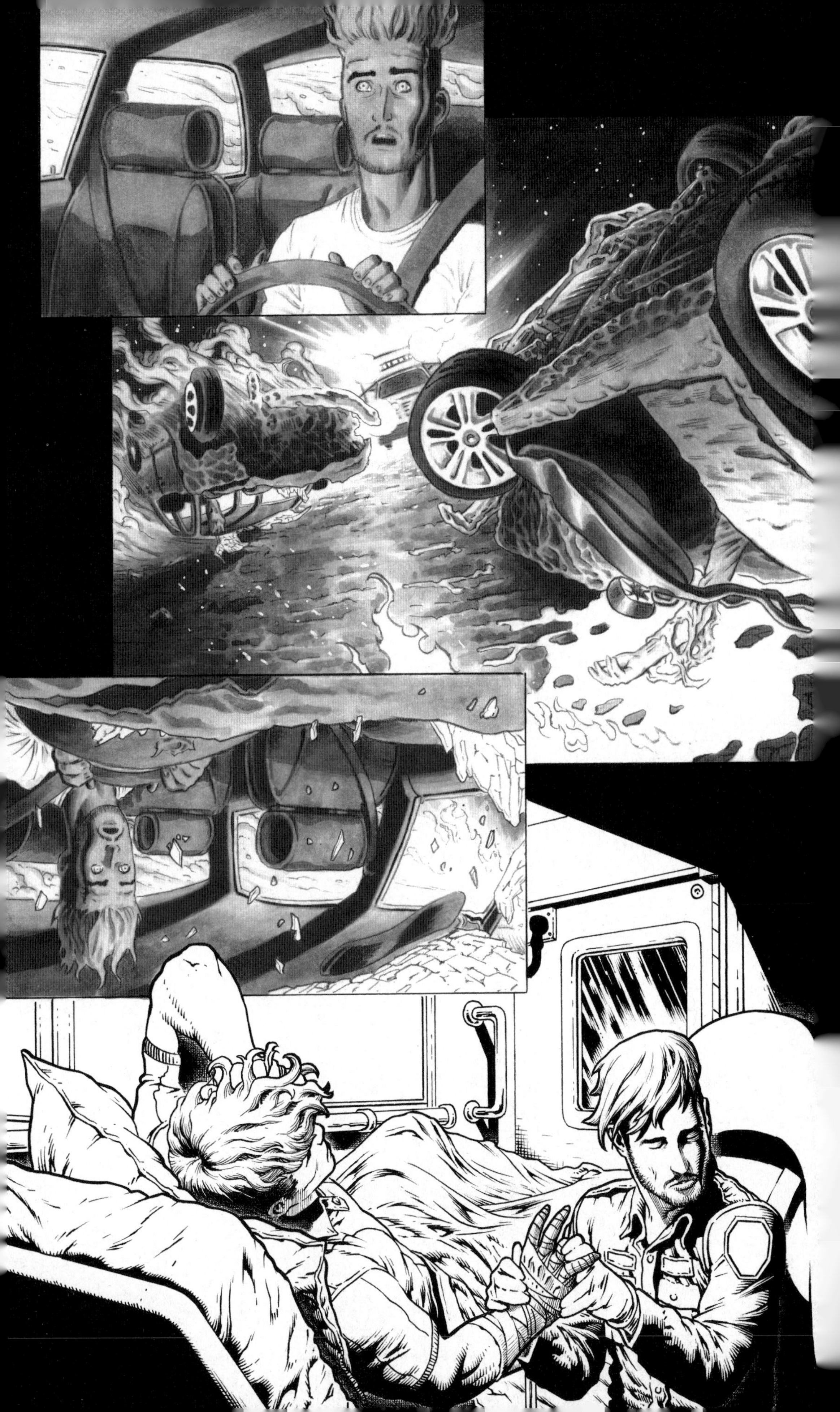

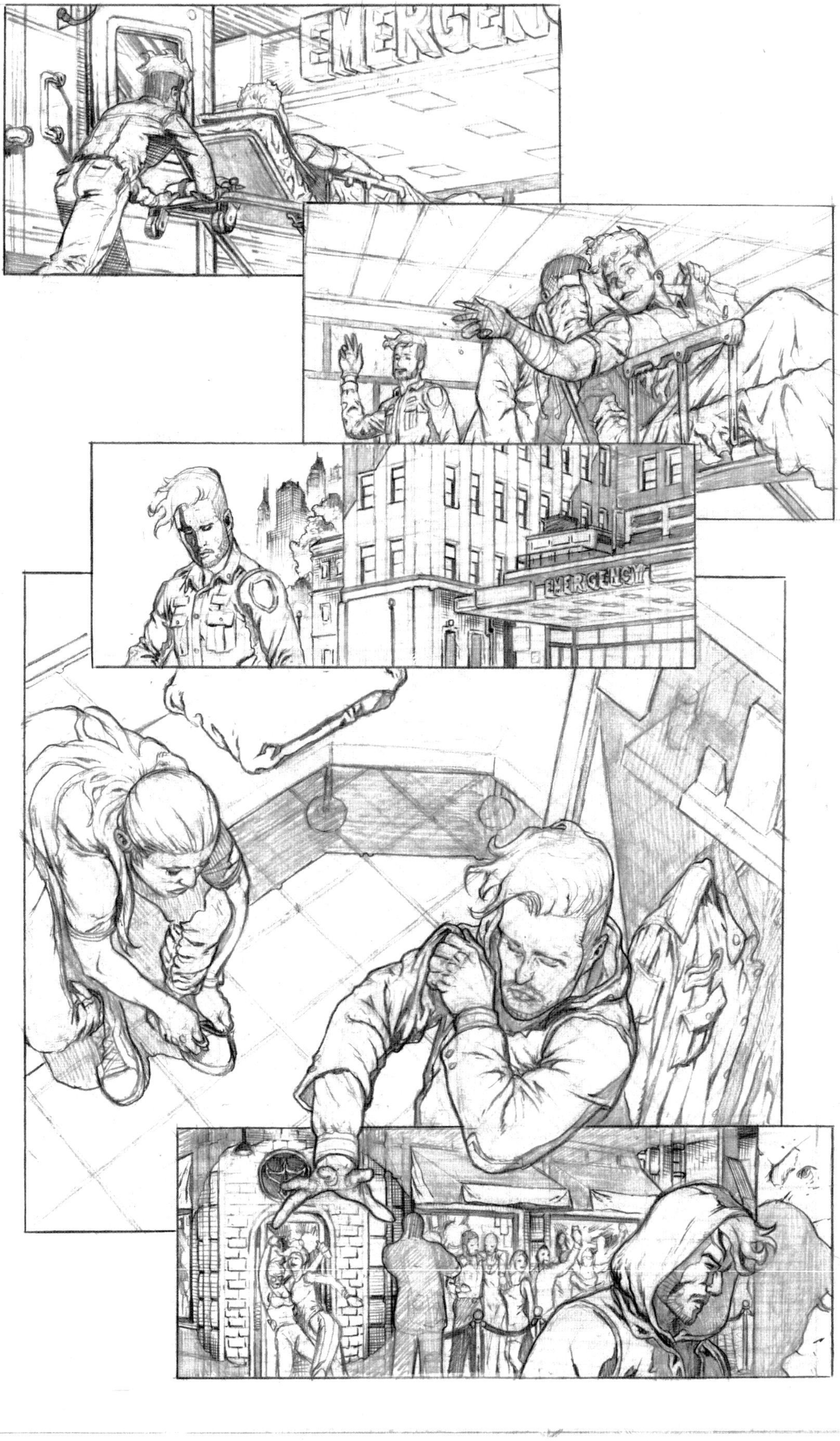
EMERGEN
EMERGENCY

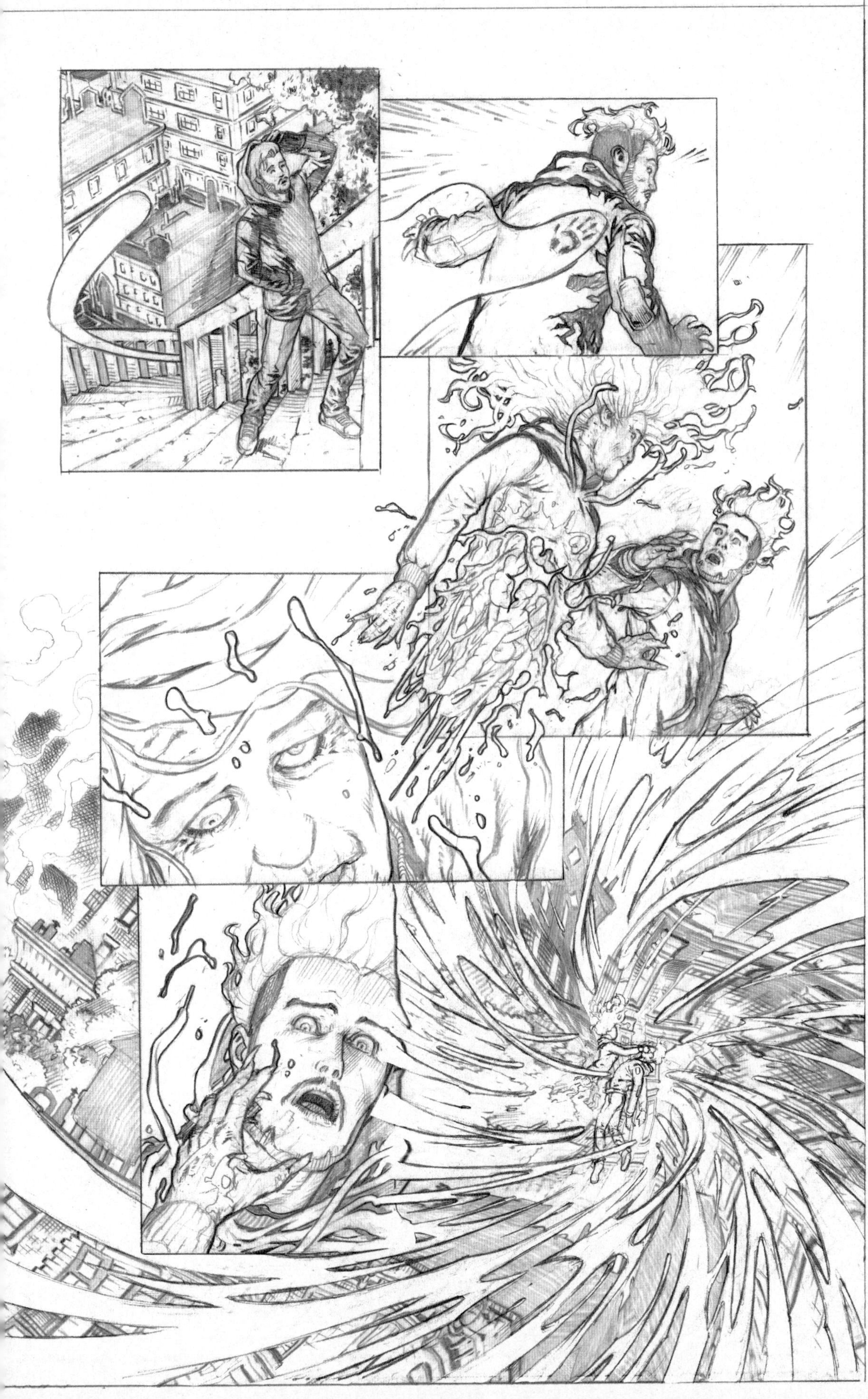

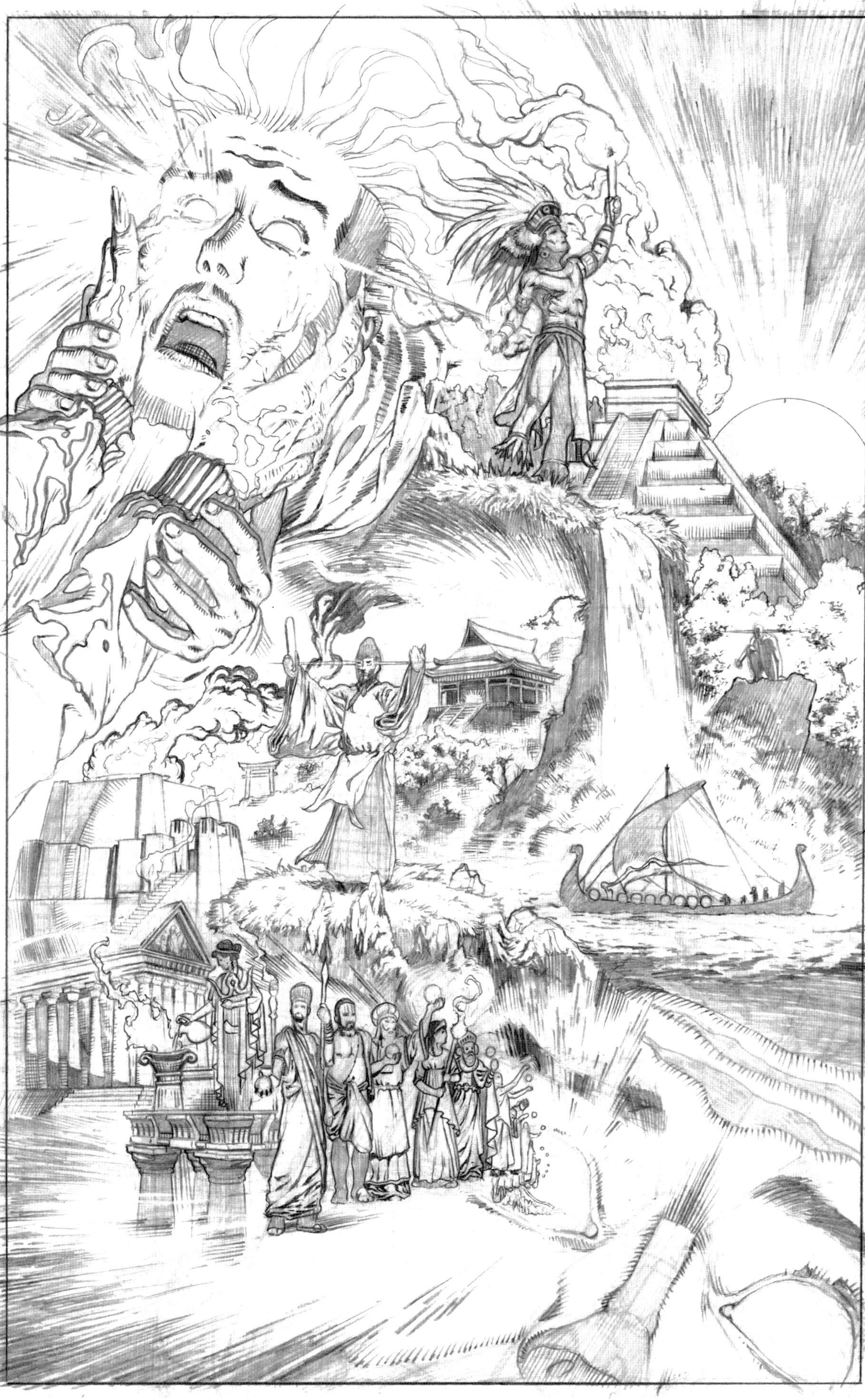

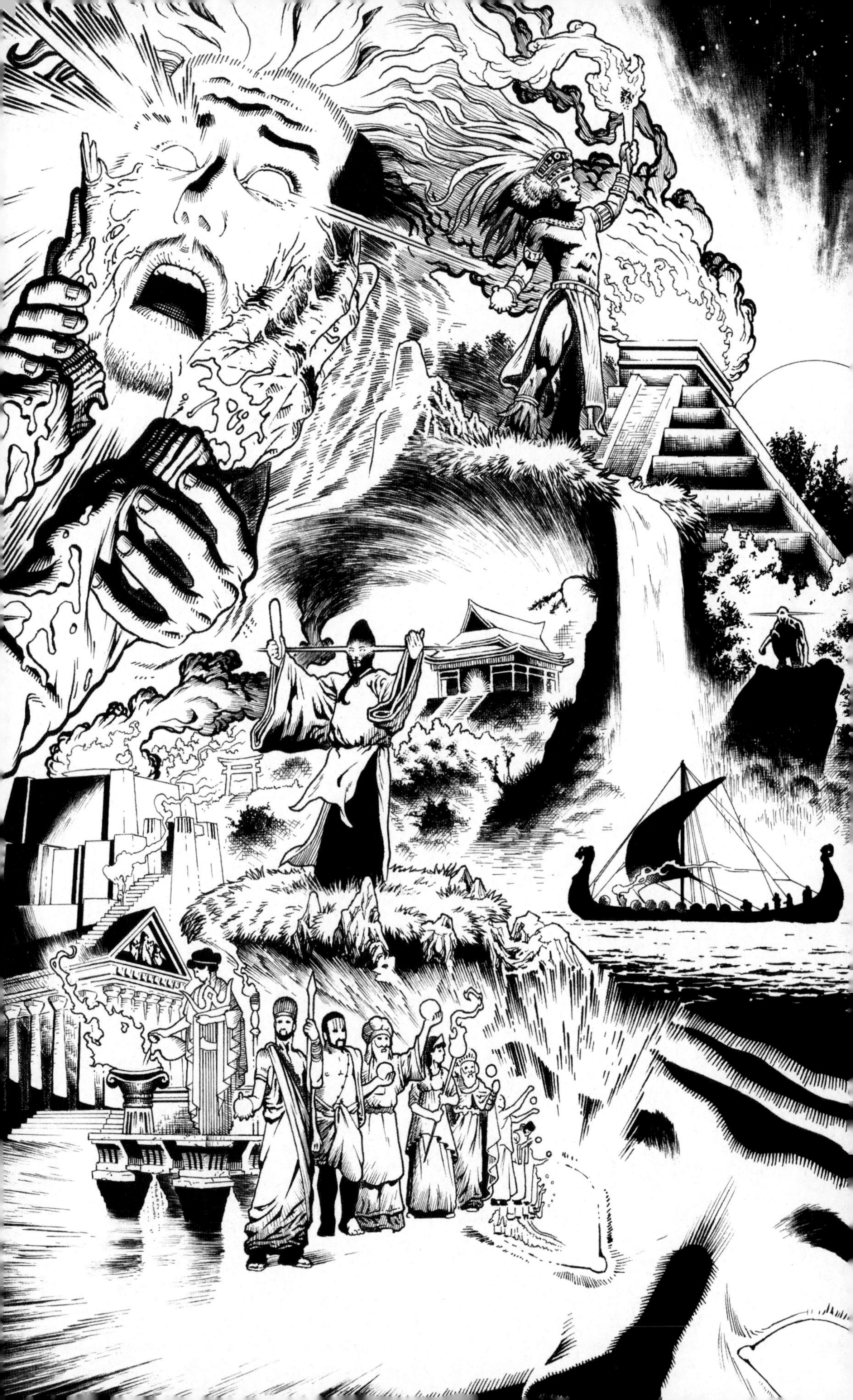

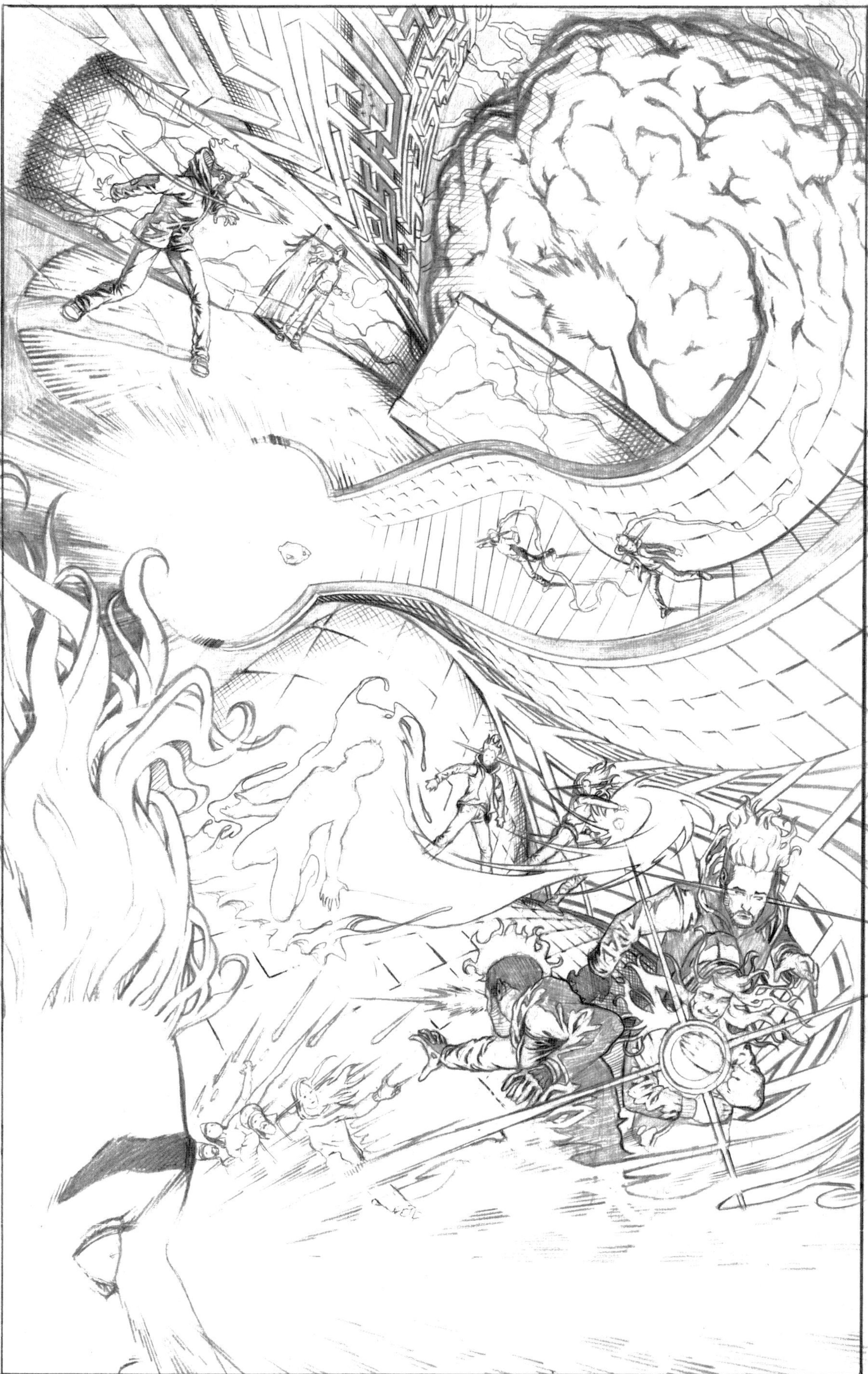

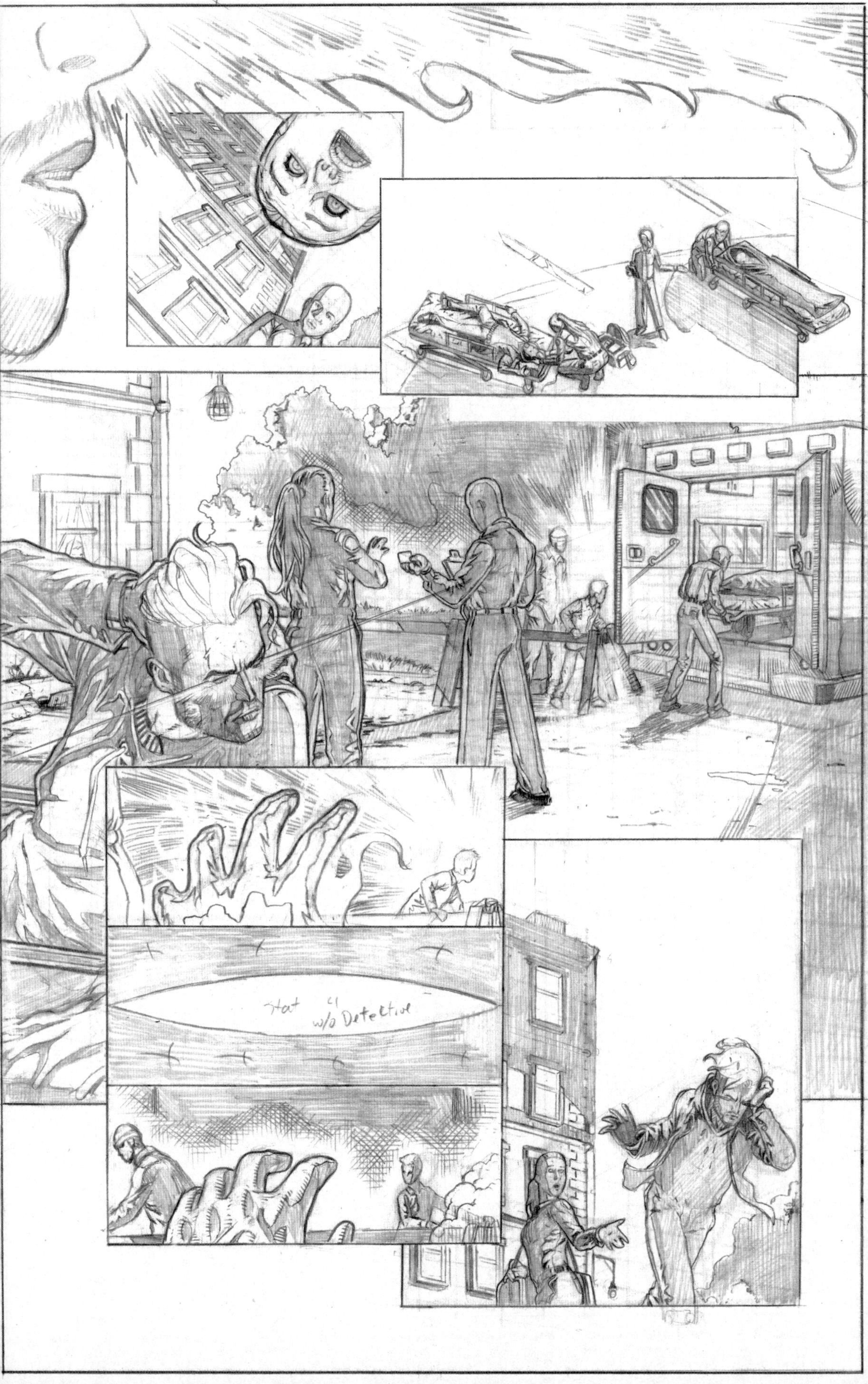
Stat
w/o Detective

PAGE 12:

Panel 1:
Sylas walks over towards the booth. We see he's woozy as he stands up, the lights all flashing around him, disorienting. He's moving as if through a drug trip, a couple standing next to him on the balcony making out casting wild light, and energy emanating off the dance floor.

Maybe we have a couple of blurry bubbles around, reflecting Tim and Antonio talking, but they're blurred out since Sylas isn't close enough to hear.

Panel 2:
Sylas makes it to Tim Williams' booth. Antonio is talking with him, and Williams clearly is just trying to be polite to a guy he assumes is a fan.

Tim Williams (Maybe do an effect where the first couple of words are blurred, then they come into focus):
Well, thank you, man. Have a good night.

Antonio:
You should meet my friend too.
This is Sylas.

Tim Williams:
Cool, nice to meet you, I'll see you around.

Panel 3:
Antonio whispers to Sylas, his hand on his shoulder, almost as if he can channel energy through Sylas.

Antonio:
Be gentle, just take a bit...

Panel 4:
On Sylas's eyes crackling.

Antonio (Caption):
Get a taste of what his life is like.

Panel 5:
Sylas's hand reaches out, and we see Tim with the blue aura around him, now that he's back to talking with his friends.

Panel 6:
Sylas's eyes go wide as he's startled by what he sees, a rush of energy coming towards him, an excessive, dangerous amount. We see Antonio falling back, as if blown away by it. The energy floods all around the bottom, creating a fluid panel border with panel 7.

Antonio :
Easy there, don't--

Panel 7:
Mostly wide, just the energy, except we can subtly make out Sylas's eyes, super wide, and crackling with the energy.

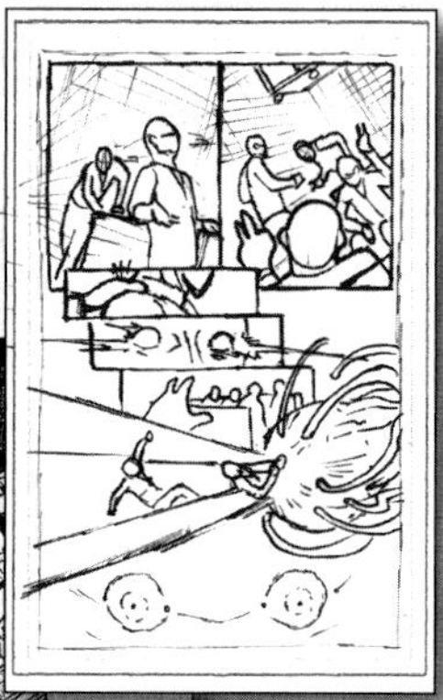

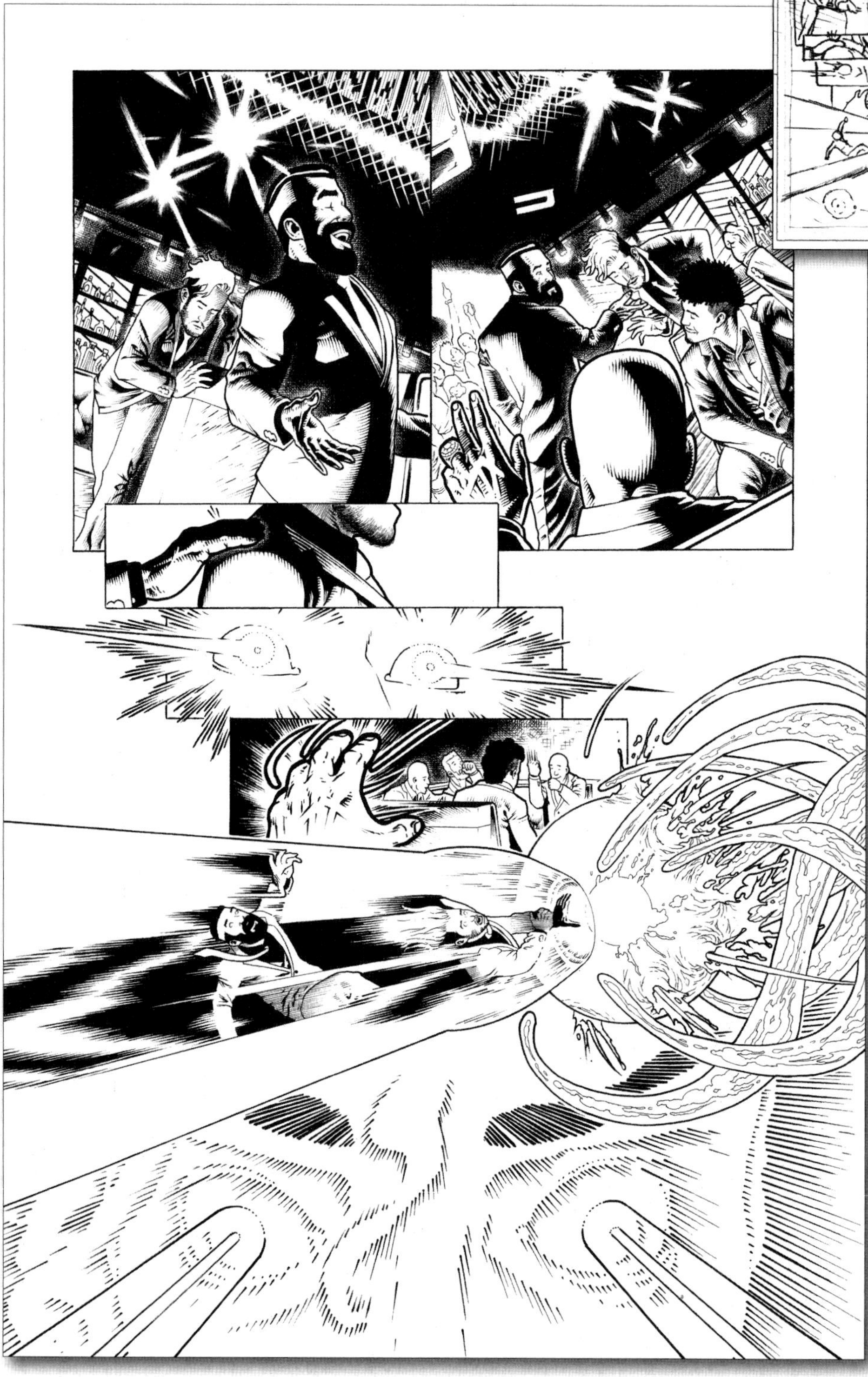

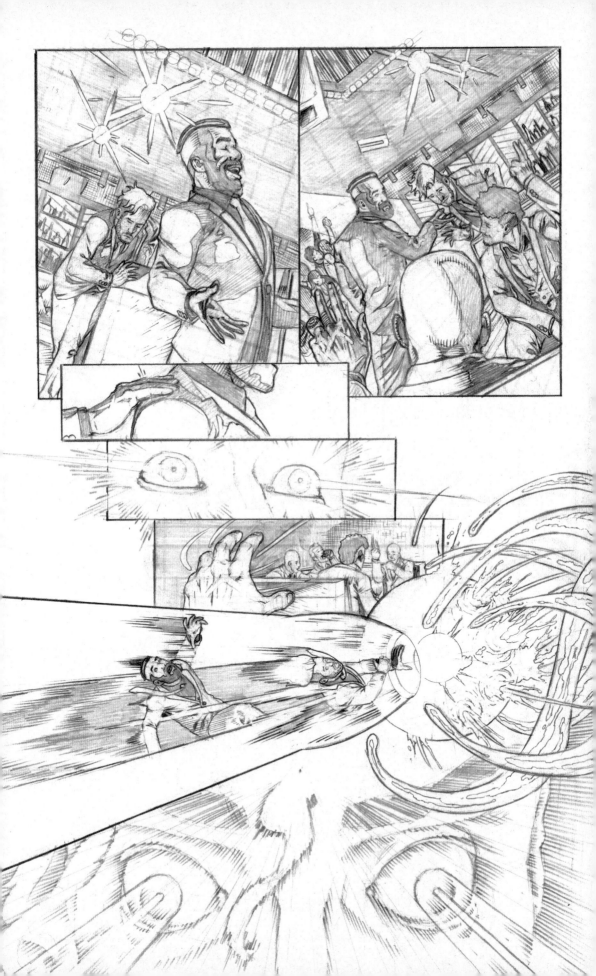

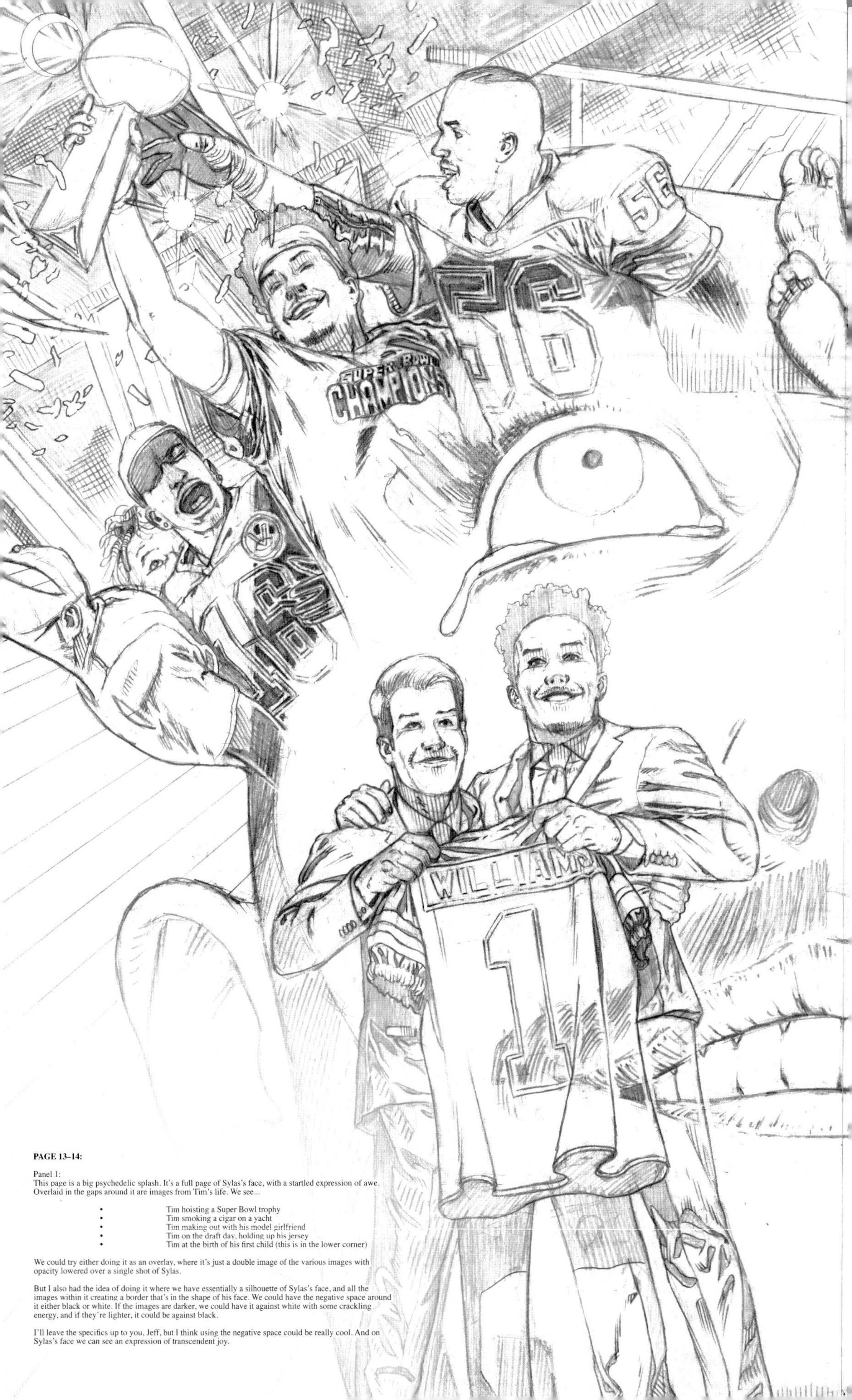
SUPER BOWL
CHAMPIONS
56
56
WILLIAMS
1

PAGE 13–14:

Panel 1:
This page is a big psychedelic splash. It's a full page of Sylas's face, with a startled expression of awe. Overlaid in the gaps around it are images from Tim's life. We see...

- Tim hoisting a Super Bowl trophy
- Tim smoking a cigar on a yacht
- Tim making out with his model girlfriend
- Tim on the draft day, holding up his jersey
- Tim at the birth of his first child (this is in the lower corner)

We could try either doing it as an overlay, where it's just a double image of the various images with opacity lowered over a single shot of Sylas.

But I also had the idea of doing it where we have essentially a silhouette of Sylas's face, and all the images within it creating a border that's in the shape of his face. We could have the negative space around it either black or white. If the images are darker, we could have it against white with some crackling energy, and if they're lighter, it could be against black.

I'll leave the specifics up to you, Jeff, but I think using the negative space could be really cool. And on Sylas's face we can see an expression of transcendent joy.

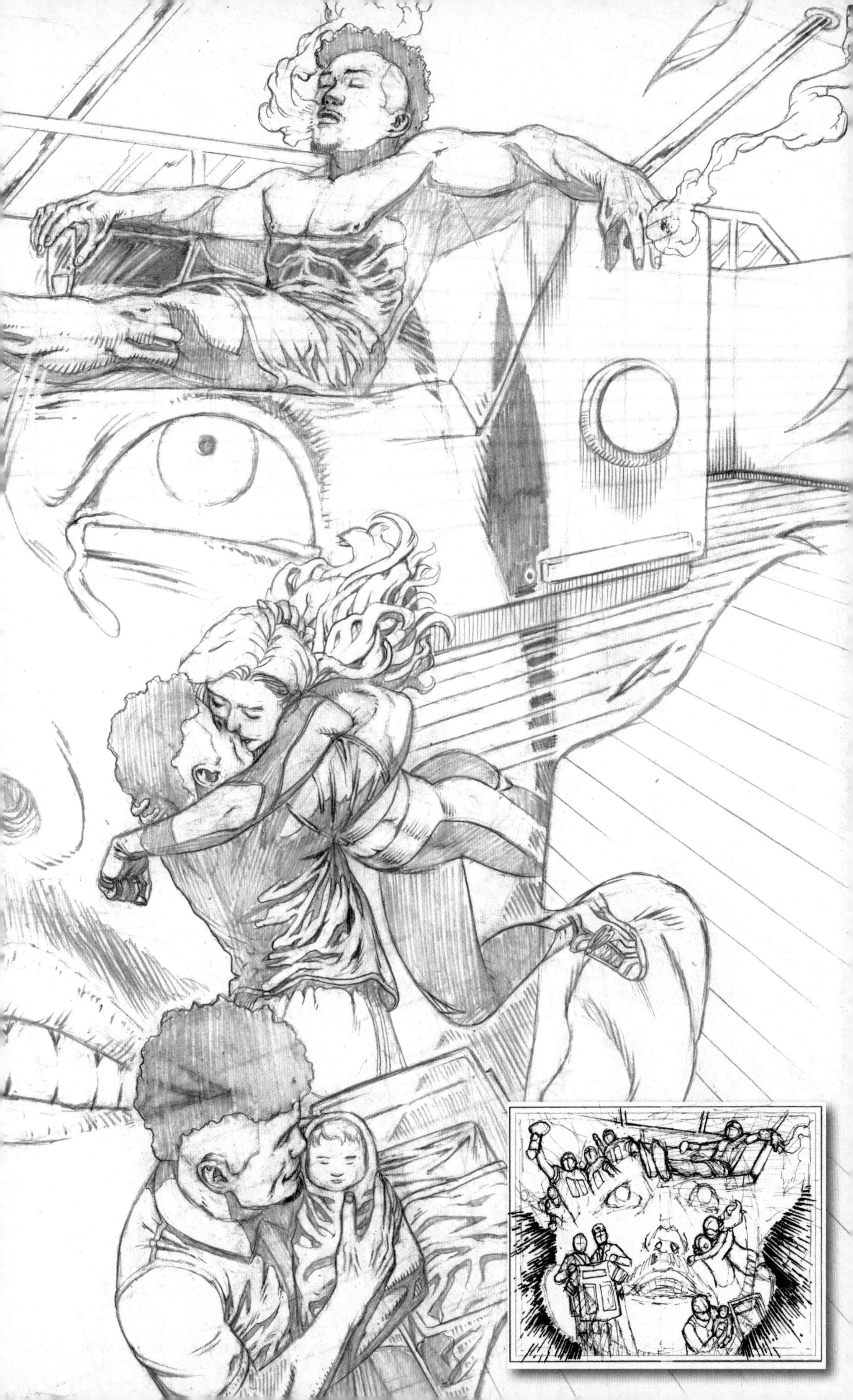

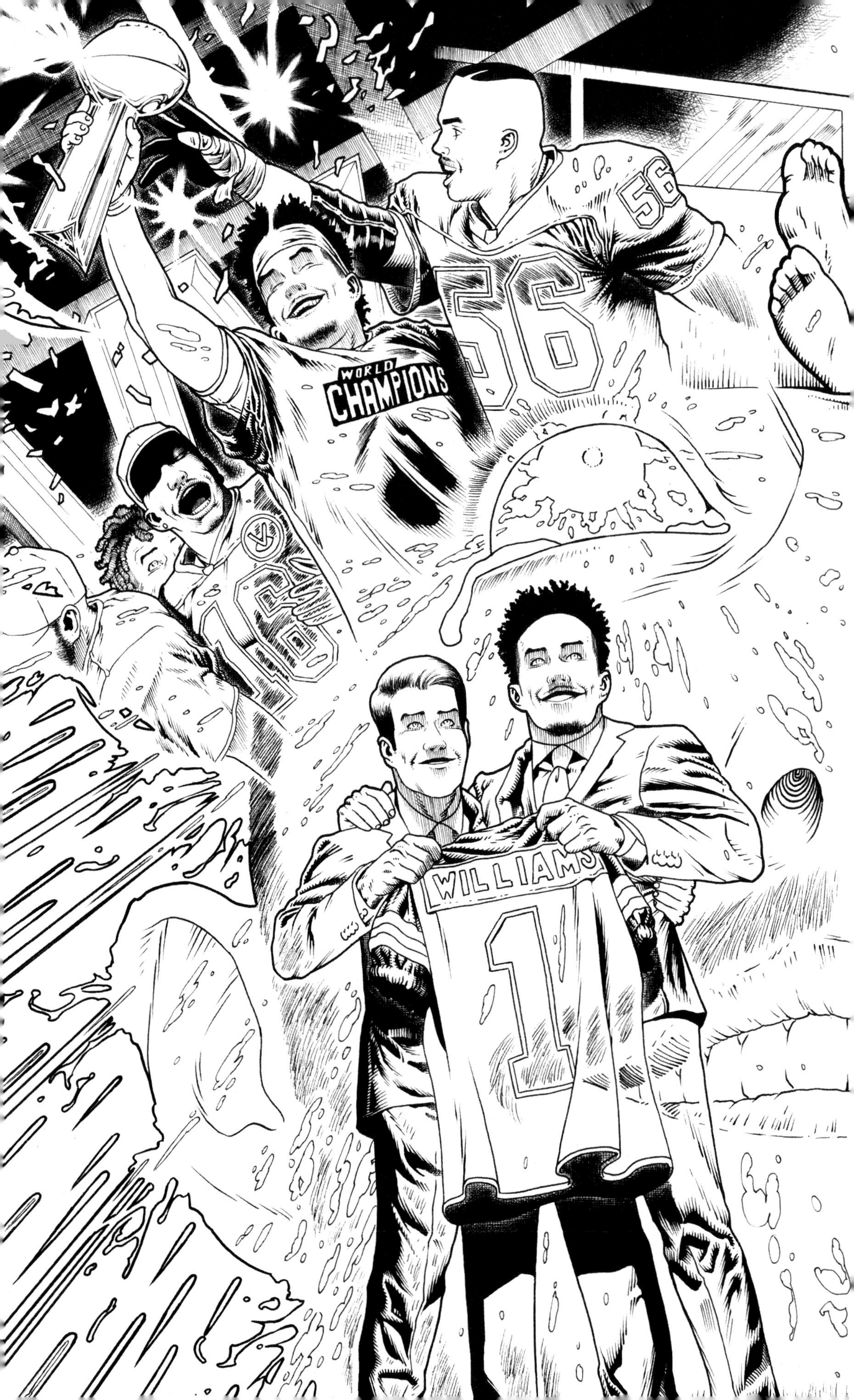
WORLD CHAMPIONS
56
56
16
WILLIAMS
1

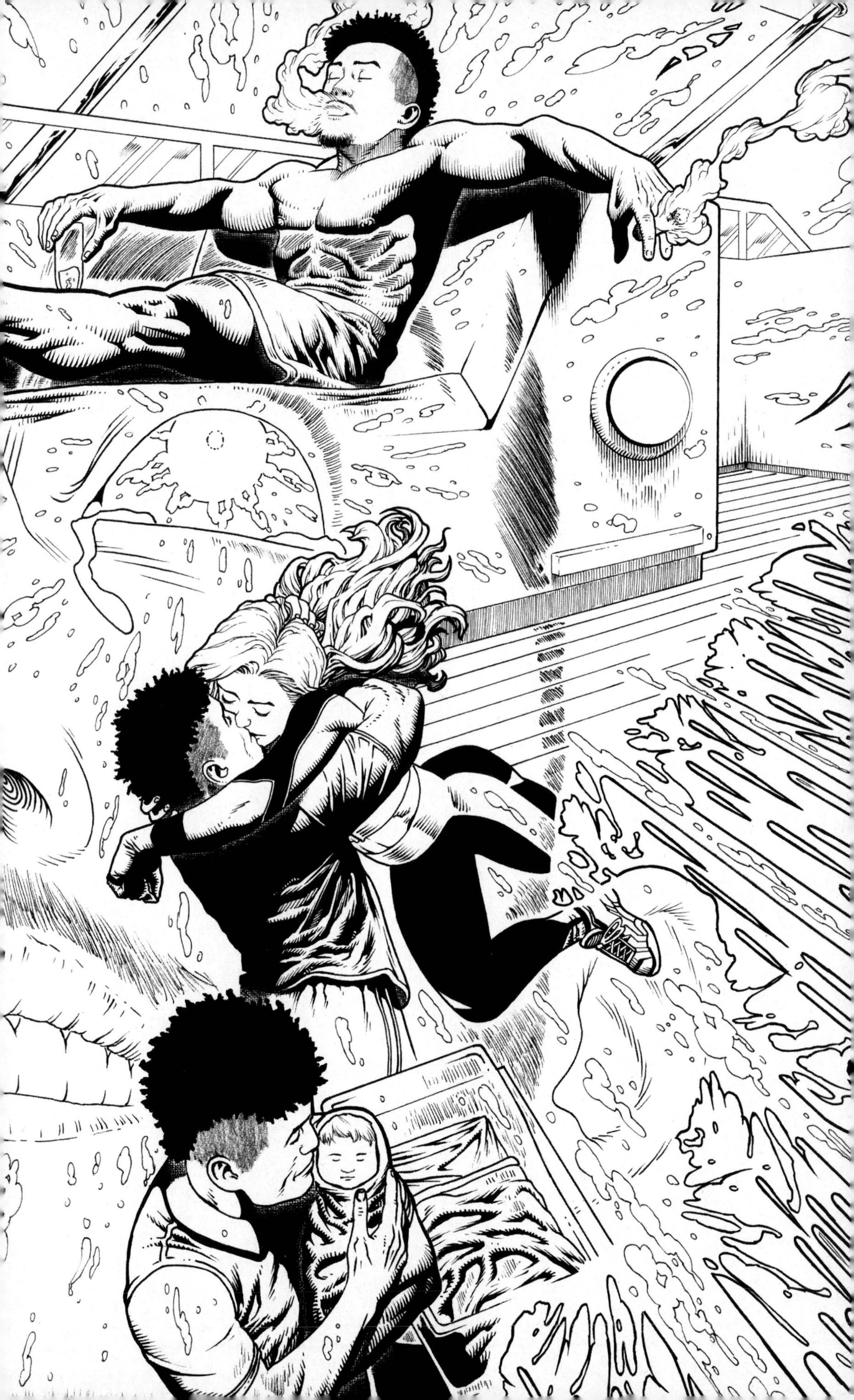

PAGE 15:

Panel 1:
Sylas, in his fancy suit sees Tim in the delivery room as his wife is giving birth. Sylas is still overwhelmingly happy. There's a strong dreamlike quality to the image, Sylas walking through a memory. Might be interesting to use a similar panel border as on the previous page, and let it flow like a double page spread. We could also build all these panels within a silhouette of Tim Williams' head, so that the page would be two faces, both containing images within them.

On this page, the structure of the images should be a bit more defined, but keep a kind of dreamy flow.

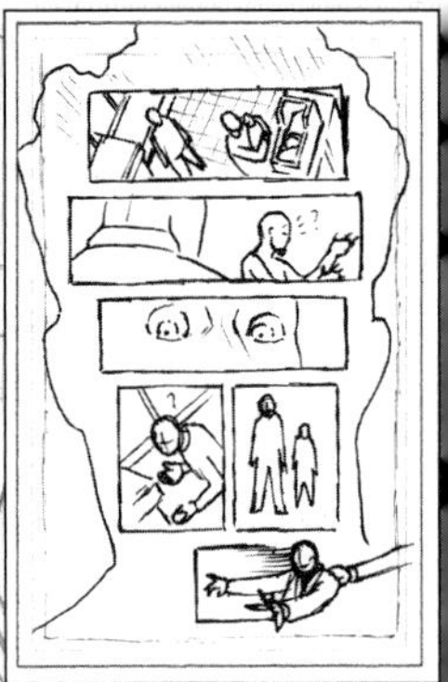

Panel 3:
Over Sylas's shoulder, he's looking where Tim was. Where Tim was once holding the baby, it's now fading away. Tim is crying, not sure why something like this is happening. His memory is literally dissipating before his eyes.

Panel 3:
Close on Sylas, tears in his eyes. He doesn't know exactly what's happening, but the joy is gone, he realizes he's done something bad.

Panel 4:
Close on Tim, looking up at Sylas. He's not so much angry as utterly tragically distraught. We see the hospital environment seemingly melting around him, the environment itself dissolving.

Panel 5:
Sylas stands in what's almost a void, staring at Tim who stares ahead numb, utterly lost, just staring off into the abyss. It's quite sad. Most of the hospital has collapsed around them, and there's just some blurs of matter left.

Panel 6:
And then a hand reaches up from behind him and pulls Sylas away. The hand is Antonio's, we see just his arm and hand as it grabs Sylas.

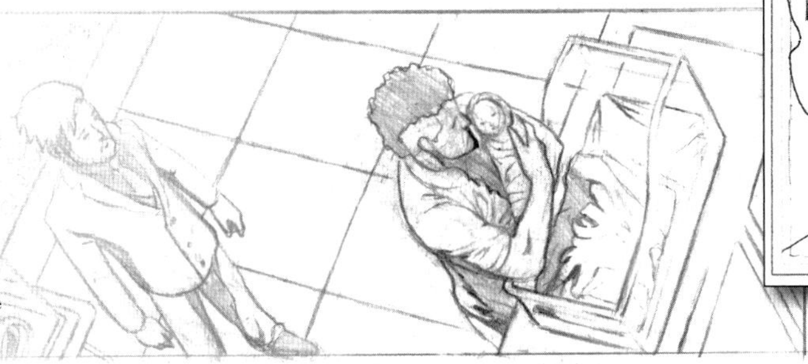

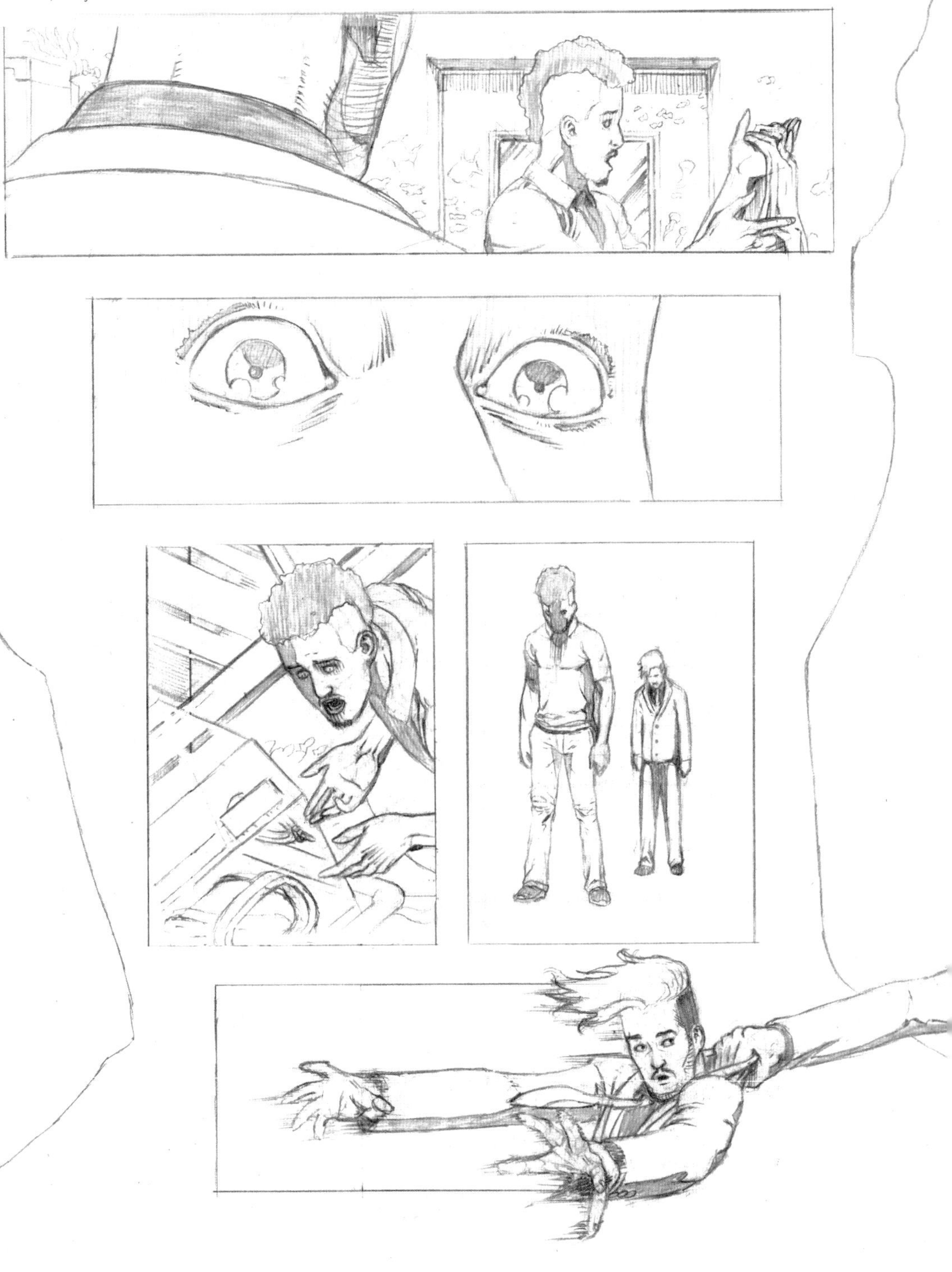

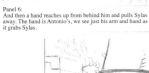

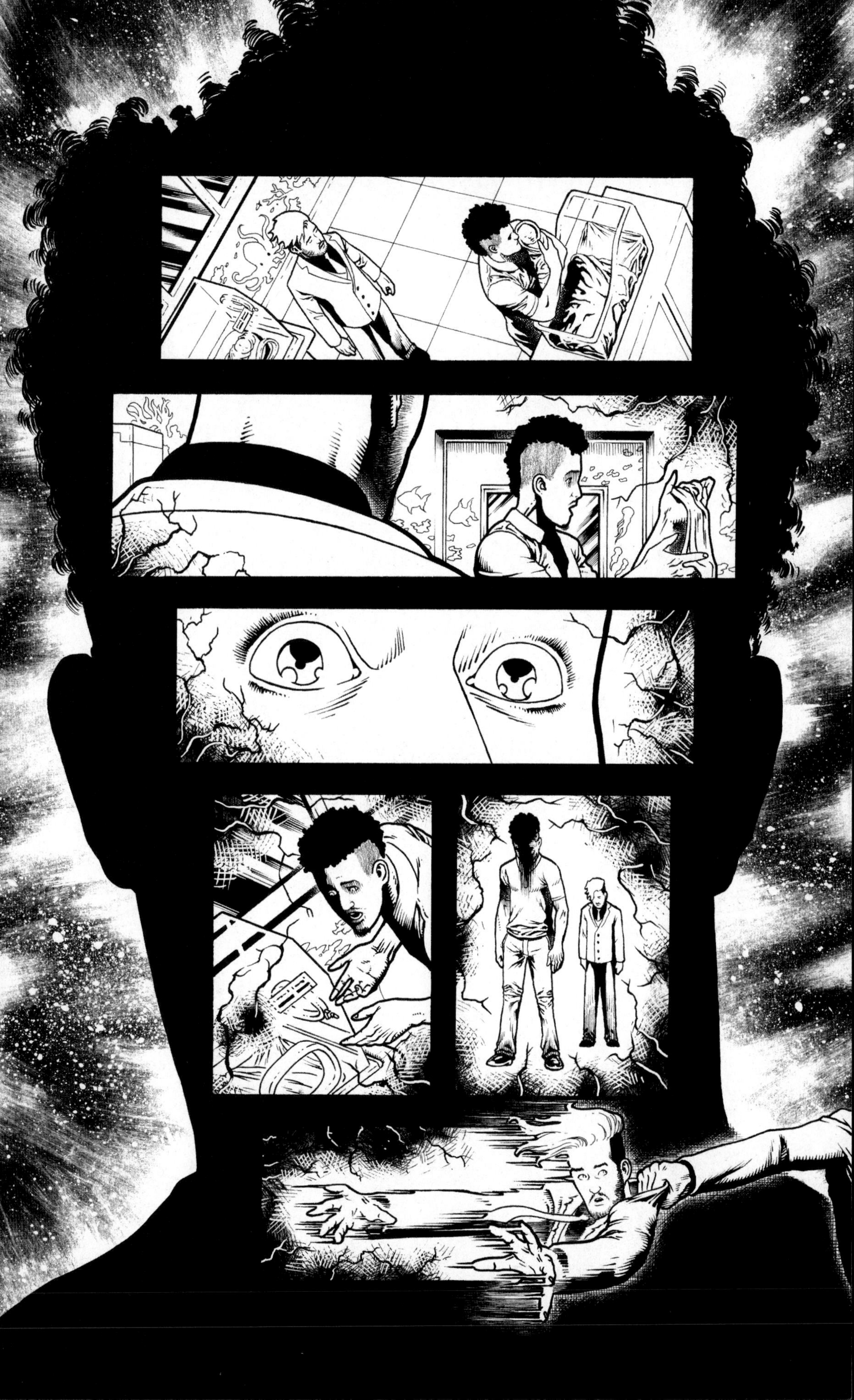

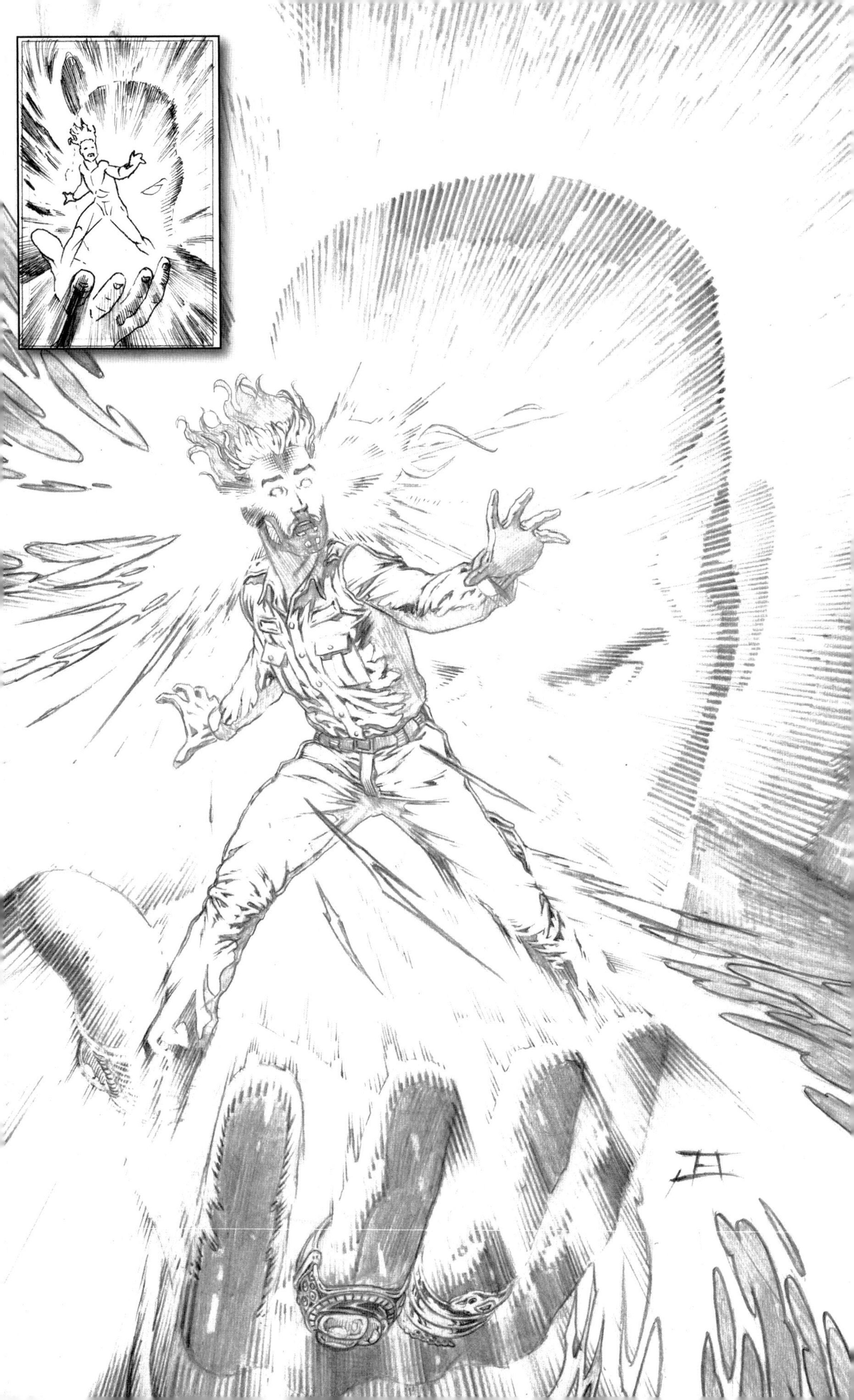

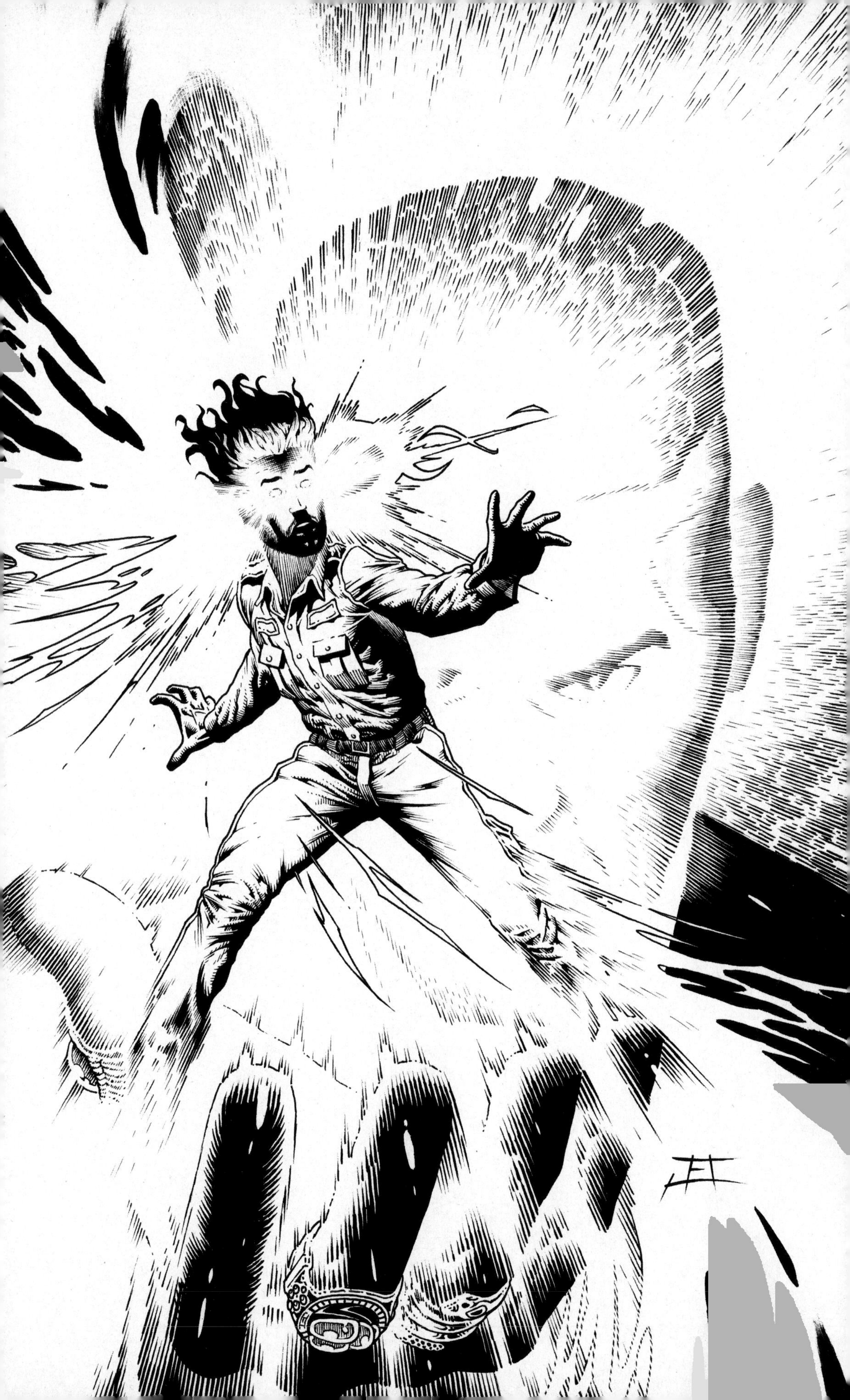

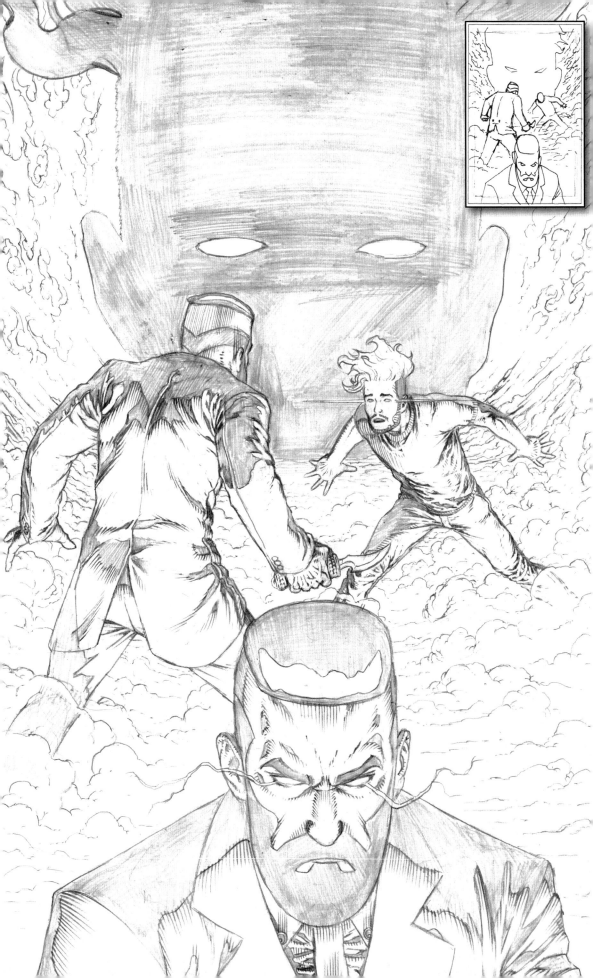

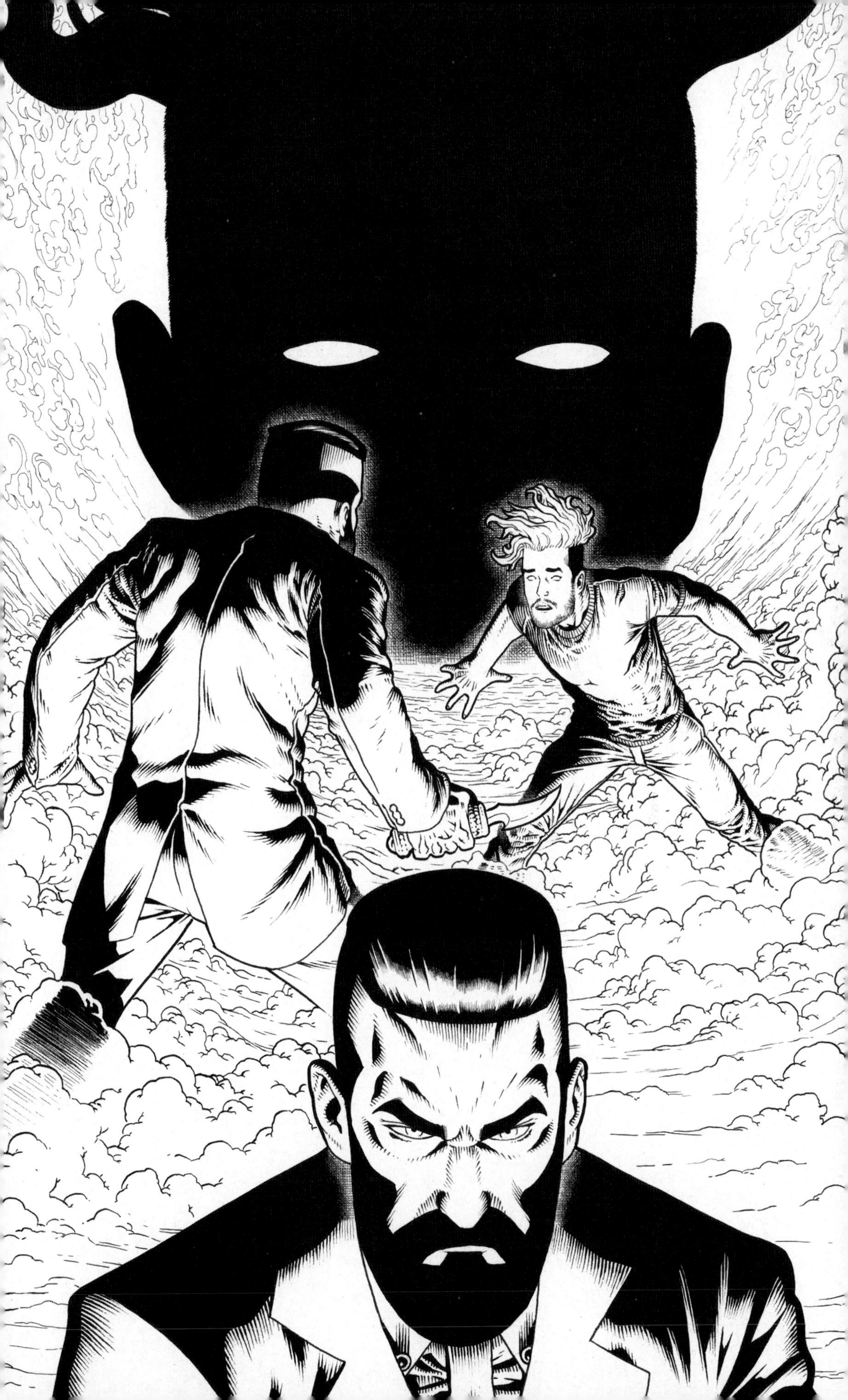

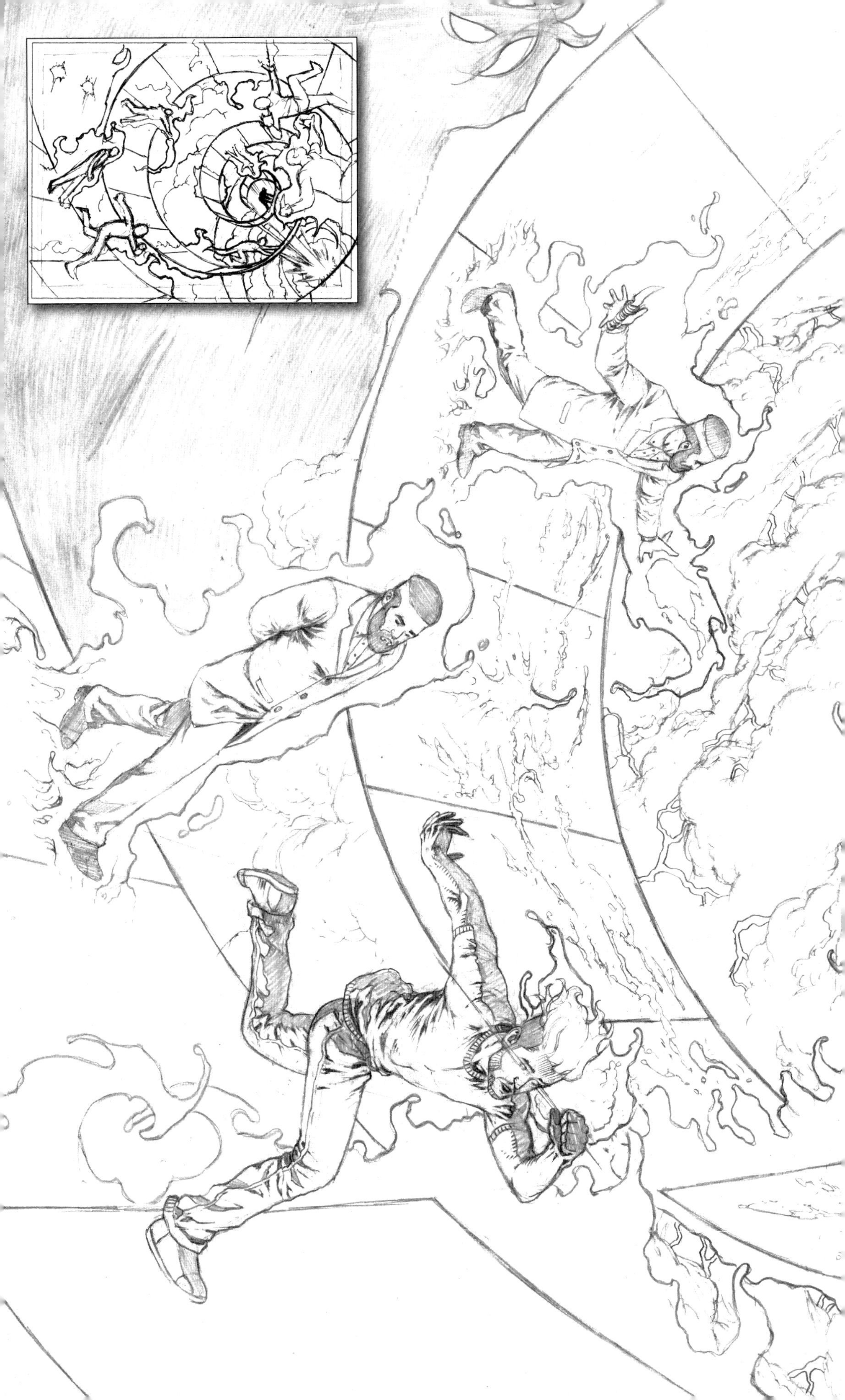

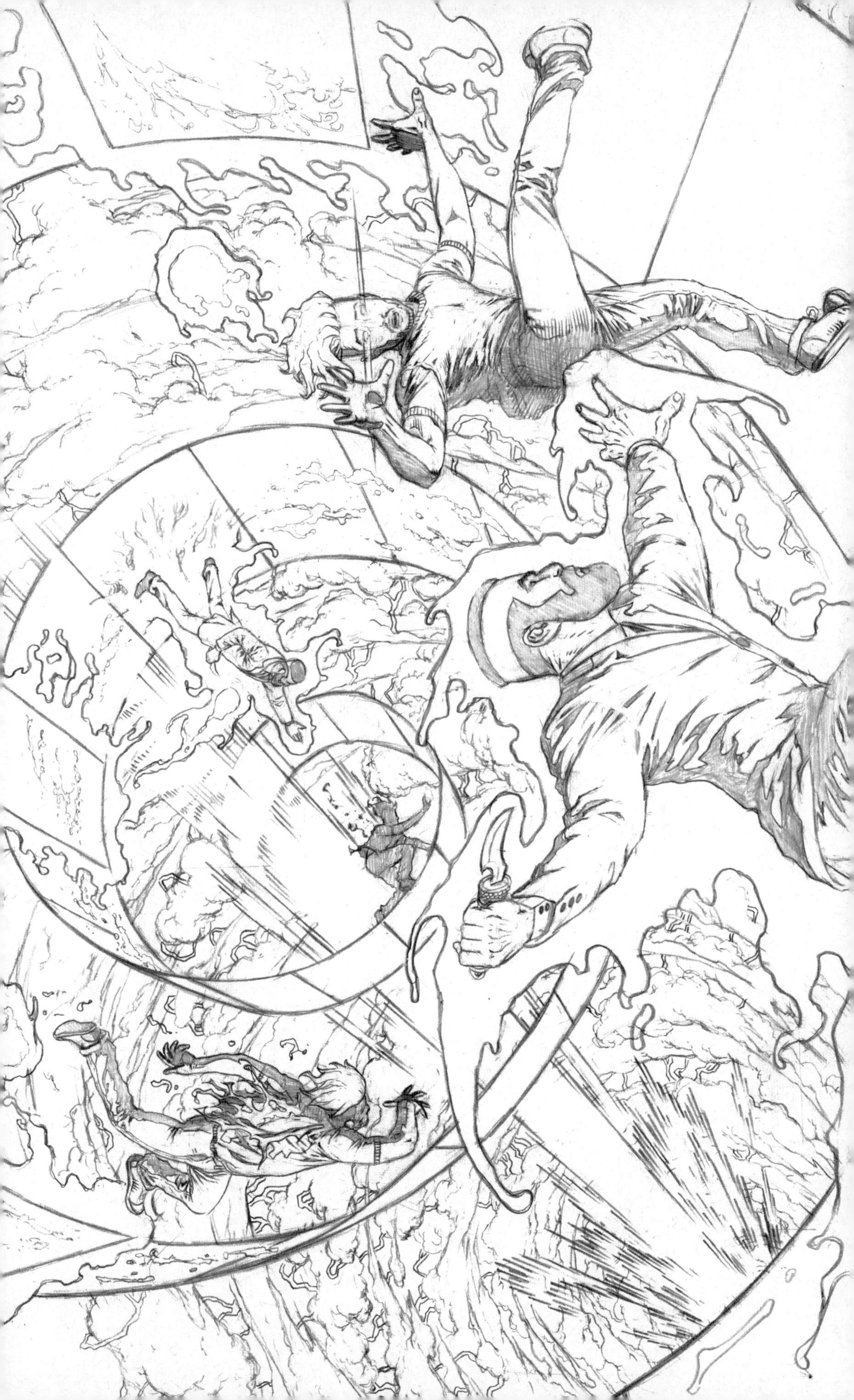

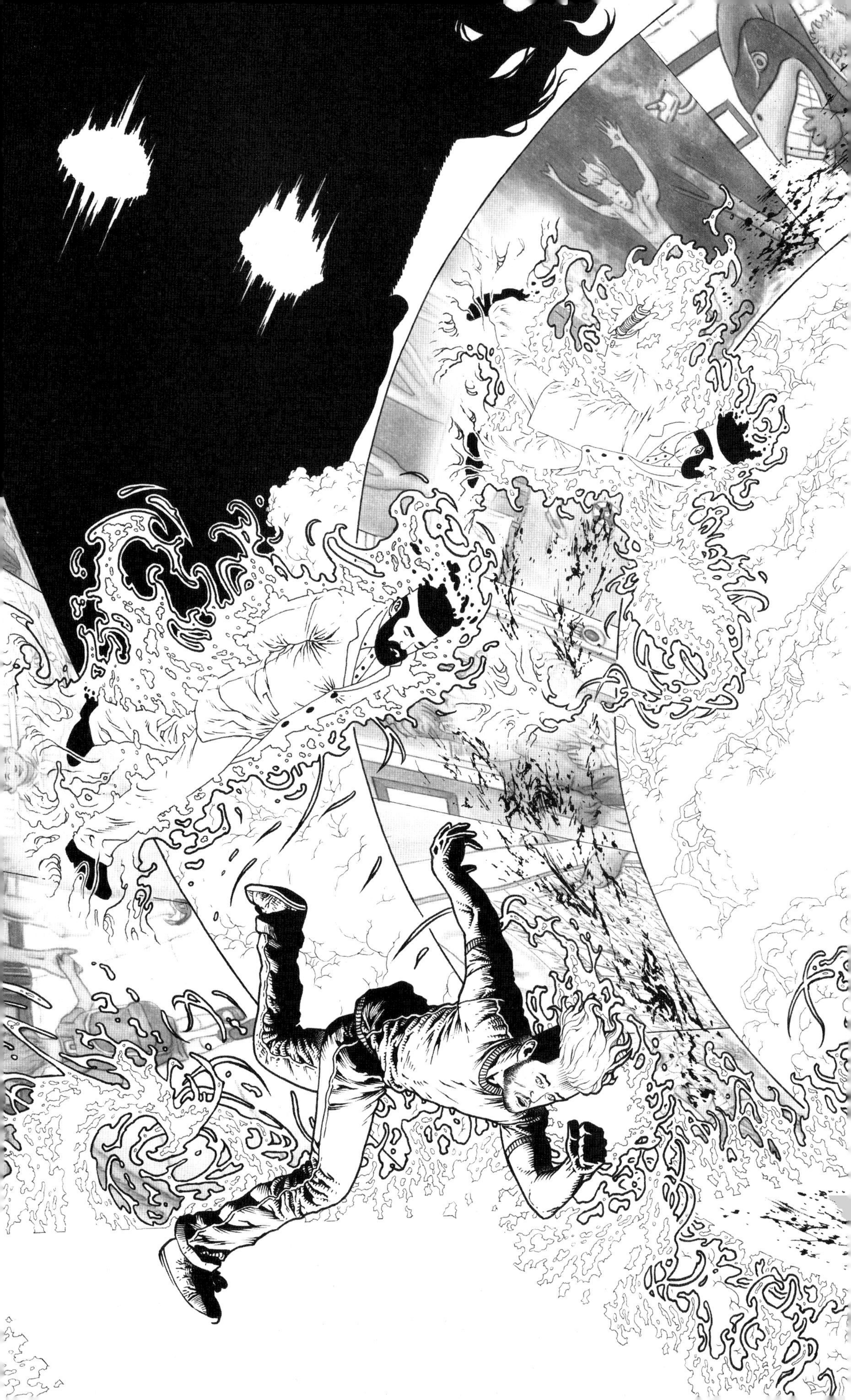

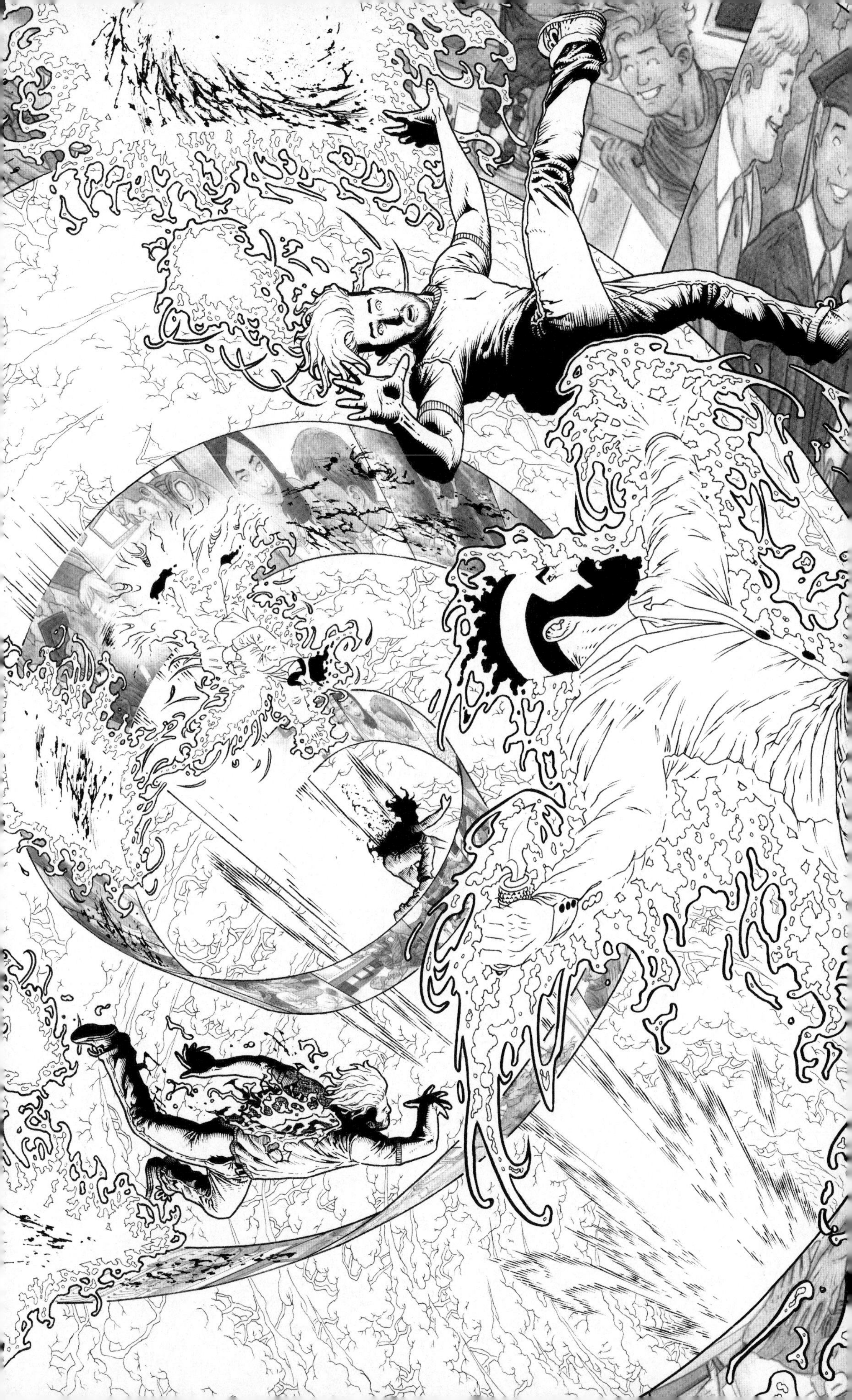

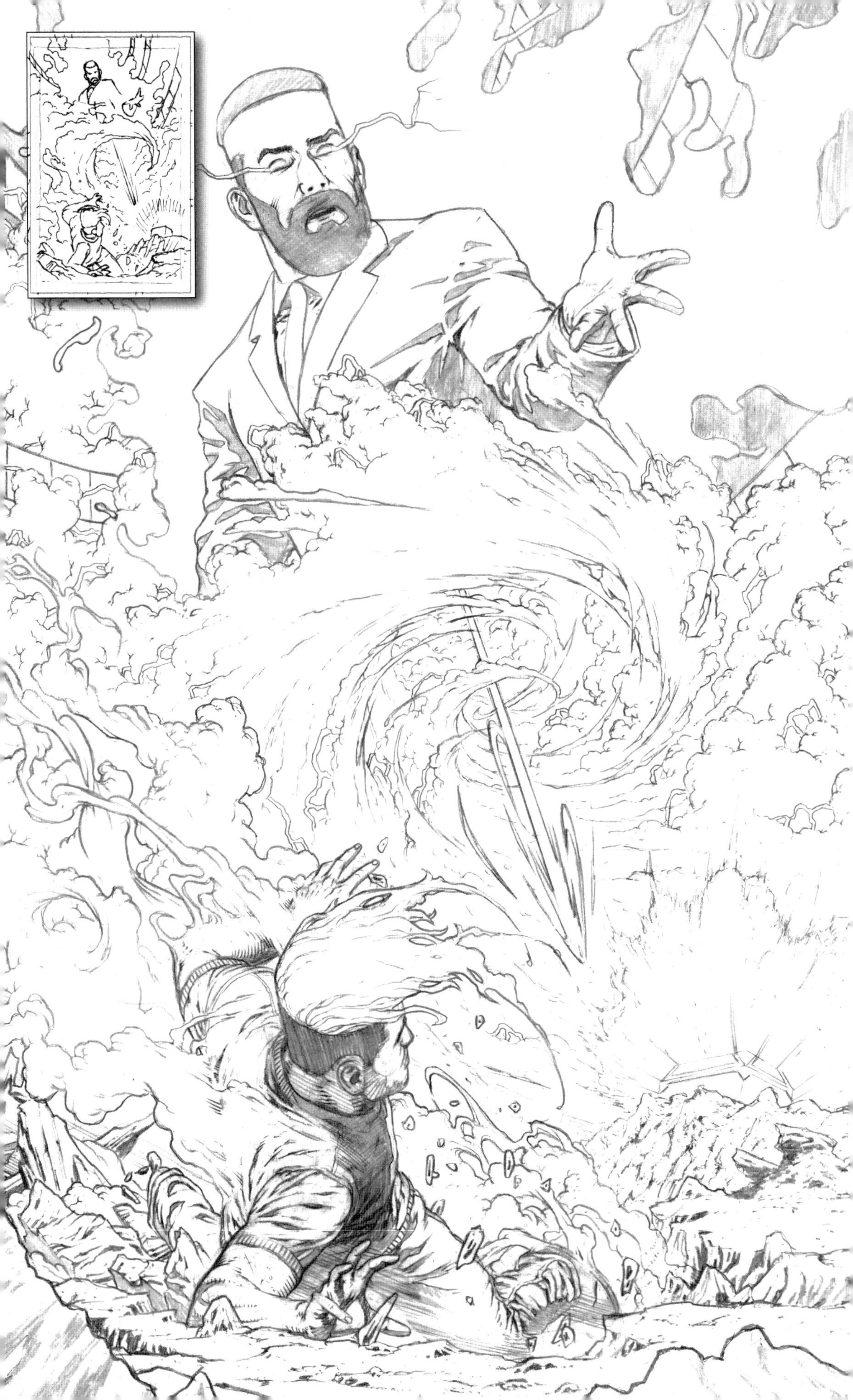

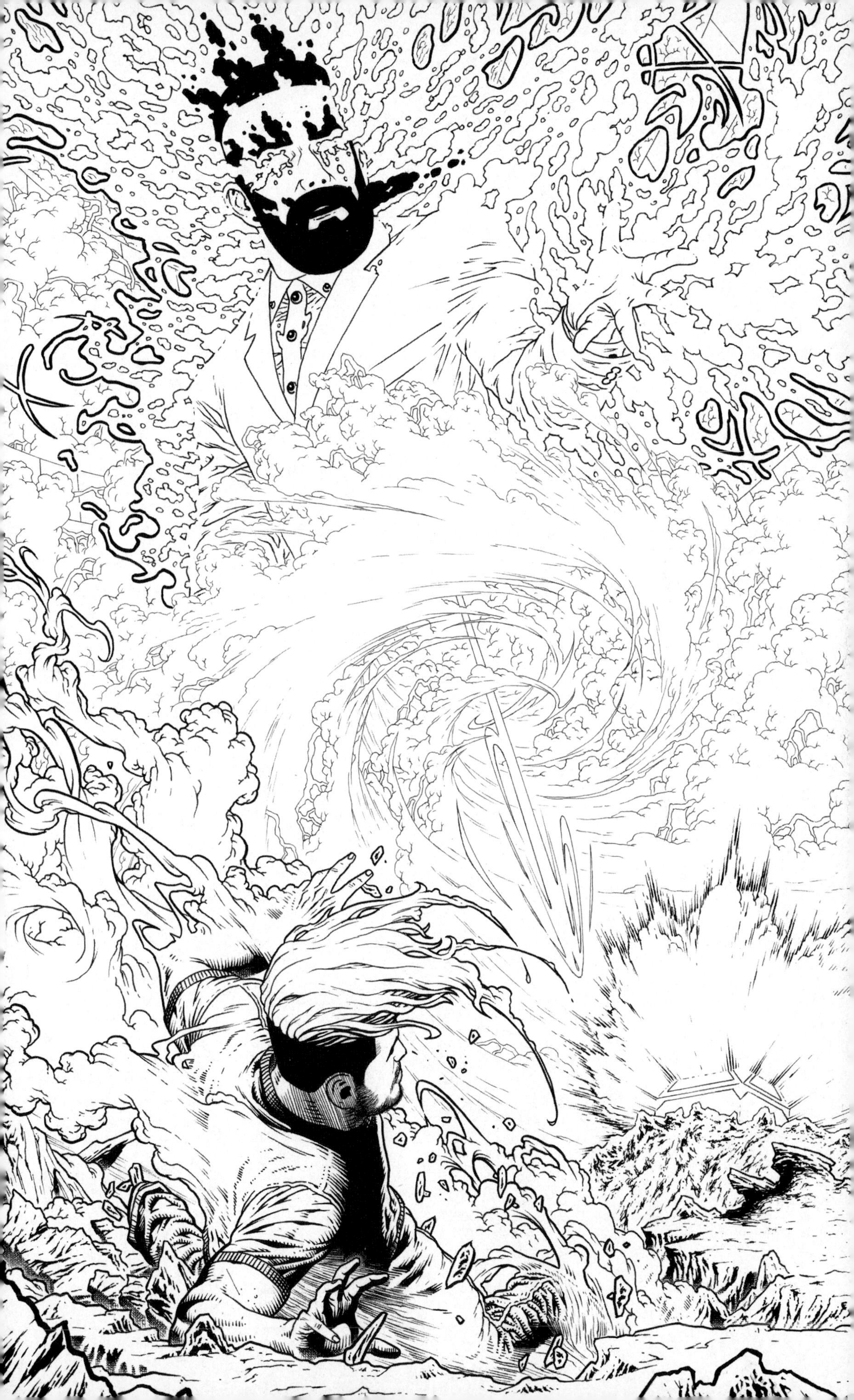

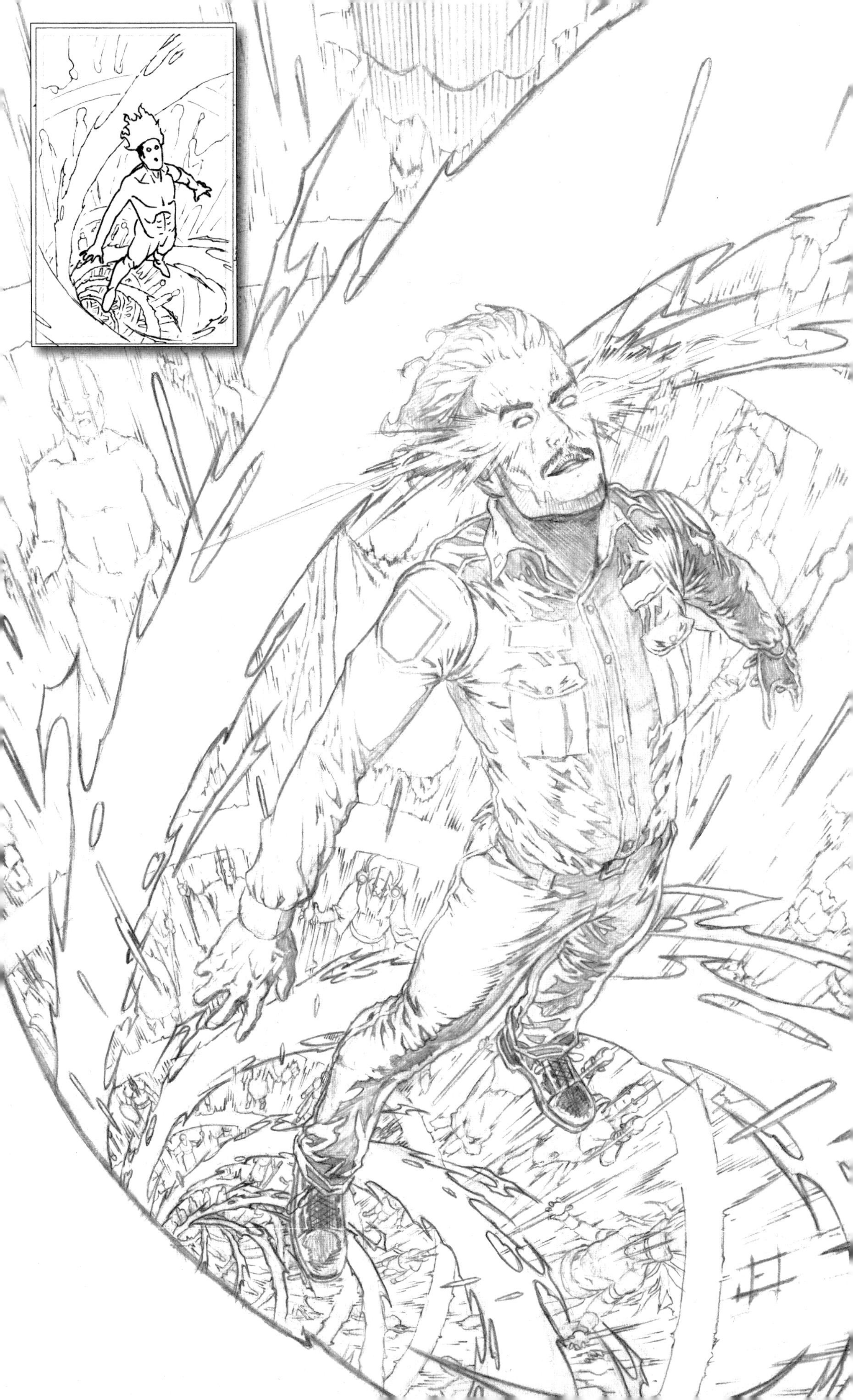

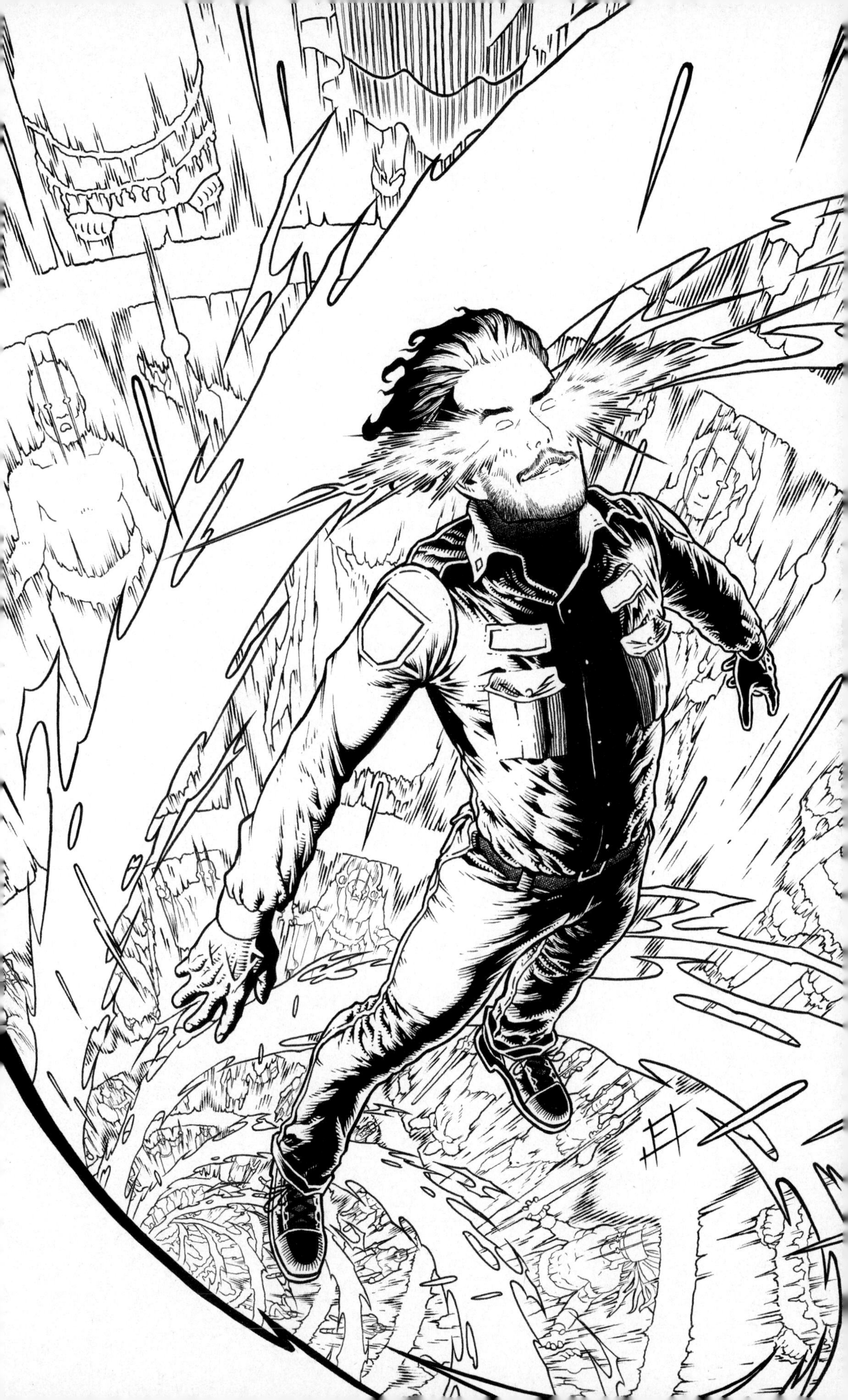

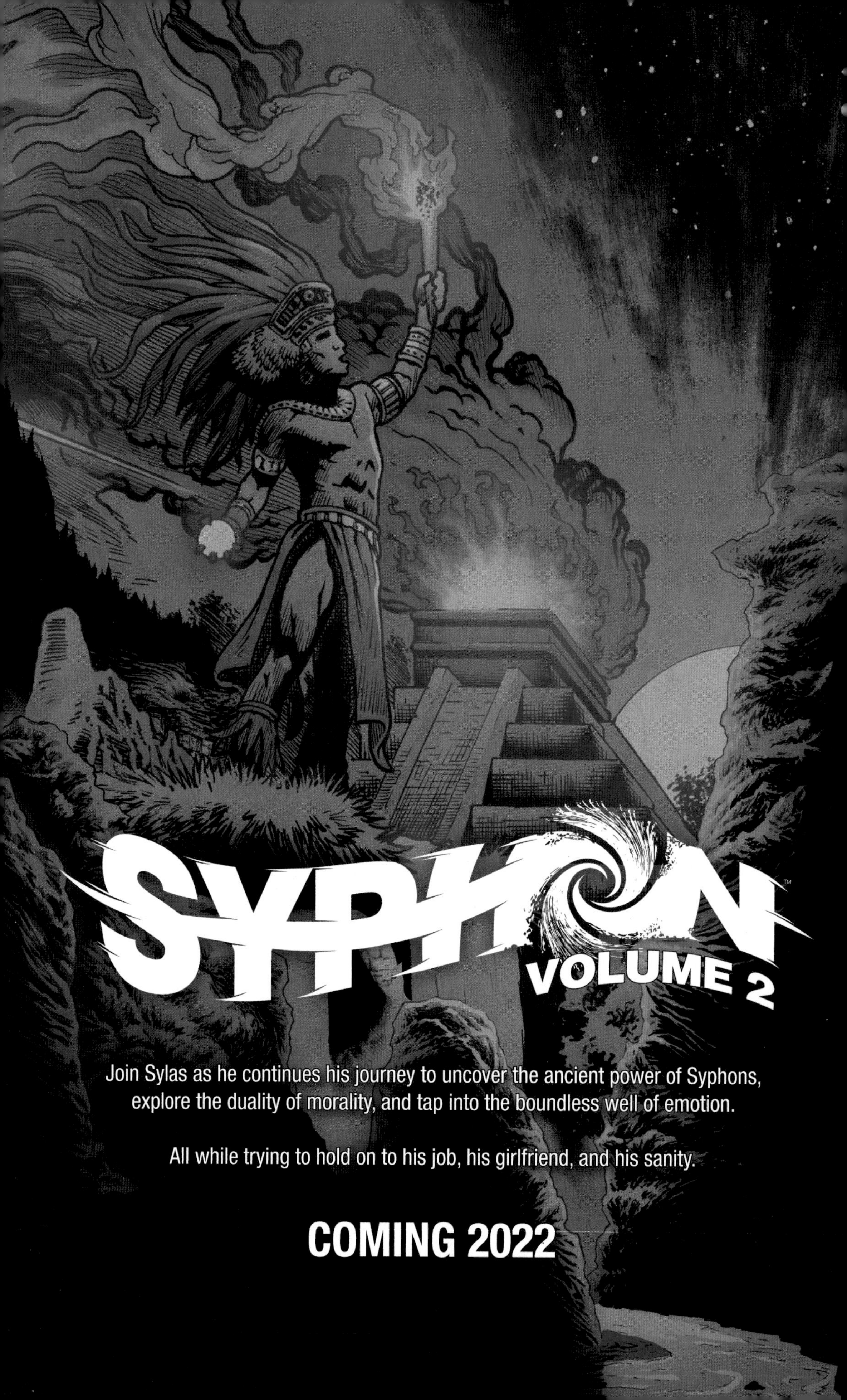
SYPHON™
VOLUME 2
Join Sylas as he continues his journey to uncover the ancient power of Syphons, explore the duality of morality, and tap into the boundless well of emotion.
All while trying to hold on to his job, his girlfriend, and his sanity.
COMING 2022

A MYTHIC FANTASY
ADVENTURE SERIES

PANTHEON

THE GODS ARE REAL

Not just one tribe, but all of them:
Mesopotamian, Norse, African, Aztec,
and Celtic, amongst others.

PANTHEON, Rise of the Djinns is the
first book in a new mythic fantasy
series that introduces unexplored
myths from around the world.

COMING IN 2022

FOR MORE INFO VISIT
WWW.MOHSENASHRAF.COM

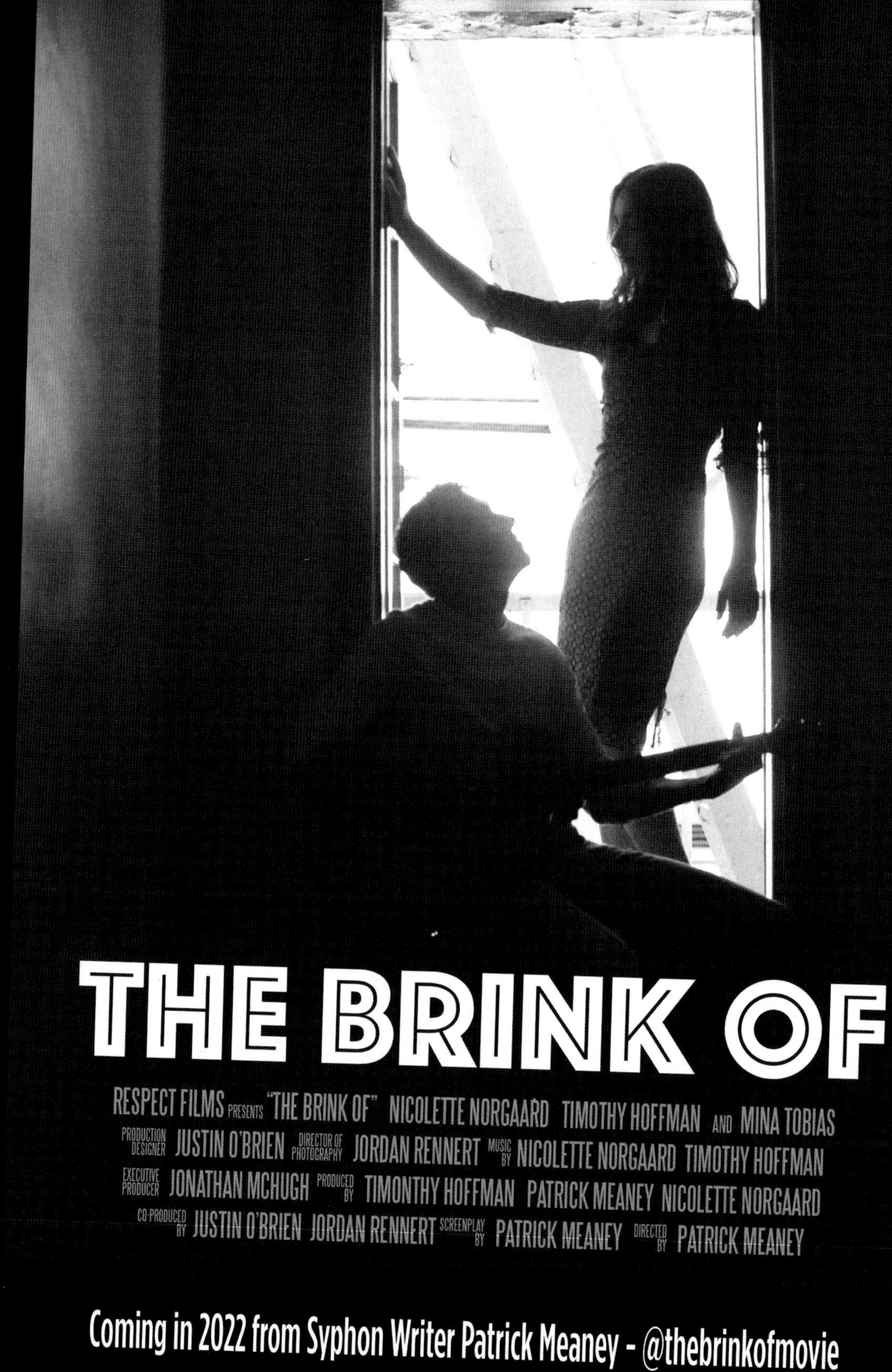
THE BRINK OF
RESPECT FILMS PRESENTS "THE BRINK OF" NICOLETTE NORGAARD TIMOTHY HOFFMAN AND MINA TOBIAS
PRODUCTION DESIGNER JUSTIN O'BRIEN DIRECTOR OF PHOTOGRAPHY JORDAN RENNERT MUSIC BY NICOLETTE NORGAARD TIMOTHY HOFFMAN
EXECUTIVE PRODUCER JONATHAN MCHUGH PRODUCED BY TIMONTHY HOFFMAN PATRICK MEANEY NICOLETTE NORGAARD
CO-PRODUCED BY JUSTIN O'BRIEN JORDAN RENNERT SCREENPLAY BY PATRICK MEANEY DIRECTED BY PATRICK MEANEY
Coming in 2022 from Syphon Writer Patrick Meaney - @thebrinkofmovie

JEFFREY EDWARDS
I L L U S T R A T I O N

Thank you from the bottom of my heart for all of your AMAZING support on Syphon!!
If you're at all interested in purchasing YOUR OWN piece of original art from Syphon,
please feel free to reach out to me through my website below:

www.jeffreyedwardsillustration.com

If you want to join my mailing list, AKA the "COMMON LIST" as the
Edweirdos call it, (Just in case you didn't know, that is the
name of my INCREDIBLE fans, and without them, I'd be nothing!) then
scroll to the bottom of the homepage of my website and you will
see a spot to sign up! Make sure that you check your email for
the confirmation email you will receive! You won't be on the COMMON LIST
if you don't confirm! And as a thank you to the COMMON LIST, you
will always get updates 24 hours ahead of everyone else!

If you'd like to catch my livestreams (typically once a week)
where I draw commissions, give away art, and just hang out, I simulcast
to both my Facebook Fan Page and my Youtube pages below:

www.facebook.com/groups/edweirdos

www.youtube.com/channel/uckc7xdlabz8vtgbxhvkpvvq

If you'd like what I do and you want to check out my other stuff,
I have Facebook, Twitter, & Instagram Pages below:

facebook.com/jeffrey-edwards-illustration-1897756840319786

twitter.com/je658

instagram.com/jeffreyedwardsillustration/

Lastly, I dedicate this book to my son, J.I.

The Top Cow essentials checklist:

A Man Among Ye, Volume 1
(ISBN: 978-1-5343-1691-1)

Aphrodite IX: Rebirth, Volume 1
(ISBN: 978-1-60706-828-0)

Blood Stain, Volume 1
(ISBN: 978-1-63215-544-3)

Cyber Force: Awakening, Volume 1
(ISBN: 978-1-5343-0980-7)

The Clock, Volume 1
(ISBN: 978-1-5343-1611-9)

The Darkness: Origins, Volume 1
(ISBN: 978-1-60706-097-0)

Death Vigil, Volume 1
(ISBN: 978-1-63215-278-7)

Eclipse, Volume 1
(ISBN: 978-1-5343-0038-5)

The Freeze, OGN
(ISBN: 978-1-5343-1211-1)

Fine Print, Volume 1
(ISBN: 978-1-5343-2070-3)

Helm Greycastle, Volume 1
(ISBN: 978-1-5343-1962-2)

Infinite Dark, Volume 1
(ISBN: 978-1-5343-1056-8)

La Mano Del Destino, Volume 1
(ISBN: 978-1-5343-1947-9)

La Voz De M.A.Y.O.: Tata Rambo, Volume 1
(ISBN: 978-1-5343-1363-7)

Paradox Girl, Volume 1
(ISBN: 978-1-5343-1220-3)

Port of Earth, Volume 1
(ISBN: 978-1-5343-0646-2)

Postal, Volume 1
(ISBN: 978-1-63215-342-5)

Punderworld, Volume 1
(ISBN: 978-1-5343-2072-7)

Stairway Anthology
(ISBN: 978-1-5343-1702-4)

Sugar, Volume 1
(ISBN: 978-1-5343-1641-7)

Sunstone, Volume 1
(ISBN: 978-1-63215-212-1)

Swing, Volume 1
(ISBN: 978-1-5343-0516-8)

Symmetry, Volume 1
(ISBN: 978-1-63215-699-0)

The Tithe, Volume 1
(ISBN: 978-1-63215-324-1)

Think Tank, Volume 1
(ISBN: 978-1-60706-660-6)

Vindication, OGN
(ISBN: 978-1-5343-1237-1)

Warframe, Volume 1
(ISBN: 978-1-5343-0512-0)

Witchblade 2017, Volume 1
(ISBN: 978-1-5343-0685-1)